ABORIGINAL PEOPLES AND SPORT IN CANADA

ABORIGINAL PEOPLES AND SPORT IN CANADA

Historical Foundations and Contemporary Issues

Edited by Janice Forsyth and Audrey R. Giles

UBCPress · Vancouver · Toronto

22 21 20 19 18 17 16 15 14 13 5 4 3 2

Printed in Canada on FSC-certified ancient-forest-free paper (100% post-consumer recycled) that is processed chlorine- and acid-free.

Library and Archives Canada Cataloguing in Publication

Aboriginal peoples and sport in Canada : historical foundations and contemporary issues / edited by Janice Forsyth and Audrey R. Giles.

Includes bibliographical references and index.
Also issued in electronic format.
ISBN 978-0-7748-2420-0 (bound); ISBN 978-007748-2421-7 (pbk.)

1. Native peoples – Sports – Canada. 2. Native peoples – Sports – Social aspects – Canada. 3. Native peoples – Canada – Social conditions. I. Forsyth, Janice Evelyn II. Giles, Audrey R.

E78.C2A1485 2013 796.089'97071 C2012-904139-4

Canada

UBC Press gratefully acknowledges the financial support for our publishing program of the Government of Canada (through the Canada Book Fund), the Canada Council for the Arts, and the British Columbia Arts Council.

This book has been published with the help of a grant from the Canadian Federation for the Humanities and Social Sciences, through the Awards to Scholarly Publications Program, using funds provided by the Social Sciences and Humanities Research Council of Canada.

UBC Press
The University of British Columbia
2029 West Mall
Vancouver, BC V6T 1Z2
www.ubcpress.ca

Contents

Part 2: Contemporary Issues

To all of the people who work so hard
to make Aboriginal sport a space to experience
all of the good things life has to offer.

Acknowledgments

Janice Forsyth

To my parents and Guy, who gave their unconditional support throughout this project. You were always there when I needed you. For you, all my love. And to my co-author Audrey, for sharing the load, offering insightful feedback, and helping me to laugh at my mistakes. Your focus and energy are what drove this book. Thank you.

Audrey Giles

A plethora of life events occurred as we assembled this text, and there are numerous people who deserve thanks for their contributions to my personal and professional lives and, most of all, for supporting me in my attempt to – as Zebedee Nungak put it – "do constructive damage to the status quo." First and foremost, I would like to thank Janice Forsyth, my co-editor and dear friend, who kept track of innumerable details and, more importantly, kept her sense of humour and always keen sense of interior design intact. Thank you for your insight and friendship.

The contributors to this book also deserve to be thanked, not only for their interesting chapters but also for their patience as they watched the text inch toward completion. Without you, we would have neither a book nor an academic community of friends. Vanessa Lodge's editorial support played a key role in ensuring that this project kept moving along. Thank you for becoming a formatting guru!

My incredible group of graduate students ("Team Giles") inspire me, make me smile on a daily basis, and make me a better academic and human being. Thank you for being you! And had it not been for the remarkable influence of two astonishing mentors, Debra Shogan and Vicky Paraschak, I likely would have chosen a very different path, not only in academia but also in my selection of furry companions. Debra and Vicky, your influence on my life has been and continues to be immeasurable.

My thanks also go to my northern friends and colleagues (especially Ian Legaree, Geoff Ray, Gary Schauerte, Deb Stipdonk, Chris Szabo, and Shane Thompson), the Remedians from my University of Alberta days, and my friends and colleagues at the University of Ottawa (particularly Erin Cressman and Shaelyn Strachan), all of whom have shown me that academia need not be a lonely (or particularly serious) pursuit. I wish that I could share this book with Rod Murray, who I like to think would have enjoyed it. Peace and much love, my friend.

I would also like to thank the talented team at UBC Press (especially Darcy Cullen and Lesley Erickson) for their fantastic guidance and assistance in all areas of this project.

Finally, my thanks go to those who make life meaningful: my sisters, Sarah and Ceinwen; my niece, Meredith; and my faithful companions in life, Tundra and Tilly. You have given me unimaginable love and joy. Thanks to Sar, for always having my back ... even when I've tiled it into a corner and think that silicone caulking may be the answer; to Cein, for showing me what tenacity really means and for finally admitting that there was no spider in my hair; to Meri-Moo, for amazing me with your cuteness and brilliance; to Tundra Dawg, for demanding endless belly rubs and allowing me to bask in your celebrity; and to Tills, for proving that it is impossible to outsmart a canine mastermind. This book is for you.

ABORIGINAL PEOPLES AND SPORT IN CANADA

Introduction

JANICE FORSYTH AND AUDREY R. GILES

Aboriginal people's involvement in Canadian sport – whether as athletes, coaches, or organizers – has been extensive and their record often marked by notable achievements. One of the first Aboriginal athletes to gain wide recognition was Tom Longboat, the Onondaga runner from Six Nations of the Grand River Reserve in southern Ontario, who catapulted to fame in the early twentieth century thanks to his accomplishments in long-distance running. Fred Sasakamoose, from Ahtahkakoop First Nation in central Saskatchewan, was taken away at a young age and sent to St. Michael's Indian Residential School in Duck Lake, where he learned how to play hockey. Then, in 1954, after several years in the junior league in Moose Jaw, Saskatchewan, he was called up to play with the Chicago Blackhawks, becoming the first known status Indian to play in the NHL. More recently, twin sisters Sharon and Shirley Firth, members of the Gwich'in First Nation in Northwest Territories, garnered attention by competing at four Winter Olympic Games in cross-country skiing (1972 Sapporo, Japan; 1976 Innsbruck, Austria; 1980 Lake Placid, United States; 1984 Sarajevo, Yugoslavia).

Ted Nolan, of the Garden River First Nation in northwestern Ontario, played for the Pittsburgh Penguins and Detroit Red Wings and was later hired as head coach for the New York Islanders and, later, the Buffalo Sabres. After Nolan won the Jack Adams Award for coach of the year in 1997, his contract negotiations with company management broke down, and he spent the next ten years working elsewhere in hockey, mostly helping Native youth to reach their potential in the sport. He returned to the New York Islanders for the 2006-07 year, leading them to the playoffs, only to be fired the following season. Although questions about racism and his checkered career in the NHL still surface in media, the NHL has yet to attempt to address them in a serious way.

Alwyn Morris, from Kahnawake Mohawk Territory in southern Quebec, won a gold and a bronze medal in pairs kayaking in the 1984 Los Angeles Summer Olympic Games. On the podium during the gold-medal presentation, he held up an eagle feather – a symbol of Aboriginality in North American culture – in recognition of the support he received from his grandparents, especially his grandfather, who had passed away a few years earlier, and to use the political platform that the Games provided to broadcast his Aboriginality to the world. Morris went on to co-found the Aboriginal Sport Circle, a national multi-sport organization for Aboriginal sport and recreation development in Canada.

Waneek Horn-Miller, also from Kahnawake, was co-captain of the Canadian water polo team that won a gold medal at the 1999 Pan American Games and that then went on to compete as a team at the 2000 Olympic Games in Sydney, Australia. She was cut from the national squad in 2003 under the pretext of team cohesion issues but challenged the claim by saying it was racially motivated – that she had been let go because of the steely determination she drew from her Mohawk culture. A case in point is the 1990 battle at Oka, where, at age fourteen, while standing alongside her people trying to defend their land from government encroachment, she was stabbed by a soldier with a bayonet that narrowly missed her heart. In the water polo dispute, all parties, including national team coaches, athletes, and Horn-Miller, agreed to arbitration using the alternate dispute resolution system for sport. In 2004, concessions were made on both sides: Horn-Miller did not return to the team, but her coaches and teammates were required to undergo cultural sensitivity training and Aboriginal sensitivity training. The two training sessions have yet to be carried out.

These are but some of the more prominent Aboriginal figures in sport whose accomplishments and challenges have been captured and circulated widely through print, television, radio, and new media. There are many more athletes whose names rarely surface in the public realm in spite of their outstanding performances. Take, for instance, Fred Simpson, an Anishinaabe athlete from Alderville First Nation in southern Ontario, who, along with

Tom Longboat, competed for Canada in the marathon at the 1908 Olympic Games in London, England. Longboat collapsed in the latter part of the race, but Simpson finished sixth overall. He subsequently turned professional, competed in many high-profile races in Canada and the United States, and then retired from competition in 1912 (Forsyth 2010). Yet, his name is largely absent from the historical record. There are also the recipients of the Tom Longboat Award, one of the most prestigious and longest-standing sports awards for Aboriginal people in Canada. Since its establishment in 1951, the Tom Longboat Award has been given to over 550 athletes, coaches, and organizers; for the vast majority of these, their sporting experiences have yet to be documented and analyzed (Forsyth 2005). A similar statement can be made about Aboriginal contestants in traditional indigenous sports and games, Aboriginal sport participants in Atlantic Canada, and the innumerable Aboriginal people who are involved in sporting activities for fun, fitness, and a sense of community: their experiences have yet to be recorded and incorporated into our broader understanding of Canadian sport.

What scholarship does exist on Aboriginal sport in Canada? Currently, information is scarce and limited mostly to a few fields of inquiry in the social sciences and humanities, mainly history, sociology, anthropology, psychology, and health. Scholars have increasingly attempted to pull the different strands of knowledge together by producing special issues of academic journals. Recent titles that have supported this trend include the *Journal of Sport History* (2008), *Pimatisiwin: A Journal of Aboriginal and Indigenous Community Health* (2007), *International Journal of the History of Sport* (2006), and *Journal of Sport and Social Issues* (2005). These publications have helped to enhance the profile and legitimacy of Aboriginal sport and recreation as an area worth studying in Canada. Indeed, several graduate dissertations on Aboriginal sport in Canada have been produced since 2005 (e.g., Forsyth 2005; Giles 2005; O'Bonsawin 2006; Lavallée 2007). Once relegated to the margins of disciplinary traditions, Aboriginal sport is emerging as an important lens through which to examine issues of individual and community health, gender and race relations, culture and colonialism, and self-determination and agency, to name but a few contemporary avenues of exploration.

Apart from this edited collection, no books on Aboriginal sport in Canada have been published to date, so students, established scholars, and the general public must wade through an array of sources in a variety of fields just to formulate a basic outline of the materials available on this topic. Not surprisingly, such conditions limit the expansion of the field, as well as constrain our knowledge of pressing issues tied to Aboriginal people and sport.

That is not to say that Canadian scholarship is completely bereft of useful information. There is small handful of outstanding texts that touch on various aspects of Aboriginal sport in Canada; however, they do not take sport-related matters as their central theme. One example is Katherine Pettipas's examination (1994) of Aboriginal cultural repression on the Prairies. Her research is significant for the way it shows how Aboriginal people in the late 1800s to the mid-nineteenth century used Euro-Canadian sports to keep their language and traditions alive in the face of overt attempts to wipe away all aspects of Aboriginal ways of life. Two of the authors in this collection expand our understanding of Pettipas's work by analyzing the challenges that occur at the interface between tradition and modernity. In "Women's and Girls' Participation in Dene Games in the Northwest Territories," Audrey Giles examines the ways in which culturally based understandings of tradition and menstrual practices shape beliefs about how Dene games should be played and who should play them. After outlining the history of Dene games, Giles shows the complexity, for both Aboriginal and non-Aboriginal participants, policy makers, and organizers, of attempting to maintain "traditional" practices in contemporary settings. In "Performance Indicators: Aboriginal Games at the Arctic Winter Games," Michael Heine explores the underlying tensions that exist when Inuit and Dene games are played in the context of a major international competition, the Arctic Winter Games. He outlines the underlying principles and values that render participation in Inuit and Dene games meaningful and teases out the intricate considerations that are involved when these principles and values are removed from their traditional cultural contexts and acted out in a formalized competitive framework. Both chapters add valuable theoretical insight to the practical problem that many Aboriginal people face: how to keep their traditions alive in the context of modern sport.

Another example of a detailed history that includes sport as part of its subject matter is Jim Miller's meticulous account (1996) of the residential school system in Canada, in which he describes the different types of physical activities that were common at schools throughout the country. Similar to Pettipas, Miller's work provides researchers with a solid jumping-off point for more detailed investigations of Aboriginal physical activity practices in educational settings. Two chapters in this volume are particularly instructive here. In "Bodies of Meaning: Sports and Games at Canadian Residential

Schools," Janice Forsyth outlines the disciplinary functions of sports and games at these institutions. Her chapter calls attention to sport's paradoxical impact on students' lives: it gave them a brief reprieve from the physically gruelling and highly regulated way of life that characterized most schools, yet this reprieve was part of an assimilative strategy that was used to discipline their "savage" ways and, in turn, transform them into "normal" Canadian citizens. In "The Quality and Cultural Relevance of Physical Education for Aboriginal Youth: Challenges and Opportunities," Joannie Halas, Heather McRae, and Amy Carpenter discuss the problems that pervade on-reserve schooling. These authors illustrate how the systemic underfunding of Aboriginal education influences the provision of infrastructure, equipment, and quality of instruction for on-reserve schools in Manitoba. They also argue that a lack of culturally appropriate curricula pervades off-reserve schools and serves to circumscribe Aboriginal students' participation in physical education in those schools. The underfunding of Aboriginal education and the lack of culturally relevant curricula result in Aboriginal students withdrawing from physical education and sport, which serves to limit their athletic development and thus also the number of Aboriginal high-performance athletes in Canada.

The existing body of Aboriginal sport scholarship in Canada can be contrasted with research produced on the American context – several notable publications have significantly advanced our understanding of Native American life and culture through analyses of sport. A dominant thread of this research is on sports and games at Native American boarding schools (Lomawaima 1994; Trennert 1998; Bloom 2000; Brayboy and Barton 2003); the issue of Native mascots in American professional and college sports leagues (King and Springwood 2001; King 2004c; Spindel 2002) also regularly generates significant scholarly attention. Several edited collections (King 2004a, 2004b, 2005) speak to the growing interest in a wide range of issues and approaches to understanding Native sport in America, and a few scholars have narrowed their attention to the issue of Native American integration in sport. For instance, Jeffery Powers-Beck (2004) examines American Indian integration into professional baseball – a trajectory that is more often associated with African American athletes. By broadening the scope to include Native Americans, Powers-Beck enhances our understanding of the practical workings of race by exposing where African American and Native American experiences in baseball intersected and diverged. In a similar vein, Donald Fisher (2002) explores the history of lacrosse in America and Canada, and shows how the game was appropriated from the Native inhabitants and then reintroduced to them as a codified sport in which their involvement was occasionally altogether restricted. Each of these contributions to American scholarship reveal a great deal about Native and non-Native relations in American life and culture through their examination of sports and games at boarding schools, the tensions surrounding the use of Indian mascots, and Indian integration into broader American society. Given the attention that Aboriginal people's involvement in sport has garnered in the United States, the dearth of research in the Canadian context seems particularly stark.

The scholarship on Native American involvement in sport is helpful – to a point. The Canadian context differs greatly from the American context because of differences in legislation, particularly the Indian Act in Canada; multiple Aboriginal identity positions constructed from complex ideas about nationhood, as expressed by the three dominant political groups in Canada, the First Nations, Métis, and Inuit; and the way in which sport is delivered to the people – in Canada, it is largely through a centralized, state-operated and -funded program, whereas there is no such form of organization in the United States. In light of this, we argue that a collection such as this one is needed to compare and contrast American issues with Canadian discourses, legislation, and organizations.

Developing a text that focuses on Aboriginal people's involvement in sport in Canada is thus an important undertaking. Within Canada, there is certainly a substantial body of research and writing on Aboriginal people and Aboriginal issues more generally. The vivacity of Native studies as a standalone field is a testament to the abundance of literature on the topic. Perhaps the dearth of academic production concerning Aboriginal people's involvement in sport is tied to a pervasive outlook that positions this area of study more as a hobby than as a field worth serious academic attention. The chapters in this collection challenge such a sentiment and reveal the extent to which sport plays an integral role in understandings of Aboriginal history, culture, identity, politics, and health, and should be studied alongside issues of land claims, cultural regeneration and survival, individual and community well-being, identity formation, gender relations, and educational outcomes and suicide among youth, to name a few key themes that resonate with current Aboriginal politics in Canada.

Issues of gender and Aboriginal involvement in major international games are two areas where this collection fills an obvious void in the literature. M. Ann Hall's chapter, "Toward a History of Aboriginal Women in

Canadian Sport," illustrates the importance of focusing our scholarly attention on Aboriginal women's sport history – an area that seems to have been overlooked in the upsurge in research on Aboriginal sport. She shows how Aboriginal women have always played an important role in the development of sport and recreation in Canada – as athletes, coaches, organizers, and administrators in both mainstream and Aboriginal systems. Her chapter highlights Aboriginal women's many sporting accomplishments while also providing an overview of the challenges they face because of race- and gender-based discrimination. In a similar vein, the issues surrounding Aboriginal involvement in major games are worth considering, especially in light of the high-stakes cultural politics that are often associated with their involvement. In "Indigenous Peoples and Canadian-Hosted Olympic Games," Christine O'Bonsawin examines the ways in which images of Aboriginal people and Aboriginality have been used in ceremonies for Olympic Games held in Canada (Montreal, Calgary, and Vancouver). In addition, she traces Aboriginal people's levels of involvement in past Olympic Games in Canada, paying close attention to the ways in which broader societal issues, including those of Aboriginal rights, have informed this involvement.

In order to engage with this text on the deepest possible level, readers must keep in mind a few things. First, it is important to understand the structure of Canadian sport, particularly as it relates to Aboriginal people, so that readers can more firmly grasp the place and importance of Aboriginal sport within the broader Canadian system. To frame the matter concisely, Sport Canada, a branch within the federal Department of Canadian Heritage, is responsible for sport development throughout the country. It strives to achieve its goals by partnering with various organizations to coordinate and deliver sport to Canadians, from the grassroots to the highest levels of competition. In other words, Sport Canada does not deliver sport; rather, it coordinates the entire sport system by creating and implementing sport policies to guide federal interests, and to foster partnerships between other national departments, government, and non-government agencies to expand its overall reach. It strategically allocates human and financial resources to ensure its objectives are met.

Sport Canada is responsible for overseeing the development of Aboriginal sport in Canada. A key partner in this system – the mainstream, government-run system – is the Aboriginal Sport Circle, a multi-sport organization that serves as the national voice for Aboriginal sport development in Canada. Established in 1995, the Aboriginal Sport Circle and its regional affiliates develop and deliver sport to Aboriginal people only. Some view the Canadian and Aboriginal sport systems as working like a double helix: there are places at which the two systems intersect, but there are others where they depart. As such, in this volume we do not refer to a singular sport system in Canada, but rather to two sport systems, specifically the mainstream Canadian sport system and the all-Aboriginal (or all-Native) sport system. As some of the chapters' authors demonstrate, the connection between the two systems is often characterized by tension.

Nowhere is this tension made clearer than in Victoria Paraschak's chapter, "Aboriginal Peoples and the Construction of Canadian Sport Policy." Here, she examines the first-known strategy of its kind in the world: Sport Canada's Policy on Aboriginal Peoples' Participation in Sport (Canadian Heritage 2005). Using the model of the double helix, Paraschak explains how the mainstream and Aboriginal sport systems provide a racialized, racializing, and at times racist sporting space for Aboriginal people. In so doing, she highlights the policy's significance for both Aboriginal and Canadian sport systems and reveals its problems and possibilities. Robert Schinke, Duke Peltier, and Hope Yungblut's chapter, "Canadian Elite Aboriginal Athletes, Their Challenges, and the Adaptation Process," builds on Paraschak's chapter by detailing Aboriginal athletes' experiences in the Canadian and Aboriginal sport systems. Schinke, Peltier, and Yungblut argue that sport psychology is not culture-free and that the culturally bound ideas found in elite sport may serve to dissuade many Aboriginal athletes from continued participation. As such, they posit, Aboriginal elite athletes have unique needs that must be acknowledged and met within both the Aboriginal and mainstream Canadian sport systems. Further building on Paraschak's chapter, in "Two-Eyed Seeing: Physical Activity, Sport, and Recreation Promotion in Indigenous Communities," Lynn Lavallée and Lucie Lévesque offer an innovative approach to understanding physical practices, one that can inform future research that focuses on Aboriginal people's involvement in sport. Drawing on social ecological theory and the medicine wheel, Lavallée and Lévesque suggest that "two-eyed seeing," which refers to incorporating the strengths of indigenous and Western perspectives to create a hybridized understanding of how to address a particular issue, can be used effectively in health promotion efforts. Importantly, such an approach emphasizes the often overlooked contributions that indigenous understandings of the world can make to the promotion of sport, physical activity, and recreation for Aboriginal and non-Aboriginal people alike.

A second issue that readers should consider is terminology. The term "Aboriginal" is a contemporary designation and here refers to individuals residing within Canada who are First Nations, Métis, or Inuit. Aboriginal people within Canada are the only individuals who have their ethno-cultural identity defined by legislation, in this case, the Canadian Constitution Act of 1982. Some sport events (e.g., the North American Indigenous Games) are Aboriginal-only events: participants must be First Nations, Métis, or Inuit. In other events (e.g., Arctic Sports at the Arctic Winter Games), most participants are from a particular Aboriginal group (e.g., in the case of Arctic Sports, the Inuit). Thus, when reading this volume, it is important to remember that although there are some commonalities among Aboriginal groups, First Nations, Métis, and Inuit also have their own unique cultural practices. It is worth mentioning too that the authors in this book often use the term "Aboriginal" interchangeably with "Native" and "Indian," depending on the era that is being discussed or the language that is predominantly used in their sources. In addition, whereas the terms "First Nations" and "Inuit" are used to refer to the broader cultural grouping, some authors use the specific ethno-cultural names, such as Cree, Mohawk, and Dene, to highlight the experiences of specific groups of people.

Aboriginal Peoples and Sport in Canada addresses several main questions: How have Aboriginal people shaped the Canadian sport system? In what ways has the Canadian sport system changed throughout the years to incorporate Aboriginal people and Aboriginal sport practices? What broader social, political, and economic contexts need to be taken into account to develop a better understanding of Aboriginal sport in Canada today? *Aboriginal Peoples and Sport in Canada* is thus the first text that provides a detailed, multidisciplinary approach to the study of Aboriginal sport in Canada. The authors in this edited collection, many of them leaders in their respective fields, draw on a wide array of materials from anthropology, history, psychology, women's studies, physical education, and sociology to examine some of the key issues that enable and constrain Aboriginal participation in sport today, as well as in the future. What emerges is a stronger understanding of the tensions that stem from cultural ideas that differ between Aboriginal and non-Aboriginal people, and among Aboriginal people, about what sport is and how it should be organized, how unequal power relations influence the ability of different groups of Aboriginal people to implement their own visions for sport, and how Aboriginal people are attempting to make sport one venue through which to assert their cultural identities and find a positive space for themselves and upcoming generations in contemporary Canadian society. *Aboriginal Peoples and Sport in Canada* is an invaluable resource for researchers and students in kinesiology, recreation, leisure, physical education, and health, and will also appeal to readers interested in gaining a deeper understanding of Aboriginal–non-Aboriginal relations in Canada.

The book is divided into two parts. Part 1 uses historical research as the basis for addressing contemporary issues. Part 2, on the other hand, uses various theoretical tools to address contemporary issues. Our aim in dividing the text this way is to highlight the importance of using history and theory to address present-day concerns.

In the final chapter, we (Forsyth and Giles) summarize the trends and issues identified in the preceding chapters, discuss the future of Aboriginal sport in Canada, and make recommendations as to how the field should proceed in an era when researchers have been urged to make their scholarly findings both accessible and practical. Nowhere has this movement been more pronounced than in the field of Aboriginal research, where Aboriginal people and their allies have challenged and changed in important ways the nature of conducting research. It is our hope that this text will challenge students and established scholars alike to shift their grasp of Aboriginal sport in Canada from static understandings of a simplified past to a more nuanced understanding of the ways in which Aboriginal people's participation in sport informs and is informed by contemporary issues in Canada.

REFERENCES

Bloom, J. 2000. *To Show What an Indian Can Do: Sports at Native American Boarding Schools.* Minneapolis: University of Minnesota Press.

Brayboy, T., and B. Barton. 2003. *Playing before an Overflow Crowd: The Story of Indian Basketball in Rebeson, North Carolina, and Adjoining Counties.* Chapel Hill, NC: Chapel Hill Press.

Canadian Heritage. 2005. *Sport Canada's Policy on Aboriginal Peoples' Participation in Sport.* Ottawa: Minister of Public Works and Government Services Canada.

Fisher, D. 2002. *Lacrosse: A History of the Game.* Baltimore: Johns Hopkins University Press.

Forsyth, J. 2005. The power to define: A history of the Tom Longboat Awards, 1951-2001. PhD diss., University of Western Ontario.

–. 2010. Out from the shadows: Researching Fred Simpson. In R.K. Barney, J. Forsyth, and M.K. Heine, eds., *Rethinking Matters Olympic: Investigations into the Socio-Cultural Study of the Modern Olympic Movement* (177-83). London, ON: International Centre for Olympic Studies.

Giles, A. 2005. Power, policies and politics: Women's involvement in Dene games in the Northwest Territories. PhD diss., University of Alberta.

King, R., ed. 2004a. *Native Americans in Sports.* Vol. 1. Armonk, NY: Sharpe Reference.

–, ed. 2004b. *Native Americans in Sports.* Vol. 2. Armonk, NY: Sharpe Reference.

–, ed. 2004c. *Re/claiming Indianness: Critical Perspectives on Native American Mascots.* Thousand Oaks, CA: Sage Publications.

–, ed. 2005. *Native Athletes in Sport and Society: A Reader.* Lincoln: University of Nebraska Press.

King, R., and C.F. Springwood, eds. 2001. *Team Spirits: The Native American Mascots Controversy.* Lincoln: University of Nebraska Press.

Lavallée, L. 2007. Threads of connection: Stories of participants involved in an urban Aboriginal recreation programme. PhD diss., University of Toronto.

Lomawaima, T. 1994. *They Called It Prairie Light: The Story of Chilocco Indian School.* Lincoln: University of Nebraska Press.

Miller, J.R. 1996. *Shingwaulk's Vision: A History of Native Residential Schools.* Toronto: University of Toronto Press.

O'Bonsawin, C.M. 2006. Spectacles, policy and social memory: Images of Canadian Indians at world's fairs and Olympic Games. PhD diss., University of Western Ontario.

Pettipas, K. 1994. *Severing the Ties That Bind: Government Repression of Indigenous Religious Ceremonies on the Prairies.* Winnipeg: University of Manitoba Press.

Powers-Beck, J. 2004. *The American Indian Integration of Baseball.* Lincoln: University of Nebraska Press.

Spindel, C. 2002. *Dancing at Halftime: Sports and the Controversy over American Indian Mascots.* New York: New York University Press.

Trennert, R. 1988. *The Phoenix Indian School: Forced Assimilation in Arizona, 1891-1935.* Norman: University of Oklahoma Press.

PART 1

HISTORICAL PERSPECTIVES ON ABORIGINAL PEOPLES IN SPORT AND RECREATION

Bodies of Meaning
Sports and Games at Canadian Residential Schools

JANICE FORSYTH

Several years ago, I interviewed a man (Bill) who had attended a residential school in northwestern Ontario, where he played on a competitive hockey team. I was interested in learning more about this team and the way the Department of Indian Affairs had used it as part of its broader strategy to integrate residential school students into the public school system in the early 1950s. We chatted for several hours. Sometimes Bill's wife would join in the conversation. Although she had attended the same school at roughly the same time, she and Bill had never met there because school officials kept male and female pupils separated. As if to emphasize the pervasiveness of this segregation, she explained that she learned about the hockey team only much later in life, through conversations with her husband. Boys and girls mostly played at different times, or, when they were outside all at once, they were restricted to opposite sides of the building so that neither could see what the other was doing. Similar to gendered activity patterns in broader Canadian society at this time, the boys were encouraged to be vigorous and competitive, while the girls were generally provided with opportunities to engage in unstructured, less physically demanding activities. These patterns served to reinforce the notion of competitive sport as a privileged male domain, a pattern that was linked to mainstream sport practices as well.

Bill enjoyed playing on the hockey team. He pulled out photos, news clippings, and memorabilia that he had collected, and told me stories about some of them; it was a small but vital assortment of artifacts that he imbued with meaning. Talking about his sports days evoked moments of pride and amusement – a sharp contrast with his recollections of schooling. Residential schools took on a somewhat different light when viewed from his sports perspective. We smiled and laughed at some of the yarns he spun about being an athlete. His was a good team that ranked highly in the province; it produced several outstanding players. And the teammates liked to have their fair share of fun, sometimes at their coach's expense. "Boys will be boys," Bill said.

Lately, Bill told me, he felt troubled by an interview he had had with a lawyer representing the Anglican Church, against which he had filed a claim under the Indian Residential Schools Settlement Agreement for abuse he suffered as a student. The lawyer had asked a lot of questions and, near the end of the meeting, posed this question: "Was there anything good at all that came from your time at school?" "Playing hockey," Bill had answered, explaining that through competitive sports he had made lifelong friends, learned how to be part of a team and experienced the value of teamwork, travelled to places he might not otherwise have seen as a youth, cherished the joys of winning, and learned from losing. The lawyer took notes, thanked him for his time, and left.

Looking at me across the table, Bill said that maybe he should not have told the lawyer his story about hockey. Could it, he wondered, be used against his claim? Would the lawyers develop a case for sport as a positive effect of the school system and use this argument to deny other applications? I, on the other hand, wondered whether he would suppress these memories, woven as they were into the general narrative structure of abuse that pervades public discussions about residential schools. If these fragments of positive memories were the only good thing that many school survivors had, what might the implications be if the story about how students used sports and games to endure their institutionalization was not shared with other survivors and their families? What impact would this silence have on attempts to bring greater understanding to the legacy of the residential school system in Canada? How important were sports and games and physical activity practices to the broader educational objectives at Indian Affairs? How can research on sports and games at residential schools provide a platform for dealing with this ugly history? At the time, I was simply at a loss for words.

Since my meeting with Bill, I have become deeply interested in the history of sports and games at Canadian Indian residential schools. My primary concern is not with the nature of abuse that has given rise to the various reports, commissions, foundations, and healing initiatives that attempt to address the social and psychological legacies that have burdened many former students and their families. Rather, my interest is in developing a better understanding of the various ways in which sports and games were used by institutional authorities to regulate and control Aboriginal bodies, and how these bodily practices were linked to the broader social, political, and economic objectives of Indian Affairs.

In this chapter, I argue that sports and games at Indian residential schools served two purposes: first, they constituted a small but important part of the federal agenda to instill a new and deeply rooted embodied sense of self among the government's young charges; second, they helped to mobilize civic support for Indian assimilation, whether it was through the residential school system in the first half of the twentieth century or the integration of its students into the public school system in the latter half. Throughout this discussion, I use key concepts informed by Michel Foucault's analytics of power, specifically discipline and bio-power, to examine the various techniques that were used to normalize Aboriginal bodies and to assess the implications of using theory to expand our understanding of the residential school system. In so doing, this chapter contributes to historical and sociological analyses of sports, games, and physical education in the public *and* the Indian residential school systems, as well as histories of Aboriginal-white relations in Canada.

Indian Residential Schools in Canada

I begin with a selective overview of the history of the residential school system in Canada, of which more is now known than it was in the early 1990s, when information about residential schools was scarce. The upsurge in research and writing on the subject is due in part to the Royal Commission on Aboriginal Peoples, a parliamentary commission that was established in 1991 to document and analyze Aboriginal-government relations from the sixteenth century onward, and to make recommendations about how to restructure those parts of the relationship that continue to adversely affect Aboriginal lives today. The five-year investigation concluded with the *Report of the Royal Commission on Aboriginal Peoples* (Royal Commission on Aboriginal Peoples 1996), a four-thousand-page document that includes a section on residential schooling. The report represents the first significant publicly funded effort to outline the history of the residential system in Canada and to expose the detrimental effects it has had on successive generations of survivors. It provides a brief overview of the entire operation, from the earliest days of missionary-sponsored schools, to the racist, gendered, and class-based ideologies that underpinned the system, to the formal policies that legitimized the development and maintenance of these institutions, to the broader social and political environments that brought about their closure. To be sure, these institutions were by no means confined to the distant past: the last institution, Gordon Residential School in southern Saskatchewan, was closed as recently as 1996.

What does the literature tell us about the Indian residential school system in Canada? Much of what we know is based on information generated about the residential model. Variously referred to as boarding or industrial schools, residential schools were generally large and situated near non-Native towns and cities, so that children from distant communities had little or no choice but to "reside" there throughout the school year, or, in many cases, year-round. St. Michael's Indian Residential School in Alert Bay, British Columbia, on the northern point of Vancouver Island, was one such school. Established in 1929, St. Michael's was an institution that accommodated two hundred male and female students from outlying areas; it was the largest school under Anglican administration at that time (Anglican Church of Canada 2008). In contrast, the day schools were much smaller, were located on or near Indian reserves, and lacked housing facilities, which meant that students returned home each day. Regardless of these differences, in the mid-twentieth century, the term "residential school" came to be used by government and church officials to refer to both types of institutions.

The basic contours of the residential system are clear. The Catholic, United, Anglican, Methodist, and Presbyterian Churches had been operating these institutions before Confederation in 1867. A good example is the Alderville Manual Labour School, established in 1838 by the Wesleyan Methodist missionaries in Upper Canada. Located in what is now southern Ontario, along the shores of Rice Lake, the school originally housed twelve students, even though they were local (Simpson n.d.). The purpose of the experiment was to see if the manual training and religious instruction would take better effect if the children were removed from their home environments. Government officials, led by Egerton Ryerson, one of the most noted men in the field of education in early Canada, deemed the trial a success, even though many of the trial institutions failed to take root, in part because of insufficient human and financial resources. It was not until the new dominion government began to support the residential model nearly two decades later that the system began to expand. As such, Alderville, and several other schools in Upper Canada, served as the prototype of the residential model adopted throughout the country in the latter half of the nineteenth century.

For more than one hundred years, from the 1880s to the 1990s, church and state attempted to inculcate a durable disposition toward a new set of cultural conditions among the 150,000 pupils in their care (*CBC News* 2010a). Students were generally between the ages of seven and fifteen years, though school registers show pupils as young as three and as old as nineteen (Miller 1996). Altogether, about 139 residential schools operated at one point or another in various parts of the country (Truth and Reconciliation Commission of Canada n.d.b). The western provinces had the greatest number of institutions; the northern territories had the most remote. Less is known about the history of residential schools in Atlantic Canada. Insofar as the facts of history tell us, New Brunswick and Prince Edward Island were the only regions where these types of schools were not established; Nova Scotia had one institution – Shubenacadie Indian Residential School. That being said, in 2010, Supreme Court Justice Robert Fowler certified a class-action lawsuit for residential school survivors in Newfoundland and Labrador: there were at least five schools in this region. However, since the federal government did not directly fund the schools, federal officials have denied any responsibility – even though the Department of Indian Affairs was responsible for the general welfare of the students at these institutions (*CBC News* 2010b). Building a better understanding of residential school history is thus a challenging task, especially when researchers generally have ignored residential schools that do not have a clear and direct link to the federal government, an oversight that is influenced in large part by contemporary politics.

Initially, the primary responsibility for schooling fell to the churches. Left largely to their own devices, religious officials implemented curricula geared toward their own practical and spiritual objectives (Miller 1996). Financial support was provided by the federal government through a per capita grant system that provided funding according to the number of students enrolled in each school. The more pupils identified on the registry, the greater the funding from Indian Affairs, the new federal department that had been given responsibility for Indian education. The per capita grant system might have seemed like a financially prudent decision to the bureaucrats in Ottawa, but in practice it led to fierce rivalries among the different denominations competing for subsidies (ibid.). This rivalry, combined with the lack of standard curricula and the means to enforce it, meant that the residential schools were chronically underfunded, in a near-permanent state of disrepair, poorly staffed, and lacking qualified teachers. It was within this social and economic context, coupled with the assimilative aims of the developing Canadian state, that an emphasis on young Aboriginal bodies arose.

Training the Student Body

Discipline and Bio-Power

French theorist Michel Foucault's analyses of power have had a profound impact on the intellectual landscape of sports studies. His work calls attention to the use of the body as a political tool that is always tied to a specific set of social and historical conditions. The range of techniques that can be used to control the body is contingent on the broader objectives of society, which are constantly shifting: a technique that is acceptable in one era may not be acceptable in another. For instance, in his examination of the prison system, Foucault (1977) documented how spectacular forms of punishment, such as public torture, were gradually replaced with "gentler" modes of control, in particular imprisonment, to coincide with civic demands for a more humane, civilized form of treatment. Thus, a key problematic underlying his work is how the state can absorb a growing and restless population into the larger body politic more efficiently and persuasively, using less force and minimizing direct control.

Foucault (1977) argued that these new modes of control produced docile bodies through the individual's internalization of techniques of self-discipline and self-control. In other words, individuals learn to regulate themselves. It is not the case that the docile body is a passive body, one that is submissive and easily managed; rather, a docile body is a body that has been rendered productive for social, political, and economic purposes. This shift from external forms of control to internalized forms of regulation reflected a major shift in the way power was deployed, such that modern power could be distinguished from pre-modern power (or sovereign power, to use Foucault's terminology) by the way people were integrated into the dominant social order (Gutting 2005): in modern societies, normalization could be secured through various forms of surveillance, not through violence (e.g., torture) or direct forms of repression (e.g., policing). From this perspective, modern power does not reside in any one individual or group but is instead diffuse and embodied, so that each individual, through a specific set of procedures, monitors and controls his or her own actions. It is this diffuse notion of modern power that I use here to explore the history of residential schools.

Two key concepts that I use for this exploration are discipline and bio-power. For Foucault, discipline is concerned mainly with the imposition of precise norms upon individual bodies (e.g., a focus on detailed movements and gestures), with the effect being the normalization of individuals into broader society through regulated practices (e.g., institutionalized levels for sports performance and standards for daily physical education). As a regulatory measure, discipline provides a set of "procedures for training and for coercing bodies" into a new form of social control (Harvey and Sparks 1991, 169). There are many types of disciplinary practices, but altogether they constitute a modern and efficient way to control a population. Bio-power is linked to discipline through the institutional use of surveillance techniques to monitor and control bodies for social, political, and economic purposes. Within the context of residential schools, physical training, physical education, and sport can be understood as forms of discipline because they provided a clear set of methods and principles to inculcate a new docility in the pupils – a docility that would presumably facilitate their integration into mainstream society. Thus, the body in modernity is worked on through various techniques of power so that it becomes what Harvey and Sparks refer to as the "invested body" whereby the body "increasingly becomes subjected to social controls and interventions (powers) aimed at channelling and managing its forces" (ibid.) without formal outside interventions.

Physical Training and Mass Displays

Physical practices linked to schooling constituted a new form of disciplinary society in Canada in the late nineteenth century. This was particularly true for indigenous people, whose cultural traditions had increasingly been subjected to intense scrutiny in an effort by religious and government agents to understand, control, and ultimately reshape those practices. The prevalent restrictions were those placed on traditional indigenous ceremonies, for instance, the potlatch and sun dance in the 1880s. There was a widespread belief among the broader population that these and other indigenous customs were uncivilized, and that indigenous people needed to engage in more productive forms of behaviour so that they could contribute to the growing Canadian state (Pettipas 1994). Yet, the prohibitions were not enough to generate new habits among the Indians; there had to be something to fill the void for this process of cultural transformation to be effective. As such, the prohibitions coincided with increasing support for Euro-Canadian sports and games. In this way, church and state attempted to fundamentally alter indigenous physical practices through a combination of regulation and provision centred on a politics of the body (Paraschak 1998). A good example is seen in the sports day celebrations that became a popular feature on many reserves in Canada, with intra- and intercommunity competitions being encouraged by residential school instructors, Indian Agents, and federal policy makers alike (Pettipas 1994; Paraschak 1998; Forsyth 2005).

The residential school system was different from previous control methods – for instance, government prohibitions – in that it introduced more efficient ways of monitoring and managing Aboriginal bodies (Kirk 1998). Various forms of physical training played a key role in this process. In the early 1900s, before the First World War, physical training was linked directly to physical health. Throughout this era, waves of communicable diseases circulated through the schools, wreaking havoc on the students, many of whom were already vulnerable to viral and bacterial infection from living in overcrowded conditions and from the poor air circulation inside the schools. Surveys and school and hospital records, among other things, were used to monitor health trends. Generally, the findings described miserable states of living. Reports showed that a significant number of students had died at these institutions, while others had been transferred to hospitals before succumbing to disease or had been sent home, where they would infect their family and community. The state of affairs became so bad that Indian Affairs had little choice but to address the high morbidity rates among the students (Kelm 2001). The introduction of physical training programs was thus seen as an efficient and cost-effective way of dealing with the recurrent health issues in the schools.

Following the model of health curricula already established throughout North America and Europe, Indian Affairs introduced calisthenic exercises to its schools in 1910 in an effort to reduce the spread of pulmonary disease among the pupils. These exercises could be performed indoors when the weather was poor because they required relatively little space and no equipment, but instructors were encouraged to move outdoors whenever possible to capitalize on the fresh air. Calisthenic exercises represented a distinctive form of modern disciplinary training and were used in an attempt to control disease. In the case of these exercises, power was exercised not by direct control of the body as a whole but through meticulous control of specific parts of the body – a type of micro-management. For instance, in the 1910 training manual issued by Indian Affairs to all residential schools, the description of the "Fundamental Standing Position" made it clear that not just any standing position would do; it had to be a particular type of standing for it to be considered "appropriate" training for students:

> [The Fundamental Standing Position] should correspond to the position of a soldier when at "attention," except that the feet are from 60 to 90 degrees instead of at 45, the heels should be together and on the same line, the feet turned out, the knees straight, the body being erect on the hips, which should be drawn slightly inwards, the chest expanded, but the abdomen held well in; the shoulders drawn well backwards and forced downwards so that they are level; the arms hanging naturally by the side in line with the heel; the head must be held erect with the chin in, the eyes looking straight to the front, and the weight of the body should rest on the balls of the feet. (Department of Indian Affairs 1910, 1)

"Healthy" bodies – that is, bodies more able to resist disease – were thus produced through specialized training. The point was not to encourage better physical health through unstructured play, but rather to achieve the results through a specific set of procedures, thereby producing "bodies that not only do what we want but do it precisely in the way that we want" (Gutting 2005, 82).

Military drill for boys and girls, another common feature of the public school system in the late nineteenth and early twentieth century (Morrow 1977), was also widely employed throughout the residential schools. Pupils marched everywhere and followed a daily routine circumscribed by the sound of whistles and bells from morning till night. Cadet training for boys was popular, and histories of residential schools usually mention some aspect of this training (Miller 1996). The link between military training and nationalism was unmistakeable, as the drills were designed to replace tribal allegiances with a sense of patriotic duty. Military techniques were incorporated into the domain of physical health where calisthenic programs were also constructed along regimented lines.

Mass gymnastic displays for boys and girls were another common form of discipline linked to bio-power. The mass exercises served dual purposes: they provided church and state with opportunities to promote assimilation and to attract new students to school. In areas where there was more than one school, the parents had some measure of control over where their children would be educated (Miller 1996). It's possible that physical training programs could help sway their opinions. Images of young bodies moving in formation could evoke ideas about health and integration and lend visible support to the ideological contention that the children were being mentally and physically prepared to meet the demands expected of them in the industrial labour force. In actuality, most families had little or no input as to where their children would be kept, nor did they have much contact with their children during the school year (Miller 1996; Milloy 1999). Thus, it is more likely that the effects of the collective symbolism produced by the mass gymnastic displays helped to secure and maintain public support for the federal agenda than helped to gain parental support for schooling. Indeed, the displays, which were often conducted in association with other public events, could produce strong, positive identifications from onlookers, as Christian ideals about race, civility, and citizenship meshed together in living tableaux (Kirk 1998). Native bodies trained to perform complicated manoeuvres before a discerning crowd thus served as a form of what Foucault (1977) termed "examination," which is a technique of observing and imposing a normalizing judgment that makes it possible to assess differences between individuals and certain populations. For instance, in June 1951, after watching a choreographed exhibition of mass gymnastic exercises hosted by Native pupils from the Kamloops Indian Residential School, one male spectator was so moved by the demonstration that he wrote to the headmaster, Reverend O'Grady, to congratulate him for the good work he was doing with the students:

> I am sure I would never forgive myself if I did not write to you and express my appreciation of the wonderful example you have presented to the public of the type of well behaved children, quiet and demure in their manners before the public. I was down at the park and viewed the whole of the display from the standpoint of a long experience in watching and enjoying any spectacle where the results of training are put before the critical eye of the public and I assure you that of all the people I have interviewed not one but has agreed with me that if all our young people were trained by the same method where learning walks side by side with decorum and good behavior, where Christian precepts are imparted, we would have no more of hoodlums and gangs. They all seem to call to mind the fact that never do we hear of organized crime emanating from charges such as it is your duty; and I have no doubt a pleasure to teach and instruct in the fundamental laws of Truth, Honesty and Christian precepts. I am not speaking of that physical training so necessary to develop the body, I am only referring to the minds

> you are so painstakingly molding and shaping so that they can take their place in society as real men and women trained in all those branches of learning which will form the necessary attributes to that future welfare. (Beete 1950)

For many spectators, the young bodies moving in formation reinforced the widespread belief that religious instruction, combined with formal schooling extolling the virtues of good citizenship, would teach the youth respect for discipline and deference to official authority (Kirk 1998).

Couched in terms of "self-improvement," Native students were subjected to regimented physical training programs designed to inculcate patriotic values and instruct male and female students in appropriate masculine and feminine behaviours. This strict interpretation suggests that Native students were treated no differently from non-Native students of the same era; however, when the prevailing attitudes toward Native peoples are taken into consideration, the idea of self-improvement takes on distinctly racial overtones. Aside from the obvious health benefits derived from organized physical activities, regimented training programs were thought to provide Native youth with much-needed lessons in life. This discourse revolved around notions of "racial uplift." Successful curricula would not only help Native students to rise above their "race" and assume positions in the labour force, they might entice them to give up their Native status as well. For Native boys, at least, these lessons could be imparted through an organized structure of competitive sports and games.

Physical Education and Sports

By the late 1940s, it was clear to the officials at Indian Affairs that a program of physical education that included Euro-Canadian sports and games could help move its agenda along (Forsyth 2005, 2007). Federal officials believed that, in addition to being a cost-effective solution for dealing with the poor health conditions in the schools, organized sports and games would facilitate the integration of Native youth into the public school system by teaching them the physical competencies that youth in the public school system were already mastering. Federal officials also believed that sports and games would help smooth the progress of Native assimilation into broader Canadian society by bringing Native and non-Native people into contact with each other through competition. As a technique of bio-power, competitive sport was an efficient way to manage the social, political, and economic problem facing the government: how to encourage Native assimilation into broader Canadian society. Thus, in 1949, Indian Affairs created the new administrative position of supervisor of physical education and recreation within its bureaucracy. This was the first position of its kind at Indian Affairs, and it marked the formal beginning of direct federal involvement in Native sport and recreation development in Canada. The federal program was never well supported and its relevance would soon dwindle as the residential school system was dismantled. By the 1960s, it would eventually become an invisible feature at Indian Affairs (Forsyth 2005). Nevertheless, the formal establishment of the program also signalled the intensification of administratively controlling young Aboriginal bodies through an organized and regularized curriculum of physical education, sport, and recreation so as to normalize their behaviours and facilitate their movement into mainstream environments.

More than fun and games, a diversified sport and recreation program was thought to teach its participants how to use their leisure time wisely (Canada 1954). Through organized activities, they would learn discipline and deference to authority, as well as how to be productive members of society. Stories of these activities were recorded from time to time in various local newspapers. In 1951, the *Sault Daily Star* reported that Jan Eisenhardt, the newly hired supervisor of physical education and recreation at Indian Affairs, had successfully negotiated with the Sault Ste. Marie city council to have one of its recreation directors spend two days per week during the summer at the Garden River First Nation Reserve, located a few miles east of the city. To Eisenhardt, the arrangement would benefit the people from both the Garden River First Nation Reserve and Sault Ste. Marie. "The Indian people's contact was with the wrong type of white man," he explained; "from contact with city children in an organized recreation scheme, the reserve children would learn a great deal of good. The city would benefit by getting better future citizens" (*Sault Daily Star* 1951, 14). The fact that Indian Affairs would cover the costs of the additional programming was an incentive that made the program more attractive to the city. In response to Eisenhardt, Alderman Peter King emphasized the economic benefits of the deal, stating that such a simple plan "would make the children better citizens at no cost to the city" (ibid.).

In the second half of the twentieth century, athletic contests – bodily practices that were linked to social, political, and economic power – became a more pronounced feature of residential schools. Schools augmented their programs to include sports competitions, which were usually limited to local or regional events. For instance, Blue Quills Indian Residential School in east-central Alberta held its first all-Native track and field meet in 1961, which presented the first opportunity for its students to interact with students from other Indian schools (Persson 1986). Federal officials encouraged school staff to promote participation, especially in team sports, because it was thought these competitions would develop leadership skills and teach cooperation (Canada 1954). To aid this agenda, Indian Affairs provided additional financial support to day and residential schools that fostered competitive opportunities involving both Indian and public schools, and encouraged Native athletes to play on local non-Native teams and leagues (e.g., Canada 1953, 1954). In 1951, Indian Affairs began providing one-time-only grants to schools that already had established sports programs and whose students were competing successfully against other Native or "white" teams. Thus, the federal government affirmed its support for using sports and games as a form of discipline in order to achieve its goal of Native assimilation.

Such was the case for the Sioux Black Hawks hockey team from the Sioux Lookout Indian Residential School, an Anglican-run institution in northwestern Ontario. In April 1951, the Department of Citizenship and Immigration and the Department of Health and Welfare co-sponsored a friendly boys competition between the bantam-aged Black Hawks and the top playground teams in Ottawa and Toronto. The primary purpose of the trip was to reward the Black Hawks for their "ability, behavior and sportsmanship" on the ice (*Evening Citizen* 1951, 20). A second reason called attention to the nationalistic purposes of sport; it was through the availability of such grants that the government hoped "to encourage hockey among Canada's Indians" (ibid.). Further to these objectives were the intangible benefits that the students would supposedly accrue from this excursion. As their coach, Bruce McCulley, explained to *The Journal*, "These three days in Ottawa will be worth three years' schooling for the boys" (*The Journal* 1951). The trip was simultaneously an educational project to introduce the youth to the nation's cultural centre, which included, among other things, tours of the national archives, national museum, and Parliament Buildings in Ottawa, and a media-generated spectacle to promote the integration of Native students into the public school system. It ostensibly demonstrated that the federal government was not only involved in an ideological campaign to produce a loyal Native citizenry by providing boys with opportunities to participate in the patriotic sport of hockey but was also encouraging Native assimilation by bringing Native and non-Native youth together in friendly, competitive play.

A poignant example of the disciplinary culture of sport in one residential school is found in Basil Johnston's 1988 autobiography, *Indian School Days*. Johnston recalls his youth at Spanish Indian Residential School (later renamed Garnier), an all-male institution that was situated on the north shore of Lake Huron in Ontario. He describes how, in the late 1940s and early 1950s, the student body was divided into four groups named after professional hockey teams – the Montreal Canadiens, Toronto Maple Leafs, New York Rangers, and Chicago Blackhawks – and which competed against each other in loosely organized events. The primary objective was to foster a competitive spirit among the students when doing regular chores. If one member failed to live up to the expectations of the Jesuit instructors, the whole team suffered for his negligence. Winning teams were usually awarded what little bit of "free time" they had earned from finishing first. Interscholastic competitions served another, more explicitly disciplinary purpose at Spanish, as they were meant to exhaust the students, thus ensuring that any remaining energy would be spent on the playing fields and not running away (Johnston 1988).

In spite of the increased importance of sports and games to government, in terms of outdoor amenities, most schools lacked such basic playground equipment as swings and teeter-totters. Space and equipment for relatively inexpensive sports such as softball, volleyball, and basketball and for jumping pits for track and field were also almost non-existent. One exception to this rule was outdoor hockey, which emerged as the most popular form of activity among Native boys in the mid-twentieth century (Miller 1996). Still, most schools lacked the necessary hockey equipment for their students to engage in competitive play. Indoor facilities at the schools were not much better. Where gym space existed, it was often too small to accommodate team sports. Some schools utilized basement halls for recreational purposes, while others made use of dining rooms. Even then, most institutions were poorly equipped for indoor games, a problem compounded by the fact that most teachers lacked the training, experience, and imagination to implement a physical education program, or were not interested in leading one. To make matters worse, the poor air circulation inside most schools detracted from the health benefits physical activities were expected to provide (Eisenhardt 1950).

Yet, even with these limitations, some schools excelled at competitive sports and games. Some institutions, such as the residential schools in Lebret and Prince Albert, Saskatchewan, developed outstanding athletic programs, and a number of their students, having honed their athletic skills in the residential school system, later moved on to professional sports careers, in particular boxing, rodeo, and hockey, or competed successfully in elite-level amateur sport, as evidenced by the long list of recipients of the Tom Longboat Award (Forsyth 2005). Established in 1951 by Indian Affairs and the Amateur Athletic Union of Canada, the administrative organization responsible for amateur sports development in Canada at that time, the Tom Longboat Award is the longest-standing and highest level of award given to Native athletes in the country. Within the context of the residential schools, the award also served a disciplinary function: as a record of achievement it represented the standard against which other athletic accomplishments could be measured. In so doing, the "record" facilitated the constant comparison of achievements relative to an abstract (and impossible to achieve) goal: the constant enhancement of performance (Heikkala 1993). The body-work for athletes at these schools would never be complete.

History of the Present

By the late 1960s and early 1970s, many of the day and residential schools had been shut down and the students placed in the public school system. This move toward integration was made possible with the 1951 revisions to the Indian Act, which permitted Indian Affairs to enter into joint agreements with provinces and territories to provide education to Native students. Once an agreement was signed, the local school board was in charge of the day-to-day mechanics of schooling, while Indian Affairs was responsible for financing the arrangement (National Indian Brotherhood 1988). The process of integration was slow to start, but by 1964 there were more than two hundred joint agreements in place throughout Canada (Hawthorn 1967). The end of the residential school system appeared in sight. What lay beyond the horizon was a need to address its legacies.

On June 11, 2008, Canadian prime minister Stephen Harper delivered a formal apology in the House of Commons to former students for Canada's role in the operation of the residential schools. Speaking about the history of that system, Harper stated:

> Today, we recognize that this policy of assimilation was wrong, has caused great harm, and has no place in our country ... The government now recognizes that the consequences of the Indian Residential Schools policy were profoundly negative and that this policy has had a lasting and damaging impact on Aboriginal culture, heritage and language. (*CBC News* 2008)

Harper's 2008 apology followed more than a decade of admissions of guilt and requests for forgiveness from the religious denominations that were involved in the endeavour, including the United Church in 1986, the Oblates of Mary Immaculate in 1991, the Anglican Church in 1993, and the Presbyterians in 1994. Much can be made of the timing of the federal statement, especially in light of Canada hosting the 2010 Olympic Games; nevertheless, it can be said that the public pronouncement is de facto recognition that the residential school system did significant harm to a great number of Native people and their families, and that these harmful legacies continue today in the form of drug and alcohol abuse, intergenerational violence, weak educational outcomes (even when supports are provided), and poor health.

In 2005, before Harper's apology, negotiations for the Indian Residential Schools Settlement Agreement (IRSSA) were initiated. Former students, among them, Bill, the hockey player whose story opens this chapter, had taken the federal government and the churches to court, winning the largest class-action settlement in Canadian history. The implementation of the compensation packages began in 2007. Former students, approximately eighty thousand survivors, were given the opportunity to opt out and pursue independent litigation or accept the Common Experience Payment for each year they were in residence (Truth and Reconciliation Commission of Canada n.d.a). The IRSSA also provided funding for several healing initiatives, including the establishment of the Truth and Reconciliation Commission. The commission was given the mandate to construct a comprehensive history of the school system, to enter into a partnership with a research centre to house the information, and to support the development and dissemination of specific projects that could potentially contribute to the remedial process.

As this chapter shows, examinations of sports and games at residential schools should be an integral part of the healing process, a view that was acknowledged by Chief Justice Murray Sinclair, the commission chair, at the 2009 national meeting of the Assembly of First Nations, the national representative group for status Indians in Canada. If we accept the basic premise on which the commission is founded, that greater understanding is a key to healing, then examining all aspects of the residential school system and raising challenging questions about the patterns that emerge from the evidence will be vital to that success. The point here is not to argue about whether Euro-Canadian sports and games were "good" or "bad" features of curricula, or to define the outcomes in positive or negative terms, but to examine how these activities played a central role in the program of assimilation and how students responded to these activities in productive and creative ways.

Creating better understanding will not be easy. Euro-Canadian physical activity practices are almost always cast in positive and patriotic terms, a view that tends to obscure their social and political effects. For instance, although the ban on traditional religious cultural practices like the potlatch and the sun dance had been quietly removed from the Indian Act in 1951, the policy remained implicitly effective by virtue of informal measures that provided financial assistance to sport and recreation activities that fit government-approved criteria, ensuring that Native energies would be channelled into physical behaviours defined as appropriate by the federal government (Paraschak 1998). These effects have not gone completely unnoticed by observers. The *Report of the Royal Commission on Aboriginal Peoples* (Royal Commission on Aboriginal Peoples 1996) noted how Indian Affairs looked to popular Euro-Canadian sports and games to help bring about fundamental changes in the values and behaviours of Aboriginal students. It was thought that participation in Euro-Canadian activities would contribute to the transformation of communal values by fostering a competitive spirit among the pupils, and hopefully, through regulated instruction, the skills they learned would translate into a desire for individual achievement and wealth. More detailed analyses of sports and games at residential school are needed. A Foucauldian approach would be useful in such an analysis because it can be used to recognize the ways in which power has been, and in some cases continues to be, exercised through sport and recreation via the control of Aboriginal bodies. Such an approach, however, also acknowledges that Aboriginal peoples are active agents in their own lives and, as such, have and continue to offer resistance to dominant exercises of power. Further, a Foucauldian approach complicates our knowledge of residential school students' experiences, as it resists metanarratives of good versus bad and thus opens up space for understanding that, within the context of these highly oppressive environments, sports and games were generally well received by the students. Most often, they remember these activities as being the only bright spot in their day. It was their time to get away from the routine and drudgery of daily chores; it was time to have fun with their friends.

Conclusion

To return to Bill's concern that opened this chapter: all of this is not to say that research should not focus on the abuse that took place at these institutions.

To be sure, there is still much work to be done to address the problems of a past that permeates the present and will no doubt shape relations between Canadians well into the future. Bill's apprehension, however, should not be read as yet another account of the painful experiences that continue to impact the lives of residential school survivors. Instead, I believe it should be viewed as a troubling self-examination of how bodily practices, in this case sports and games, are implicated in former students' understandings of their experiences at residential schools.

Competitive sports provided many Aboriginal students with avenues for positive self-expression and identification (Bloom 2000), but the techniques used to monitor and control their bodies also transformed Aboriginal physical practices into something that could be talked about and classified, and thus categorized for administrative purposes. Therefore, Bill's positive identification with playing hockey must also be understood as a form of bio-power, which is linked to discipline, that provided institutional authorities as well as the participants themselves with valuable information about the effectiveness of these activities to render Aboriginal bodies "normal," or presumably ready for integration. Sports and games were thus pivotal sites through which power was legitimized and exercised through Aboriginal bodies in the residential school system.

Lastly, this chapter has shown how a Foucauldian-inspired analysis can be a productive way to think about the process of healing without getting caught up in the binary logic that pervades discussions about the history of residential schools in Canada. The institution of schooling produced its own set of practices that both enabled and inhibited the already embodied sense of self the students brought with them to these institutions. Residential school survivors, not unlike other athletes, should take pride in their sporting accomplishments without fear of having those achievements used against them when telling their stories about schooling. Indeed, their experiences can be understood as the expression of creative responses to conditions of marginalization and duress. In this regard, Foucauldian-inspired analyses might provide a way to better understand a complex and, at present, controversial past. And it is precisely this level of analysis, one that uses theory to map the contours of the physically active body, that is required if we are to move beyond the positive and negative discourses that constrain our ability to address the "history of the present" (Roth 1981) with which Canadians are now faced.

REFERENCES

Anglican Church of Canada. 2008. St. Michael's Indian Residential School – Alert Bay, BC, Milestones. http://www.anglican.ca/.

Beete, G. 1950. Letter from Kamloops resident to Reverend Father O'Grady, preceptor, Kamloops Indian Residential School, British Columbia. June 25. Private collection.

Bloom, J. 2000. *To Show What an Indian Can Do: Sports at Native American Boarding Schools*. Minneapolis: University of Minnesota Press.

Canada. 1953. *Report of Indian Affairs Branch for the Fiscal Year Ended March 21, 1953.* Ottawa, ON: Department of Citizenship and Immigration. Library and Archives Canada, Indian Affairs Annual Reports, 1864-1990, ArchiviaNet.

–. 1954. *Report of Indian Affairs Branch for the Fiscal Year Ended March 31, 1954.* Ottawa: Department of Citizenship and Immigration. Library and Archives Canada, Indian Affairs Annual Reports, 1864-1990, ArchiviaNet.

CBC News. 2008. PM cites "sad chapter" in apology for residential school. June 11. www.cbc.ca/canada/.

–. 2010a. A history of residential schools. June 14. http://www.cbc.ca/news/.

–. 2010b. N.L. residential school lawsuit can proceed. June 9. *CBC News*. http://www.cbc.ca/news/.

Department of Indian Affairs. 1910. *Calisthenics and Games: Prescribed for Use in All Indian Schools*. Ottawa: Government Printing Bureau.

Eisenhardt, J. 1950. *Tentative Plans in Regard to the Program of Physical Education, Sports, Games and Recreation for the Indian Population.* Report prepared for Philip Phelan, superintendent of Education, Indian Affairs Branch. Section B, Item 1(a)(ii), Residential Schools, Indoor Facilities. Private collection.

Evening Citizen. 1951. Twelve Indian puck-toters here for bantam series. April 12, p. 20. Private collection.

Forsyth, J. 2005. The power to define: A history of the Tom Longboat Awards, 1951-2001. PhD diss., University of Western Ontario.

–. 2007. The *Indian Act* and the (re)shaping of Canadian Aboriginal sport practices. *International Journal of Canadian Studies* 35: 95-111.

Foucault, M. 1977. *Discipline and Punish: The Birth of the Prison.* Translated by A. Sheridan. New York: Pantheon Books.

Gutting, G. 2005. *Foucault: A Very Short Introduction.* New York: Oxford University Press.

Harvey, J., and R. Sparks. 1991. The politics of the body in the context of modernity. *Quest* 43: 164-89.

Hawthorn, H.B. 1967. *A Survey of the Contemporary Indians of Canada: A Report on the Economic, Political, Educational Needs and Policies; Part 2.* Ottawa: Indian Affairs Branch.

Heikkala, J. 1993. Discipline and excel: Techniques of the self and body and the logic of competition. *Sociology of Sport Journal* 10: 397-412.

Johnston, B. 1988. *Indian School Days.* Toronto: Key Porter.

Kelm, M. 2001. *Colonizing Bodies: Aboriginal Health and Healing in British Columbia, 1900-1950.* Vancouver: UBC Press.
Kirk, D. 1998. *Schooling Bodies: School Practice and Public Discourse, 1880-1950.* London, UK: Leicester University Press.
Miller, J.R. 1996. *Shingwaulk's Vision: A History of Native Residential Schools.* Toronto: University of Toronto Press.
Milloy, J. 1999. *A National Crime: The Canadian Government and the Residential School System, 1879-1986.* Winnipeg: University of Manitoba Press.
Morrow, D. 1977. The Strathcona Trust in Ontario, 1911-1939. *Canadian Journal of History of Sport and Physical Education* 8(1): 71-99.
National Indian Brotherhood. 1988. *Tradition and Education: Towards a Vision of Our Future.* Vol. 1. Ottawa: National Indian Brotherhood and Assembly of First Nations.
Paraschak, V. 1998. "Reasonable amusements": Connecting the strands of physical culture in Native lives. *Sport History Review* 28(1): 121-31.
Persson, D. 1986. The changing experience of Indian residential schooling: Blue Quills, 1931-1970. In J. Barman, Y. Hébert, and D. McCaskill, eds. *Indian Education in Canada,* vol. 1, *The Legacy* (150-67). Vancouver: UBC Press.
Pettipas, K. 1994. *Severing the Ties That Bind: Government Repression of Indigenous Religious Ceremonies on the Prairies.* Winnipeg: University of Manitoba Press.
Roth, M.S. 1981. Foucault's "history of the present." *History and Theory* 20(1): 32-46.
Royal Commission on Aboriginal Peoples. 1996. *Looking Forward, Looking Back: Report of the Royal Commission on Aboriginal Peoples.* Vol. 1. Ottawa: Minister of Supply and Services Canada. http://www.collectionscanada.gc.ca/.
Sault Daily Star. 1951. Sault agrees to assist Garden River sports plan. July 4, p. 14. Private collection.
Simpson, M.J.M. n.d. A history of the Rice Lake Indians by Mary Jane Muskrat Simpson – The Alderville Residential School. http://www.totemconsulting.ca/.
The Journal. 1951. Bush-to-bank-streak leaves boys bug-eyed. April 12. Private collection.
Truth and Reconciliation Commission of Canada. n.d.a. About us, residential schools. http://www.trc-cvr.ca/.
–. n.d.b. Residential school locations. http://www.trc.ca/websites/.

2 Indigenous Peoples and Canadian-Hosted Olympic Games

CHRISTINE M. O'BONSAWIN

On three occasions – the 1976 Montreal Summer Olympic Games, the 1988 Calgary Winter Olympic Games, and the 2010 Vancouver Winter Olympic Games – the International Olympic Committee (IOC) has awarded the coveted Olympic Games to Canadian cities. In each case, Canadian Olympic organizers have included indigenous imagery in their events and marketing to promote a celebratory sense of civic and national identity. For example, in the closing ceremony of the 1976 Montreal Games, "Indian hosts" entertained audiences, both live and televised, as they performed, danced, and escorted athletes and Olympic dignitaries around Montreal's Olympic Stadium. In the case of the 1988 Calgary Games, indigenous symbolism went beyond the ceremonies to be incorporated into the medal designs and sponsored exhibitions. Most recently, organizers for the 2010 Vancouver Games went further still by achieving "unprecedented Aboriginal participation in the planning and hosting" of the Games and by encouraging indigenous people to participate as athletes, volunteers, employees, entrepreneurs, artists, performers, spectators, and cultural ambassadors (Aboriginal Participation 2009). In each of the three Games, indigenous people and indigenous imagery served the organizational and political needs of the Canadian organizing committees; however, this inclusion has not always been celebratory. In fact, on many occasions, the use of indigenous imagery in Canadian Olympic programs has been accompanied by controversy and tensions as indigenous people and their supporters challenged and protested inaccurate and appropriated representations. Beyond summarizing the use and inclusion of indigenous imagery in the Olympic programs of Montreal 1976, Calgary 1988, and Vancouver 2010, this chapter offers a critical reflection on what is often considered to be the imprudent use of indigenous imagery in the programs of Canadian-hosted Olympic Games.[1]

1976 Montreal Summer Olympic Games

The 1976 Montreal Summer Olympic Games were held from July 17 to August 1. These being the first Games to be held on Canadian soil, Montreal organizers were without a national Olympic model to emulate. Fortunately, the success of Montreal Expo 67: Man and His World provided Olympic organizers with a blueprint for hosting the Games. In both instances, the inclusion and exhibition of indigenous people and symbols were an essential part of strategy.

In the planning of Expo 67, tensions arose concerning the exhibition of indigenous people and cultures. Since its formation in 1961, the National Indian Council (NIC), a representative national body for Indian and Métis rights, lobbied Expo 67 organizers for inclusion; the NIC was eventually granted control (albeit for a short period) over its own independent Indian exhibit. The NIC proposed that its exhibit present distinctively indigenous perspectives regarding the historic oppression and ongoing mistreatment of First Nations people in Canada. By 1964, increased conflict and disorganization within the NIC led Expo 67 organizers to ask the Department of Indian Affairs and Northern Development (DIAND), the federal department responsible for Indian administration in Canada, to intervene by working in partnership with the NIC to develop the exhibit. Growing conflict within the NIC had gravely limited its ability to use the Expo to advance indigenous interests within Canada and worldwide (Rutherdale and Miller 2006). DIAND filled the void and produced an exhibit that aligned with its century-long policy of assimilation by promoting narratives of a romantic, yet doomed, Indian past. Internal conflicts would eventually split the NIC into two Aboriginal political organizations: the Canadian Métis Society (which was renamed the Native Council of Canada in 1970, and again renamed the Congress of Aboriginal Peoples in 1993) and the National Indian Brotherhood (now the Assembly of First Nations).

Despite the tenuous partnership between the NIC and DIAND, the Indian Pavilion offered a groundbreaking approach in the world's fair model, as it allowed for indigenous and settler people to jointly explore their arduous relationships in historical and present-day Canada (Brydon 1997). Whether or not they were aware of competing tensions surrounding the exhibit, fairgoers were presented with what Rutherdale and Miller (2006, 160) described as a "balanced theme of Indians 'joining the mainstream' with assertions of First Nations' pride, grievance, and entitlement." These tensions became obvious in the education display, where DIAND's portrayal of smiling Indian youth was positioned alongside and in sharp contrast to indigenous messages that described residential schools as alienating and harmful for their children. Furthermore, indigenous works of art, which the NIC hoped would serve as educational instruments showing the beauty and sophistication of indigenous histories and cultures, contrasted with DIAND's preference for the enduring ethnographic prototype, which positioned Indian artifacts as simple and primitive. In the end, DIAND's traditional theme of Indian assimilation was overshadowed by indigenous expressionism as the Indian Pavilion "awakened non-Native Canadians to both the plight of Aboriginal peoples and their increasing unwillingness to suffer in silence" (ibid., 148).

Following the success of Expo 67, and in an effort to once again turn the world's attention to Montreal, Mayor Jean Drapeau successfully lobbied the IOC to bring, for the first time in the history of the movement, its coveted Olympic Games to Canada. In an attempt to commemorate and showcase indigenous cultures in the Olympic program, and to enhance Canadian national identity at home and abroad, Montreal organizers strategically included indigenous people and imagery in the closing ceremony at a time when Canadian indigenous and government relations were operating under heightened tensions.

In the 1970s, Canadian prime minister Pierre Elliott Trudeau was trying to implement the pillars of his new nation-building project, which included efforts toward bilingualism, multiculturalism, and a renewed federalism. Under Trudeau's vision of liberalism, the rights of indigenous people were entrenched in a discourse of multiculturalism that proposed equality among all Canadians. Within this framework, indigenous rights could coexist only in relation to the individual rights and freedoms of all Canadians. For example, in the late 1960s, Trudeau worked in partnership with the minister of Indian Affairs and Northern Development, Jean Chrétien, to develop what would eventually become the *Statement of the Government of Canada on Indian Policy (1969)*, commonly referred to as the White Paper. Essentially, this policy initiative proposed to abolish DIAND, the Indian Act (legislation outlining the federal government's relationship to Indians), Indian status, and treaty obligations. The proposal was tantamount to a Liberal attempt at assimilation. In short, Trudeau's government was recommending the incorporation of indigenous people as an ethnic minority into Canada's national fabric by eliminating their special historical status (Turner 2006). This policy was ultimately rejected by indigenous people and their supporters, but it highlights hegemonic thinking that called for the dismissal of indigenous rights. Consequently, it may be argued that indigenous influence, consultation, expressionism, and activism at this time, and at events such as the Montreal Olympic Games, could be suppressed under the rhetoric of Trudeau's "multiculturalism" campaign.

Numerous scholarly accounts detail the economic disparities and political activism associated with the 1976 Olympics in Montreal. In contrast, nominal attention, public or academic, has been paid to the inclusion of indigenous people and imagery in these Games. When indigenous issues are mentioned, it is normally within the context of the well-organized and festive closing ceremony, with its record-breaking attendance. A case in point is *Selling the Five Rings: The International Olympic Committee and the Rise of Olympic Commercialism* (Barney, Wenn, and Martyn 2004). In it, the authors recount how "brightly costumed Indians, representing 'all the tribes of Canada,' entered the stadium accompanied by 'native' music piped through the stadium sound system – entering the five interlocking rings by the young women in white, they erected a large teepee in the centre of each" (ibid., 124). This quote conveys a massive celebration that included Canada's indigenous populations in a significant way, which is to some extent true. That being said, such descriptions further reinforce the unequal power relations that have always existed between Olympic organizers and volunteer performers, in this case, Aboriginal people. Indeed, a closer examination of the closing ceremony for the 1976 Games, as well as footage from the CBC's official television coverage of the event, reveals an interesting yet troubling dynamic.

In the hours leading up to the closing ceremony, the Montreal Olympic Games Organizing Committee (COJO) provided the media with the official program guide, titled the *Closing Ceremony Programme: Games of the XXI Olympiad Montréal 1976*, a document that served as a reference and interpretation tool for national and international media. As the national television rights holder for Canada, CBC was responsible for transmitting visual images of and providing commentary on the ceremony. The commentary relied heavily on well-worn stereotypes to convey evocative images to the world, though sometimes the broadcasters strayed from the script altogether. For example, the *Closing Ceremony Programme* stated:

> To the accompaniment of tribal music of the North American Indians, played on traditional instruments, 75 Indians enter the arena via the northwest gate in the form of an arrowhead ... They, in turn, are followed by the parade of teams, with an escort provided by a further contingent of Indians. All the Indian tribes of Canada are represented ... The shield-bearers and flag-bearers form a semi-circle behind the rostrum and the athletes and the escort of Indians gather in the five interlocking rings. (Montréal Olympic Games Organizing Committee 1976, 21)

The program incorrectly identified "all the Indian tribes of Canada" as being represented, but CBC commentators specified that the indigenous participants were, in fact, representatives from nine First Nations in Quebec, including "the Abenaki, the Algonquin, the Atikamekw, the Cree, the Huron, the Mi'gmaq, the Mohawk, the Montagnais, and the Naskapi" (*CBC News* 1976). And yet, even though CBC commentators demonstrated basic knowledge about tribal affiliations, they did not mention that of the approximately 450 "Indian hosts" only 200 were Aboriginal people. As Forsyth (2002) points out, the other 250 "Indian hosts" were non-indigenous members from a local dance troupe who were hired for the closing performance. Organizers cited an overextended Olympic budget as grounds for not bussing indigenous representatives in from the surrounding communities for regular practices. The 250 non-indigenous performers, dressed and painted to look like "Indians," were responsible for leading the indigenous participants into the stadium in a supposedly "traditional" Native dance.

Forsyth (2002) goes on to show how the nine First Nations were invited to participate in a commemoration ceremony that, in fact, emphasized and reinforced their marginal political positions in Canadian society: "Although Olympic organizers stated publicly that the Closing Ceremony was being held to honor Canada's Aboriginal peoples, the organizers did not consult with the populations who they proposed to respect in the construction of the program. From start to finish, the celebration was designed *by* Olympic organizers *for* Aboriginal peoples" (72, emphasis in original). For the closing ceremony, every spectacular element, from the entry to the exit, was developed by non-indigenous planners. It is well documented that Canadian choreographer Michel Cartier developed the dance performances, and

Canadian composer André Mathieu devised the musical inspiration, which included the musical score *La Danse Sauvage* (*The Savage Dance*) (Montréal Olympic Games Organizing Committee 1976).

In view of those facts, Forsyth (2002, 72) asks, seeing as "these images were culturally demeaning and fraught with ideological implications, why would Aboriginal peoples participate?" There are several possible answers to this query. First, some First Nations communities participated in the Montreal Games to follow up on a promise made by local politicians. In light of the successful Indian Pavilion at Expo 67, Mayor Drapeau agreed to call upon local First Nations for future events. Second, some First Nations, such as the people from Kahnawake, a Mohawk community located a few kilometres outside Montreal, have a long and proud history of showmanship such that performing in events like Expo 67 and the Olympic Games were a means for them to connect to a part of their indigenous cultural heritage (Forsyth 2002). Third, participation in international events provided a platform for political expression and resistance, as was the case with Expo 67.

Unlike Expo 67, however, indigenous people were not included in the organizing and planning of Olympic events and programs, even where indigenous representations were prominently featured. There are numerous possibilities for this exclusion. It can be argued that an overextended Olympic budget limited consultations with concerned groups. It is also possible that the strict Olympic formula for carrying out the Games, as dictated by the IOC, did not provide adequate instructions for, or even allow, Olympic organizing committees to dialogue and consult with concerned groups. As well, with these being the first Olympic Games to be hosted in Canada, organizers did not have a clear organizational blueprint to follow. It could also be argued that excluding indigenous people from consultations was indicative of shifting political attitudes of the day, which appeared to favour liberal ideals of individual rights and freedoms (i.e., the 1969 White Paper and the constitutional reform process throughout the 1970s) over unique historical rights owed to the indigenous Canadians. Or, indigenous exclusion was a combination of some or all of the above explanations. Regardless of the rationale, and despite Olympic organizers' claim to be honouring the indigenous people of Canada, it is clear that organizers did not consult with the people whom they professed to be celebrating. From a scholarly and pragmatic point of view, the model put in place for indigenous involvement in the 1976 Games was a problem because it served as the standard that future Olympic organizers would use to present a unique Canadian identity to the world.

For the 1988 Winter Olympic Games in Calgary, indigenous imagery was again central to Canada's assertion of a distinct, sophisticated, and diverse national character. Whereas organizers for the 1976 Montreal Games did not consult with indigenous groups, organizers for the 1988 Games did, but developed a haphazard model for interacting with and trying to involve indigenous representatives. As such, at the 1988 Games, Aboriginal inclusion went beyond the ceremonies as indigenous people, and specifically their imagery, were prominently featured in the lead-up to and throughout the staging of the Games.

1988 Calgary Winter Olympic Games

The Games in Calgary were held from February 13 to 28, 1988. Organizers for this western Canadian show adopted a different organizational model from organizers for Montreal. In Calgary, organizers consulted with some indigenous people on the inclusion of indigenous symbols in the Olympic program. For example, the interests of Treaty 7 nations (consisting primarily of Blackfoot territories in southern Alberta) were represented by Sykes Powderface, a prominent speaker on Aboriginal treaty rights. In the lead-up to the 2002 Salt Lake City Winter Olympic Games, and with mounting American Indian disappproval of Olympic organizing initiatives, Powderface was asked by Salt Lake media to reflect on his experiences with the 1988 Games. He explained how pressure from indigenous people and indigenous communities greatly influenced the organizing committee's eventual decision to include indigenous people in the planning of the 1988 Games (Dyreson 1998). Prior to the Calgary Games, Powderface was hired by the Treaty 7 nations to serve as a liaison with the Olympiques Calgary Olympics '88 (OCO '88), the organizing committee for the Games, and to manage Olympic and band funds (Wamsley and Heine 1996). Despite the appearance of amiable working relationships between Olympic organizers and indigenous groups, tensions quickly arose in the planning stages of the Games as non-Olympic-aligned indigenous people and their supporters campaigned against the incorporation of indigenous insignia into Olympic programming.

It was a small indigenous community of approximately five hundred people from northern Alberta – the Lubicon Lake Indian Nation – that presented the biggest hurdle for organizers keen to put on a good show. In brief, the historical struggles of the Lubicon Cree can be traced to June 1899. At this time, a treaty commission travelled to northern Alberta and arrived at Lesser Slave Lake in order to commence Treaty 8 negotiations with indigenous populations. One month later, negotiations were complete, even though the commissioners were well aware that not all populations had been reached. As a result, a second commission was appointed in the summer of 1900 to treaty with those who had been missed in the first round of negotiations (Ferreira 1992). In a report filed in December 1900, Commissioner J.A. Macrae noted, "There yet remains a number of persons leading an Indian life in the country north of Lesser Slave lake, who have not accepted treaty as Indians, or scrip as half-breed, but this is not so much through indisposition to do so as because they live at points distant from those visited, and are not pressed by want. The Indians of all parts of the territory who have not been paid annuity probably number about 500" (ibid., 3). The Lubicon Lake Cree were among the estimated five hundred; however, we now know that the actual number of indigenous people in northern Alberta far exceeded this number.

By the late 1930s, the Lubicon were actively seeking formal recognition under Treaty 8. Even so, as Goddard (1991) has suggested, with the onset of the Second World War, settling treaty was a low priority for federal officials, whose attention and budgets had been redirected to the war effort. Moreover, by this time significant amounts of Crown lands, including Lubicon territory, had been transferred to the provinces, further complicating treaty negotiations for indigenous groups throughout Canada. By the 1950s, oil exploration began in northern Alberta, and with the establishment of all-weather roads into the northern regions by the 1970s, indigenous people were suffering from drastically changing environments and lifestyles. During the Lubicon's struggle to secure treaty while also protecting their territories from the encroachment of settlers and the illegal sale of their lands to petroleum companies, their social conditions drastically deteriorated – to the point where they found themselves in an intolerable state of affairs. By the mid-1980s, the Lubicon were facing a 93 percent decline in their annual trapping income, high rates of alcoholism, a tuberculosis crisis, and malnourishment in the community (Ferreira 1992). In an attempt to protect the Lubicon Cree from further encroachment, and in an effort to engage the federal and provincial governments in treaty negations, the chief of the Lubicon Cree, Bernard Ominayak, brought the interests of this small indigenous nation to national and international forums. In 1986, Ominayak and the Lubicon focused their attention on the largest international event in the world – the Olympic Games.

Under the leadership of Chief Ominayak, the Lubicon Cree called for an international boycott of the 1988 Calgary Games. It quickly became clear to the Lubicon Cree and their supporters that the international sport community would not understand, nor empathize with, the hardships and sufferings of this small indigenous nation. Rather than call upon the international sport community, the Lubicon Cree decided to call for a boycott of a cultural (non-sport) Olympic event – a Native art display titled *Forget Not My World: Exploring the Native Canadian Heritage*, which was to be hosted by the Glenbow Museum in Calgary during the Games (Ferreira 1992). The primary objective of this exhibit was "to bring together, for the first time, the best examples of native Canadian material culture from collections around the world" (McManus 1991, 202). However, as Wamsley and Heine (1996, 174) acknowledge, for Chief Ominayak, the absurdity of this proposal was evident: "[The] irony of using a display of North American Indian artifacts to attract people to the Winter Olympics being organized by interests who are still actively seeking to destroy Indian people seems painfully obvious." In an attempt to garner public national and international support, the Lubicon Cree carried out an aggressive letter-writing campaign requesting potential lending museums to decline invitations from the Glenbow Museum and to withhold artifacts. Beyond condemning the fundamental purpose of the exhibit, the Lubicon further criticized the curatorial makeup and display proposals, sponsorship, and the lending and borrowing policies implemented for the exhibit through their aggressive letter-writing campaign.

The Glenbow Museum established a curatorial committee, under the leadership of head curator Julia D. Harrison. The committee comprised six regional specialists who were responsible for the curatorship of six cultural-area designations, including the Atlantic – East Coast (Ruth Holmes Whitehead), the Northern Woodlands (Ruth B. Phillips), the Northern Plains (Ted J. Brasser), the Northern Athapaskan – Western Subarctic (Judy Thompson), the Inuit-Arctic (Bernadette Driscoll), and the Northwest Coast (Martin J. Reid) (Harrison 1988). Lubicon opposition called attention to the fact that whereas all of the non-indigenous "experts" were fully paid for their work, the Native Liaison Committee worked on a voluntary basis. Meanwhile, despite the national focus of the exhibit, the Native Liaison Committee was composed primarily of indigenous representatives from Treaty 7 nations (McManus 1991). Furthermore, organizers were criticized for their configuration of the "visitor path," which symbolically traced the footsteps of early Europeans on a path of colonial settlement from the east to the west. The proposed title, *Forget Not My World: Exploring the Native Canadian Heritage*, was quickly changed when exhibit critiques suggested that it patronizingly implied that indigenous people (and their respective cultures) had disappeared from the Canadian cultural landscape (Phillips 2002). In an effort to position the exhibit in a more celebratory climate, organizers promptly changed the title to *The Spirit Sings: Artistic Traditions of Canada's First Peoples.*

As for the sponsorship of the proposed exhibit, Lubicon opponents drew attention to the fact that the exhibit was being sponsored by the very entities violating and renouncing Lubicon interests. The total budget for the display was $2.6 million, with major donations from Shell Canada ($1.1 million), the Olympic Arts Festival ($600,000), and the federal government ($300,000). The federal government's support came by way of the Canadian Museum of Civilization, which entered into a collaborative organizational process with the Glenbow Museum for this Olympic event (Wolosen 1988). The Lubicon Cree and their supporters particularly criticized the financial support from Shell Canada and the federal government, suggesting that it was both ironic and hypocritical that these two entities were sponsoring a Native art display that claimed to be "celebrating" indigenous material culture when, in fact, both were benefiting from the expropriation and exploitation of indigenous lands, including non-surrendered Lubicon lands (Ferreira 1992).

Lubicon opposition to *The Spirit Sings* also called attention to the Glenbow's borrowing of 665 "stolen" artifacts from museums around the world: the majority of these objects had been expatriated from their indigenous owners and lands more than three hundred years earlier. Some people questioned the incongruity of celebrating artifacts that had been taken hundreds of years previously and brought to Europe to, in part, satisfy public consumption of indigenous curios (Crossingham 1987a, 3). *The Spirit Sings* caused significant distress for some indigenous people, as many of the objects were sacred and not intended for public display. Some groups turned to the law to address what they saw as ongoing historical injustice. For instance, the Mohawk Council of Kahnawà:ke filed an injunction against the Glenbow Museum because a False Face mask, a sacred object in Mohawk culture, was included in the display. The mask was removed for a two-week period while Glenbow officials appealed the court order. The final verdict was in favour of the Glenbow Museum, and the mask was placed back on display. However, when the Canadian Museum of Civilization hosted *The Spirit Sings* exhibit from June 30 to November 6, 1988, it opted not to display the mask. It was (and continues to be) a principle of the Museum of Civilization not to display False Face masks, as stipulated in a 1981 policy prohibiting the exhibition of this sacred Mohawk object (Young Man 1990).

At the conclusion of *The Spirit Sings*, Glenbow officials were responsible for returning all borrowed artifacts to the lending museums. Despite the fact that many of these objects had been taken from their original owners and territories, Glenbow officials made no effort to establish a process of repatriation to return the objects to their rightful owners. Indigenous people throughout Canada and elsewhere have since pressed for the return of important objects through processes of repatriation. According to Truscott (2006, 1), repatriation for indigenous people involves "appeals for the return of their cultural property[, which] is fuelled by a strong belief that the spirits of the dead cannot rest until returned to their 'Country,' but is also part of a general reassertion of control over their cultural heritage, whether archaeological sites, sacred landscapes or cultural material, and practice in cultural centres and keeping places."

Critics believed that decisions made by the Glenbow Museum curatorial officials constituted a second and more disgraceful wave of thievery of indigenous artifacts, as these objects were being returned to their country of origin on a temporary basis only. Not only did the Glenbow Museum make no effort to establish a process of repatriation, it made no effort to assist indigenous people in entering such a process themselves with the lending institutions. Consequently, at the conclusion of *The Spirit Sings* exhibit, Glenbow officials dutifully returned all artifacts to their "legal" owners – the lending museums (McManus 1991).

The Lubicon Cree and Glenbow officials disagreed as to whether or not the letter-writing campaign was, in fact, effectual. Shortly after the conclusion of the exhibit, Glenbow officials declared their belief that the Lubicon's strategies did not diminish the overall success of the display. Harrison, the head curator, published an article in *Anthropology Today* titled "*The Spirit Sings* and the future of anthropology." In this piece, Harrison (1988, 8) defended the actions of the Glenbow by suggesting that the museum "undertook to be socially responsible rather than politically active." In terms of public response, Harrison cited statistical evidence of the exhibit's overall success. She pointed out that of the 110 museums contacted by the Lubicon Cree, only 12 supported the boycott initiatives. She also noted that "the total number of tickets sold was 126,506, which is the largest number of people that have ever visited a Glenbow exhibition. It more than doubled the museum's previous record. The opening was one of the largest the Glenbow has had with an estimated 3,500 people in attendance" (ibid.). Although Harrison acknowledged that about 150 protesters attended the opening of the exhibit, she went on to criticize the media's failure to make note of "the much larger number attending inside the museum" (ibid.). Harrison admitted that the Lubicon Cree had successfully garnered the support of international organizations such as the World Council of Churches and the European Parliament. Still, she dismissed the credibility of this support by pointing out that neither of these entities contacted the Glenbow Museum for clarification on the matter.

From the perspectives of the Lubicon Cree and their supporters, the events surrounding the boycott unfolded much differently than Harrison depicted. First, whereas Harrison claimed that twelve museums declined invitations to participate, the Lubicon asserted that twenty-three museums supported the boycott by refusing to lend artifacts to the Glenbow Museum. Second, the Lubicon Cree and the media maintained that there were approximately 200 protestors present at the opening of *The Spirit Sings* exhibit as opposed to the Glenbow's estimated 150 (Goddard 1991). Finally, according to the Lubicon Cree, they had the support not only of international organizations such as the World Council of Churches and the European Parliament but also of prominent organizations such as the Assembly of First Nations, World Council of Indigenous Peoples, National Congress of American Indians, Indian Association of Alberta, Métis Association of Alberta (now the Métis Nation of Alberta), and the Grand Council of the Crees in Quebec (Wamsley and Heine 1996). With such national and international support, the federal government was forced back to the treaty negotiating table only two weeks after the Lubicon Cree had announced its boycott of the Calgary Games (Ominayak 1989).

Chief Ominayak stated, in the end, that the Lubicon had achieved what they had set out to do: bring international attention to a dire local matter. Beyond the support of international museums and protestors, the Lubicon Cree had gained the support of prominent indigenous leaders and academics from all over Canada, including Matthew Coon Come, then chief of the Quebec Cree (later elected grand chief of the Assembly of First Nations), who was among the protesters at the opening of the exhibit. At this event, Coon Come publicly stated, "I say if we share the flame, we should share the blame, and we must share the shame. It is a national shame for the Canadian people to allow the governments of Alberta and Canada to continue the bureaucratic warfare" (Goddard 1991, 158).

In addition, Bruce Trigger, professor of ethnology and honorary curator of ethnology at McGill University's McCord Museum, resigned from his curatorship when the McCord's Board of Governors rejected his request to withdraw its materials from *The Spirit Sings*. In late 1988, Trigger responded to Harrison's positional piece in *Anthropology Today*. In his statement, Trigger defended his decision to resign from the honorary curator position and questioned the ongoing political and social mistreatment of indigenous people in Canada. Trigger (1988, 9) quoted his own resignation letter to the McCord Museum, which stated:

> It is a national disgrace that almost 500 years after the first Europeans explored the shores of Canada, the descendants of its first inhabitants should remain more marginal to our national life, more politically powerless, and more impoverished than any other ethnic group. Native People cannot be expected to stand forever at the end of the line; their interests [need] to be considered when everyone else's have been satisfied. It is also unacceptable that attempts should be made to continue to subject these people to a paternalistic regime in which non-Native Canadians decide what is in the best interests of Native People.

Trigger went on to criticize not only the actions of the Glenbow, which had failed to initiate a process for repatriation, but also the failures of all museums that stored indigenous artifacts in backrooms and as personal possessions. He further argued that there had been a grave setback to any form of rapprochement when museums such as the Glenbow willingly ignored indigenous requests to manage their own cultural heritage (Trigger 1988).

Although Chief Ominayak and the Lubicon Lake Cree directed the majority of their energies to *The Spirit Sings* exhibit, there were other events in the cultural program of the Calgary Olympic Games that warranted attention from the Lubicon and their supporters. Similar to the controversy surrounding the exhibit, the torch run was criticized for being sponsored by Petro-Canada, as this conglomerate was invading indigenous territories (including Lubicon lands) across Canada. The Olympic flame began its cross-Canada journey in St. John's, Newfoundland, in November 1987, where it was met by a small group of protesters from the Native Peoples' Support Group of Newfoundland and Labrador (a provincial coalition working in support of Native rights in Newfoundland and Labrador, as well as throughout Canada). This group distributed approximately one hundred pamphlets outlining the arduous contact history and ongoing plights of the Lubicon (Booth 1987). In December 1987, the Mohawk Council of Kahnawà:ke declared its solidarity with the Lubicon. Before the torch was to travel through the Mohawk community of Kahnawake, officials at Petro-Canada contemplated whether to reroute the relay in order to avoid what they thought could be a violent protest (Crossingham 1987a). Members of Kahnawake assured relay organizers that they would use this opportunity to peacefully show their unity with the Lubicon Cree, and promised that no aggressive or violent tactics would be used. On December 11, 1987, seven hundred Mohawk supporters lined the streets, some holding signs that read "Share the Blame" and "Justice for the Lubicon," as the Olympic torch travelled through Kahnawake. Alwyn Morris, gold and bronze kayaking medallist from the 1984 Los Angeles Summer Olympic Games and member of Kahnawake, declared his support for the Lubicon in front of the assembled crowd that was protesting the Olympic torch run (Crossingham 1988). The Peguis Cree First Nation from Manitoba also announced that it would support the Lubicon by joining the torch protest when it arrived at the Ontario-Manitoba border in mid-January. In the end, Lubicon supporters and protesters were present along the relay route in every province except Prince Edward Island (Booth 1987).

Despite widespread support for Lubicon interests, the concerns of protesters were often silenced and at times ridiculed by the corporate elite and Olympic organizers. For example, Frank King, former chairman of OCO '88, criticized protest action along the torch route:

> As I stood in the cold night watching the uplifting effect the flame had on people, I thought back to several occasions when the supporters of the Lubicon Lake Indian land claims tried to bring public opinion to their side of the dispute by waving banners and signs at some of the flame celebrations. The so-called Lubicon "boycott" of our Games succeeded in drawing governments back to the bargaining table. Most Canadians would love to see this and hundreds of other Native land claims settled fairly. If this process is speeded up because the Olympics produced a platform for the Lubicon people, good. But the negative placards of Lubicon supporters along the torch relay route seemed out of place and ineffective. The public and the media moved unsympathetically around the protesters, and the message lost momentum. Under the glow from the ubiquitous Olympic-torch candles, people hugged and shook hands in friendship. There was no room for defiance or confrontation here, and the protesters' message was overwhelmed. (King 1991, 234)

Along the torch route, protesters had difficulty attracting media attention, specifically television. Petro-Canada had assigned its own videographers to record the events and then edited the footage before distributing it to networks (Goddard 1991). The media too dismissed Lubicon activism. On more than one occasion, the *Calgary Herald* published derogatory accounts of Lubicon protests along the torch relay route. One cartoon depicted a group of indigenous people getting burned as they blockaded the route. Cartoonist Vance Rodewalt defended his drawing, stating, "I don't believe that being a minority, even a suppressed minority, gives that minority the license to disregard the law and become a major pain in the butt" (Crossingham 1987b, 1).

In an effort to ensure that the Calgary Olympics maintained its apolitical veneer, members of OCO '88 coordinated the Native Involvement Program and the Native Participation Program. According to Wamsley and Heine (1996), the Native Involvement Program was "designed to 'continue to try to gain some native friends – specifically the Treaty 7 peoples' (to which the Lubicon are not a party). Federal Olympic coordinator Gerald Berger noted that these strategies served to keep the Olympic organizing committee, as he phrased it, 'non-political'" (ibid., 175). The Native Participation Program was established in mid-1987 with the purpose of supporting indigenous involvement in the Games. Through this initiative, OCO '88 organized a Native trade show, a Native youth conference, and powwow competitions (Wamsley and Heine 1994). For the most part, these programs and events were to be celebratory in nature; however, criticisms soon came from local indigenous groups concerning OCO '88 indigenous initiatives, particularly suggestions and decisions to incorporate indigenous imagery into the Olympic program.

In the early planning stages, Calgary Exhibition and Stampede Ltd. suggested to members of OCO '88 that an "Indian attack and wagon-burning" be part of the opening ceremony (Wamsley and Heine 1996, 173). The organizing committee did not incorporate this iconic western spectacle into the show, but it did optimize on the allure of Indian imagery. Accordingly, the 1988 Calgary Olympics were officially opened in a celebration that purported to commemorate the Province of Alberta and the Great Canadian West. As part of the show, organizers incorporated indigenous sounds, sights, and images into its colourful display of "western hospitality." Similar to the 1976 Montreal Olympics, television commentators interpreted the spectacle for the television-viewing public. Indigenous participants in the

Calgary opening ceremony came from Treaty 7 nations, including the Kainai (Blood), Aapátohsipikáni (Northern Peigans), Tsuu T'ina (Sarcee), and Nakoda (Stoney). When they entered the arena on horseback, the stadium announcer asked that the audience "please welcome *our* Native Albertans" and further acknowledged that these representatives came from "the tribes of Treaty 7 of 1877 – a treaty still in effect and *honoured* today" (ABC 1988, emphasis added). Paternalistic commentary reflected Canada's long political governance over and oppression of indigenous people, which was achieved through the administration of long-standing institutions such as the Department of Indian Affairs (now Aboriginal Affairs and Northern Development Canada) and the Indian Act 1876 (which remains in place to this day, notwithstanding its several amendments). In reporting to its American audience, commentators from ABC correctly identified the representatives as coming from "the Peigan, the Blood, the Sacree, and the Stoney tribes" (ibid.). Commentators for this American network went on to make various unfounded claims, including that Canada is "particularly proud of having dealt with its Indians – [there were] no Indian wars in western Canada in the 1800s of any significance" and "there are actually more Indians in North America now than at the time of Christopher Columbus" (ibid.). Television cameras panned the various displays that decorated McMahon Stadium, including a massive teepee that overarched the Olympic Cauldron. Throughout the ceremony, the audio recordings captured the sounds of indigenous vocals and drums, which became more audible when the young torch bearer ascended the stadium steps to light the Olympic cauldron.

Furthermore, on the reverse side of the Olympic medal was a profile illustration "of an athlete crowned with an olive wreath and an Indian with a headdress composed of ski sticks, skis, skate blades, a bobsleigh, a hockey stick, a luge and a rifle" (International Olympic Committee 2009). Stern criticism about this design was levelled by indigenous people. As Wamsley and Heine (1996, 173) have pointed out, "Greg Smith of the Peigan tribe, for one, argued that the medal design, while purporting to 'show the international community that Indians [were] a part of the games,' was in fact a deliberate attempt to distract attention from the Native resistance to the Games." Although Smith fittingly positions this as a distraction technique on the part of Calgary organizers, it is important to further consider the appropriateness of distorting, and thus misrepresenting, the cultural importance of this object.

An examination of the 1988 Calgary Winter Games reveals that both indigenous people and their imagery played a more prominent role in the Olympic program, particularly the cultural program, of these Games than the 1976 Montreal Summer Olympic Games. Whereas indigenous people and their imagery appeared to have been relegated to the closing ceremony of the 1976 Montreal Games, Calgary organizers seemed to be more interested in featuring indigenous people and culture. This inclusion was, no doubt, affected by the nationalist needs of Games organizers, but also by political distractions brought on by the Lubicon Cree and their supporters. In the case of Vancouver 2010, Canada had the opportunity to once again host the coveted Olympic Games, and once again Olympic organizers turned to indigenous people and cultures to support nationalistic and political agendas of Games operations. The next section demonstrates how organizers for the 2010 Vancouver Winter Games far surpassed the efforts put forth by Montreal and Calgary organizers to ensure that indigenous people and their cultures were prominent features of Games programming. Yet the inclusion of indigenous people and indigenous imagery appears to, once again, have been steeped in nationalist ideology and political controversy.

2010 Vancouver Winter Olympic and Paralympic Games

The Vancouver Olympic Organizing Committee for the 2010 Olympic and Paralympic Winter Games (VANOC) diverged from organizing models of Olympic Games previously hosted in Canada, as it proactively ensured that indigenous collaboration, participation, and representation were all visible components in the Games' planning, hosting, and legacies. Throughout the entire process, organizers made significant attempts to ensure that the participation of indigenous people and the celebration of their cultures were prominent and visible expressions of the Games. Accordingly, there were many instances where indigenous participation and collaboration were highly celebrated in the planning and hosting phases. Beyond acknowledging VANOC's positive initiatives, it is important to recognize the political realities that existed for indigenous people at the time, particularly in British Columbia, and critically consider indigenous opposition to the Vancouver Games.

For the most part, indigenous opposition to the 2010 Games rallied under a public campaign calling for "No Olympics on Stolen Native Land." Supporters of this campaign argued there was a pressing political reality in British Columbia that could not be forgotten in both the organizing and hosting of the 2010 Games, which was that the Games were being hosted on unceded and non-surrendered indigenous territories, or what some people considered to be stolen Native lands. With the exception of small tracts of land on Vancouver Island that were negotiated under the Douglas Treaties between 1850 and 1854, and a small portion of land in northeastern British Columbia that became part of Treaty 8 in 1899, the majority of the province remained (and is presently) unceded and non-surrendered. However, in the lead-up to the Games, interest in these negotiations was given new life and the pace accelerated as the federal and provincial governments attempted to work with third-party interests (i.e., oil, lumber, and fishing corporations) to establish land surrender agreements with indigenous populations. The entire process was complex and made more confusing for observers by the fact that the agreements were often misrepresented as treaties, a consequence of the name given to the entire process, the British Columbia treaty process. Although some "treaties" (read "land surrenders") were expedited for the purpose of the Games, and some indigenous leaders supported the new political-economic arrangements, the process was met with considerable resistance as indigenous leaders throughout the province questioned its integrity. To be sure, there was (and remains) a legitimate reason to be concerned since the word "treaty," which suggests a contract made between nations, was never employed in the text of any of the agreements negotiated (Alfred 2001).

In 1999, the IOC adopted *Olympic Movement's Agenda 21: Spot for Sustainable Development,* the IOC's plan for sustainable development and environmental safety. The plan was based on the United Nation's global action plan *Agenda 21,* which was accepted by consensus on June 14, 1992, by 182 governments at the UN Conference on Environment and Development (UNCED) in Rio de Janeiro. The Vancouver Olympic bid was put forth shortly after the IOC endorsed *Olympic Movement's Agenda 21.* One of the plan's priorities in advancing the goals of the Olympic Movement is to strengthen the role of "major groups" in the development and implementation of the Games, including women, youth, and indigenous people. According to the document, "Indigenous populations have strong historical ties to their environment and have played an important part in its preservation. The Olympic Movement ... intends: to encourage their sporting traditions; to contribute to the use of their traditional knowledge and know-how in matters of environment management in order to take appropriate action, notably in the regions where these populations originate; [and] to encourage access to sports participation for these populations" (International Olympic Committee 1999, 45). As Helen Lenskyj (2007) suggested, the *Olympic Movement's Agenda 21* merely serves as an invitational guide that bid, candidate, and host cities can take or leave. It does not officially oblige these entities to develop and implement the guidelines. Nevertheless, it can be argued that through this initiative, host cities are encouraged to develop cordial relationships with indigenous groups.

In an effort to fulfill its sustainability mandate, VANOC implemented an Aboriginal Participation and Collaboration program, the intent of which was to "achieve unprecedented Aboriginal participation in the planning and hosting of the 2010 Olympic and Paralympic Winter Games. We'll do this by developing strong relationships with Aboriginal peoples – First Nations, Inuit and Métis – and the support of [Olympic] Partners" (VANOC 2009a, 1). As VANOC acknowledged, *Olympic Movement's Agenda 21* supported the role of indigenous people in the Olympic Movement and in the organizing of the Games. However, despite being the first host city to implement the IOC's global action plan, VANOC remained notably challenged by the lack of direction the foundational document provided. Looking at the 1988 Calgary Winter Olympic Games (as well as the 2002 Salt Lake City Winter Olympic Games), Vancouver Olympic organizers pointed out that indigenous participation had traditionally been relegated exclusively to the cultural program, notably the ceremonies. In an effort to "go beyond" and "set the bar higher," as Calgary 1988 organizers had intended, VANOC established the Aboriginal Participation and Collaboration program. The program was built on five initiatives, including Partnership and Collaboration, Sport and Youth, Economic Development, Cultural Involvement, and Awareness and Education (VANOC 2009a). The goal of the Partnership and Collaboration initiative was to build relationships with the Four Host First Nations (FHFN), the Greater Vancouver urban Aboriginal community, Aboriginal people in British Columbia and Canada, and indigenous people of the world. The Sport and Youth initiative included a statement of cooperation with the Aboriginal Sport Circle (the national body for Aboriginal sport development in Canada), programs administered by 2010 Legacies Now, Aboriginal Youth Talent Identification events, the Aboriginal Youth Sport Legacy Fund, and the "Find Your Passion in Sport" poster campaign. Economic Development focused on an Aboriginal procurement strategy, Aboriginal licensing and merchandise, and Aboriginal tourism. The Cultural Involvement component promoted the adoption of the official emblem (logo), as well the staging of the 2006 handover ceremony in the closing ceremony of the 2006 Turin Winter Olympic Games. Furthermore, the Awareness and Education initiative focused primarily on communication strategies and media relations (VANOC 2009a). Despite these considerable efforts, there were a number of tensions regarding representational issues stemming from these initiatives.

In April 2005, VANOC unveiled "Ilanaaq," as the official emblem of the 2010 Winter Games was called. According to Olympic organizers, this emblem was a contemporary interpretation of an inuksuk, which is of great cultural importance to the Inuit people in Canada's North since it transmits important messages about their northern landscape and the people who inhabit it (Heyes 2002). The emblem was designed by the Vancouver-based Rivera Design Group. VANOC was heavily criticized for the emblem on two fronts: first, for not having consulted with local indigenous groups about the construction of the emblem and, second, for its selection of an emblem that was foreign to the landscape and cultural heritage of the people from the Northwest Coast. Indeed, indigenous people throughout the host province and indeed Canada protested the use of the inuksuk as the official emblem of the Games. Even community members from the FHFN (the Lil'wat, Musqueam, Squamish, and Tsleil-Waututh First Nations), on whose traditional lands the Games were being held, criticized the use of the Inuit symbol.

Upon attaining the rights to host the 2010 Games, VANOC immediately formalized its relationship with the four communities and then implemented the FHFN Protocol Agreement, which outlined the obligations between the organizing committee and its indigenous partners. The agreement was the first of its kind in Olympic history; it was also the first time the IOC recognized an indigenous group, the FHFN, as an official Olympic partner. However, partnerships are often fraught with challenges, and the Olympic-indigenous pairing experienced its fair share of problems. In particular, the adoption of the inuksuk caused many to reconsider VANOC's sincerity in honouring its relationship with the FHFN. Squamish hereditary chief Gerald Johnston publicly condemned the use of the logo, suggesting that its selection was in bad faith and that it was "akin to Russians planting their flag on the Parliament Buildings or the White House without permission" (*Daily Vancouver* 2005). The Inuit also voiced their discontent over the logo, arguing that it dishonoured the traditional functions of inuksuk and risked turning them into commodities that could be sold for tourist consumption (Heyes 2002). As scholar Scott Heyes (2002, 134) explained, "Inuksuit cannot be extracted from their setting, for to do so would be to Westernise them ... Inuksuit are living entities, but they may soon become 'artifacts' encased in glass cabinets if marketing continues unchecked." Despite ongoing opposition and dissatisfaction, VANOC refused to rescind its controversial adoption of the inuksuk and went on to suggest that Ilanaaq symbolized a deep appreciation for Canada's indigenous heritage, as well as the joy that all Canadians shared in celebrating winter (VANOC 2009b). Having publicly legitimized its use of the inuksuk for the Games, VANOC proudly promoted and endorsed the emblem to onlookers worldwide.

Then, in November 2007, VANOC unveiled its official Olympic mascots: Quatchi (a Sasquatch), Sumi (an animal spirit bear), Miga (a sea bear), and Mukmuk (a Vancouver Island marmot). Designers from Vancouver-based Meomi Design suggested that a significant source of inspiration for these designs came from local Aboriginal mythology (VANOC 2009c). The designers candidly acknowledged that the four mascots were loosely based on Northwest Coast indigenous legends of transformation, but they remained vague as to whether they engaged in an open process of consultation with local indigenous people – the most obvious group being the FHFN – about whether, or how, these symbols could be developed to support the Games. Similar to the criticisms surrounding the use of the inuksuk, VANOC was again heavily criticized for failing to consult with indigenous people about its use of indigenous symbols and for exploiting indigenous symbols for self-promotion and economic gain.

Indigenous people were also involved in the handover ceremony at the closing of the 2006 Winter Olympic Games in Turin, Italy. The handover ceremony is where the next hosts (in this case, Vancouver) are symbolically given responsibility for the Games. At the commencement of VANOC's performance in Turin, chiefs of the FHFN invited the world to their territories through a traditional Coast Salish Uts'am (Witness) ceremony. As Squamish leader telàlsemkin/siyam (chief Bill Williams) explained, to be called to the Uts'am or Witness is an exceedingly important local protocol, as it "is the actual cornerstone of our Longhouse tradition of what we call 'Chicayx.' Chicayx is our foundation of our law of how things get done. And in order to verify our law, we need people not just within our family, our community, but people from outside our community to come in and to verify that the event is taking place" (Doods 2007, 6).

The intent of the Uts'am ceremony is to call individuals to be a witness of an important event, of which the details can be recalled, shared, or verified at a later date. For the 2006 handover ceremony, each of the thirty-three thousand people in the audience received a special medallion designed by Squamish artist Jody Broomfield. After the indigenous leaders left centre stage, VANOC used the opportunity to tell its version of the history of Canada. This was imparted to the world through four segments: "The Witness," "The Kids," "The Teens," and "The Adults." This metaphorical maturation process was based on the easy-to-digest narrative of the modernization of Canada, where the country and its people had grown up, progressing from primitiveness to civilization to a fully urban and industrialized society, ready to share its history and prosperity with the world via the Olympic Games. During the eight-minute performance, members of Cirque du Soleil, École nationale de cirque, and Les 7 doigts de la main built a massive structure of snow-like blocks, so that at the end of the presentation, and with the strategic use of light and shadows, the structure was transformed to reveal Ilanaaq, the official emblem of the 2010 Olympics.

In the lead-up to the Games, VANOC and its partners made further attempts to incorporate and showcase indigenous people, cultures, and symbols. In October 2007, VANOC unveiled the designs for the 2010 Olympic medals. The medals were a collaborative effort between Corrine Hunt, a Vancouver-based artist of Komoyue and Tlingit heritage; Omer Arbel; the Royal Canadian Mint; Teck Resources; and VANOC's in-house design team. Each medal was cropped differently, and thus unique, though Hunt selected the orca whale motif for the Olympic Games medal and the raven motif for the Paralympic Games medal. Beyond the significance of these animals to Northwest Coast indigenous cultures, the designs were each inspired by Northwest Coast artistic traditions. For instance, the orca whale, representing strength, dignity, and teamwork, was designed in the style of the Northwest Coast bentwood box; the raven, associated with transformation and healing, as well as determination, creativity, and teamwork, appeared in a three-part composition in the style of a totem pole (VANOC 2009d).

Also in October 2007 it was announced that the Hudson's Bay Company (HBC), the official supplier of Canadian Olympic apparel, had selected a "knock-off" Cowichan sweater rather than authentic sweaters made by Coast Salish knitters. This decision caused debate in Coast Salish, Olympic, and public circles. Although the HBC insisted that the sweater included in the Olympic clothing line was not Cowichan-like, Coast Salish people argued that it was in fact a carefully crafted imitation of the highly popular Cowichan sweater. The HBC acknowledged that it had considered commissioning the Coast Salish people to knit these sweaters for the Olympic line but because of the HBC's strict deadlines for marketing and promotion, it was decided that the Coast Salish knitters would not be able to produce enough sweaters to meet the demands generated by Olympic tourism (Constantineau 2009). After much publicity, the HBC and Cowichan and other Coast Salish representatives reached an agreement to have the Cowichan sweaters sold in the First Nations Pavilion, as well as The Bay's flagship store in Vancouver (*CBC News* 2009).

Lastly, there was the Olympic torch relay, the Canadian leg of which began in Victoria. Starting on October 30, 2009, the Olympic torch travelled from Victoria through a thousand communities across Canada, including 115 First Nations communities, before arriving at its final destination in Vancouver. In Victoria, the relay was met by approximately four hundred protesters gathered in Spirit Square, in Centennial Square, for the Anti-Olympic Festival of Resistance. For this event, No2010 Victoria – which served as an umbrella group for Victoria's activist community and operated in solidarity with the No2010 Committee in Vancouver – organized a demonstration, which included representatives from local indigenous nations, grassroots organizations, and local supporters. After the initial rally, protesters followed the Olympic torch as it travelled through the streets of Victoria. The route was eventually changed as a result of significant protest action (No2010 2009). In the ensuing months, indigenous communities throughout the country, including the Mohawks of Kahnawake, protested the relay going through their land. They had protested the relay in 1988 on account of the Lubicon issue. For the 2010 Games, the Mohawks protested the presence of the RCMP as the foundation of the Vancouver 2010 Integrated Security Unit, the main security force employed for the Games, on the basis of a long and difficult history with this police force, as well as the fact the RCMP would function as a non-indigenous police force patrolling Mohawk territory, when the Mohawks had their own security force in place (Rakobowchuk 2009). Protesters in Kahnawake cited solidarity with the indigenous nations of British Columbia as one reason for resisting the arrival of the torch in their community. Cheryl Diabo, a member of the Mohawk Traditional Council, stated, "We don't support the torch coming through Kahnawake because of the land that's being destroyed in B.C. (for the Olympics) ... We support our native sisters and brothers who stood in line in our defence in 1990 during the [Oka] crises we faced, it's only natural that we do the same" (ibid.). Even though VANOC spent millions of dollars trying to secure indigenous cooperation, even going so far as to hire former grand chief of the Assembly of First Nations, Phil Fontaine, to win the support of communities along the route, the torch met with considerable resistance across Canada.

Indigenous programming proved to be a prominent aspect in both the protocol and cultural displays of the 2010 opening ceremony. For this performance, for example, the chiefs of the FHFN were all recognized members of the official Olympic party; a formal welcome to the territory from the FHFN was offered; the Aboriginal peoples of Canada, including representatives from the Northwest, the Inuit, the Métis, the Prairies, and the East, provided an official welcome; indigenous peoples danced in celebration as the parade of athletes took place; and throughout the duration of the ceremony numerous indigenous artistic and cultural images were incorporated, such as welcome poles, a drum, a spirit bear, and Aboriginal depictions of constellations, whales, and salmon, to name a few. Many Canadians expressed an overwhelming satisfaction with the performance of the opening ceremony, particularly in regard to the significant representation of indigenous peoples and imagery. Yet others were troubled by issues of cultural appropriation as well as by what some believed to be an overrepresentation and saturation of indigenous content within the opening ceremony performance (O'Bonsawin 2010a).

There is no doubt that organizers of the 2010 Vancouver Games achieved "unprecedented Aboriginal participation." As this chapter makes clear, indigenous people and their cultural imagery were included in almost all facets of the Games, and in particular the cultural program. This was evident through the adoption of the inuksuk as the official emblem, the mascots, the 2006 Turin handover ceremony, the Olympic medals, the Cowichan-like sweaters, the torch relay that travelled through almost a quarter of First Nations communities in Canada, and the opening ceremony. Yet, despite significant efforts to incorporate indigenous people and imagery as part of the Games, Olympic organizers, arguably, once again failed to adequately dialogue with indigenous people about their aims and aspirations for involvement. This occurred despite implementation of *Olympic Movement's Agenda 21* and VANOC's partnership with the FHFN (the first Olympic organizing committee in history to establish an official partnership with indigenous people). In spite of VANOC's concerted efforts to promote these relationships as cordial, there remained tensions and controversies surrounding indigenous inclusion in Olympic Games – issues that future organizers should try to address and ameliorate.

Conclusion

In consideration of historical and political realities in British Columbia, as well as obvious tensions within the Aboriginal Participation and Collaboration program, we must assess whether the 2010 organizing process sufficiently moved beyond the 1976 Montreal and 1988 Calgary Olympic models. The 1976 Montreal Summer Olympic Games enthusiastically incorporated indigenous people and dramatic imagery into its cultural programming, notably the closing ceremony. Here, Montreal organizers overtly failed to consider partnering with indigenous groups, let alone organize a program that respected local customs and imagery. For the 1988 Winter Olympic Games in Calgary, after controversy surrounding the livelihood and well-being of indigenous people in Alberta, organizers unofficially partnered with the Treaty 7 nations to address some of their representational issues, leaving the far more substantial (political, economic, environmental) issues untouched. In the case of the 2010 Vancouver Winter Olympic Games, organizers made use of the Olympic Movement's Agenda 21 by forming a partnership with the FHFN early in the organizing process. Still, VANOC received significant criticism for its appropriation of, and attempt to profit from, indigenous symbols. Despite varying efforts to incorporate indigenous people and imagery into official Olympic programs, all three organizing committees (1976, 1988, 2010) have been heavily criticized for failing to follow a respectful process of dialogue and for misappropriating indigenous cultures.

What are the similarities that cut across all three Games in Canada? First, indigenous criticism and opposition to Olympic Games must be contextualized within the framework of their historical, political, and social oppression. Through the authority of its charter, the Olympic Movement has the capability of doing many things, particularly contravening in national policies and the laws of host nations. In the case of Vancouver 2010, the most obvious example of the IOC's determination to sidestep national laws was its decision to exclude women's ski jumping from the athletic program, as well as VANOC's efforts, which ultimately failed to establish protest zones for activists and Olympic opponents. Both initiatives challenged Canada's Charter of Rights and Freedoms, which includes clauses protecting gender equality and the freedom of speech in Canada (O'Bonsawin 2010b). As one of the most powerful not-for-profit, non-governmental organizations in the world – an organization that has more member nations than the United Nations – the IOC could perhaps do a better job of living up to its much vaunted values. For instance, under the present governing structure and policies of the Olympic Movement, there are currently no formal mechanisms in place to evaluate the social, political, and economic climate of a potential host city and country, though numerous evaluations exist for how well a host city is doing (especially economically) after the Games have left town. At present, the very presence of the Olympic Games in particular regions of the world potentially serves as a further impediment to the rights of marginalized people, rather than a mechanism for social change. For now it seems the hosting of future Olympic Games in Canada will attract similar criticism and opposition from indigenous people and their supporters as they continue to resist the ongoing political mistreatment and injustices they face, as well as the obvious appropriation of indigenous imagery within the Olympic framework – a resistance well worth investigating and perhaps even supporting.

NOTE

1 This chapter recognizes that the terms "Aboriginal," "First Nations," "First Peoples," "Indian," "Indigenous," and "Native" have all been used to collectively address the original inhabitants of Canada. For purposes of consistency and inclusiveness, the author employs the term "Indigenous," as it represents an identity that is not geographically or socially defined. Since this chapter offers comparative critiques with the hosting of Olympic Games elsewhere, the term "Indigenous" is employed in an attempt to accurately represent an experience, which is "shaped and lived in the politicized context of contemporary colonialism" (Alfred and Corntassel 2005, 597).

REFERENCES

ABC News. 1988. 1988 Calgary Olympic Winter Games opening ceremony telecast. February 13.

Alfred, T. 2001. Deconstructing the British Columbia treaty process. *Balayi: Culture, Law, Colonialism* 3: 37-65.

Alfred, T., and J. Corntassel. 2005. Being indigenous: Resurgences against contemporary colonialism. *Government and Opposition* 4(4): 597-614.

Barney, R.K., S.R. Wenn, and S.G. Martyn. 2004. *Selling the Five Rings: The International Olympic Committee and the Rise of Olympic Commercialism*. Salt Lake City: University of Utah Press.

Booth, K. 1987. Lubicon supporters protest torch run. *Windspeaker* 5(37): 3.

Brydon, S. 1997. The Indians of Canada at Expo 67. *American Indian Art Magazine* 22(3): 54-63.

CBC News. 1976. 1976 Montreal Olympic Summer Games closing ceremony. CBC/Radio-Canada, Ottawa, August 1.

–. 2009. Cowichan Tribes reach Olympic sweater deal. October 28. http://www.cbc.ca/.

Constantineau, B. 2009. Olympic sweater not a Cowichan, Hudson's Bay says. *Vancouver Sun,* October 9. http://www.vancouversun.com/.

Crossingham, L. 1987a. Heated debate at IAA meeting. *Windspeaker* 5(6): 3.

–. 1987b. Lubicon Olympic boycott: Cartoon centre of controversy. *Windspeaker* 5(8): 1, 3.

–. 1988. Mohawk nations supports Lubicon band. *Windspeaker* 5(22): 3.

Daily Vancouver. 2005. Squamish chief calls 2010 Vancouver Olympic logo "ilanaaq" "aggression." http://2010.dailyvancouver.com/.

Doods, K.E. 2007. *Uts'am/Witness: Witnessing Ten Years of Transformation.* Vancouver: Roundhouse Community Centre.

Dyreson, M. 1998. Olympic Games and historical imagination: Notes from the faultline of tradition and modernity. *Olympika* 7: 25-42.

Goddard J. 1991. *Last Stand of the Lubicon Cree.* Vancouver: Douglas and McIntyre.

Ferreira, D.A. 1992. Oil and Lubicons don't mix: A land claim in northern Alberta in historical perspective. *Canadian Journal of Native Studies* 12(1): 1-35.

Forsyth, J. 2002. Teepees and tomahawks: Aboriginal cultural representation at the 1976 Olympic Games. In K.B. Wamsley, R.K. Barney, and S.G. Martyn, eds., *The Global Nexus Engaged: Past, Present, Future Interdisciplinary Olympic Studies – Sixth International Symposium for Olympic Research* (71-76). London, ON: International Centre for Olympic Studies.

Harrison, J.D. 1988. "The Spirit Sings" and the future of anthropology. *Anthropology Today* 4(6): 6-9.

Heyes, S. 2002. Protecting the authenticity and integrity of Inuksuit in the Arctic milieu. *Études/Inuit/Studies* 26(2): 133-56.

International Olympic Committee. 1999. *Olympic Movement's Agenda 21: Sport for Sustainable Development.* International Olympic Committee. http://www.olympic.org/Documents/Reports/.

–. 2009. Calgary 1988 – The medal. http://www.olympic.org/uk/.

King, F.W. 1991. *It's How You Play the Game: The Inside Story of the Calgary Olympics.* Calgary: Script.

Lenskyj, H.J. 2007. *Olympic Industry Resistance: Challenging Olympic Power and Propaganda.* Albany: University of New York Press.

McManus, G. 1991. The crisis of representations in museums: The exhibition "The Spirit Sings." In S.M. Pearce, ed., *Museum Economics and the Community,* 2nd ed. (202-5). London, UK: Athlon.

Montréal Olympic Games Organizing Committee. 1976. *Closing Ceremony Programme: Games of the XXI Olympiad Montréal 1976.*

No2010. 2009. Demonstrators disrupt 2010 Olympic torch relay. October 21. http://no2010.com/.

O'Bonsawin, C. 2010a. A Coast Salish Olympic welcome: The Vancouver opening ceremony and the politics of indigenous participation. In R.K. Barney, J.

Forsyth, and M.K. Heine, eds., *Rethinking Matters Olympic: Investigations into the Socio-Cultural Study of the Modern Olympic Movement* (255-64). London, ON: International Centre for Olympic Studies.

–. 2010b. "No Olympics on stolen Native land": Contesting Olympic narratives and inserting indigenous within the discourse of the 2010 Vancouver Games. *Sport in Society* 13(1): 143-56.

Ominayak, B. 1989. Aboriginal land rights in Canada – myth and reality. *NISTO – Lubicon Lake Indian Nation*. http://nisto.com/cree/lubicon/.

Phillips, R. 2002. A proper place for art or the proper arts of place? Native North American objects and the hierarchies of art, craft, and souvenir. In L. Jessup and S. Bagg, eds., *On Aboriginal Representation in the Gallery* (45-72). Hull, QC: Canadian Museum of Civilization.

Rakobowchuk, P. 2009. Olympic organizers reach deal with Mohawks to drop RCMP escort for torch relay. *Chronicle Journal,* December 8. http://www.chroniclejournal.com/.

Rutherdale, M., and J. Miller. 2006. "It's our country": First Nations' participation in the Indian Pavilion at Expo 67. *Journal of the Canadian Historical Association* 17(2): 148-73.

Trigger, B. 1988. Reply by Bruce Trigger to Julia Harrison's article – "The Spirit Sings" and the future of anthropology. *Anthropology Today* 4(6): 6-9.

Truscott, M. 2006. Repatriation of indigenous cultural property. Paper prepared for the 2006 Australian State of the Environment Committee, Department of the Environment and Heritage, Canberra. http://www.environment.gov.au/.

Turner, D. 2006. *This Is Not a Peace Pipe: Towards a Critical Indigenous Philosophy.* Toronto: University of Toronto Press.

VANOC (Vancouver Olympic Organizing Committee for the 2010 Olympic and Paralympic Winter Games). 2009a. Aboriginal participation. Vancouver Olympic Organizing Committee for the 2010 Olympic and Paralympic Winter Games. http://www.olympic.org/vancouver-2010-winter-olympics.

–. 2009b. Olympic Games emblem. Vancouver Olympic Organizing Committee for the 2010 Olympic and Paralympic Winter Games. http://www.olympic.org/vancouver-2010-winter-olympics.

–. 2009c. Vancouver 2010 mascots introduced to the world. Vancouver Olympic Organizing Committee for the 2010 Olympic and Paralympic Winter Games, http://www.olympic.org/vancouver-2010-winter-olympics.

–. 2009d. Vancouver 2010 medals each a one-of-a-kind work of contemporary Aboriginal art. 2009. Vancouver Olympic Organizing Committee for the 2010 Olympic and Paralympic Winter Games. http://www.olympic.org/vancouver-2010-winter-olympics.

Wamsley, K.B., and M. Heine. 1994. "Calgary is not a cowboy town": Ideology, the Olympics, and the politics of identity. In R.K. Barney and K.V. Meirer, eds., *Critical Reflections on Olympic Ideology: Second International Symposium for Olympic Research* (78-83). London, ON: International Centre for Olympic Studies.

–. 1996. "Don't mess with the relay – It's bad medicine": Aboriginal culture and the 1988 Winter Olympics. In R.K. Barney, D.A. Brown, G.H. Macdonald, and S.G. Martyn, eds., *Olympic Perspectives: Third International Symposium for Olympic Research* (173-98). London, ON: International Centre for Olympic Studies.

Wolosen, R. 1988. The spirit sings in Calgary: Despite protests, organizers bring Indian art back home. *Alberta Report,* February 15, p. 41.

Young Man, A. 1990. Review of "The Spirit Sings: Artistic traditions of Canada's First Peoples." *American Indian Quarterly* 14(1): 71-73.

3 Toward a History of Aboriginal Women in Canadian Sport

M. ANN HALL

Canadian sport history, still today gendered and racialized, has often ignored Aboriginal women. Canadian women's sport history, although recognizing Aboriginal women to some extent, has concerned itself more with white women's participation. Aboriginal sport history speaks eloquently about male sporting heroes and experiences, a vantage point that often ignores its heroines. Native women's history in Canada, although certainly an exciting and developing field, is mainly silent about sport.[1] As Janice Forsyth (2007, 163) suggests, "It is time that Aboriginal female realities are acknowledged, documented, and addressed through research, policy, and practice, and their stories integrated into existing accounts of Aboriginal sport and women's sport."

The history of Aboriginal women in Canadian sport cannot simply be grafted onto the traditional histories of Canadian women's sport because the experiences of Aboriginal women are not necessarily the same as those of white women. In my book *The Girl and the Game: A History of Women's Sport in Canada*, significant events, or turning points, in the history of primarily white women in Canada were used to shape and define the eras around which the story of women's sport was told (Hall 2002). The First World War, for example, brought about two major goals of the earlier suffrage movement: prohibition and the right to vote. Working-class women flocked to the cities in search of employment and, once employed, they sought recreational opportunities for their spare time. Many turned to sport through a grassroots movement that established the first women's athletic clubs, organizations, and leagues. Rather than cancelling competitions during the war, they often continued their games and tournaments to support patriotic causes or to raise money for the war effort. With so many men away, women took on more organizational responsibilities in the private sport clubs, which gave them more confidence to establish and continue to run their own sport clubs and organizations after the war.

White women's sport in Canada also flourished during the Second World War because women used sport to raise money for various war-related projects and agencies, to entertain the home-based troops, and to provide healthy recreation for girls and women. Women often took over the coaching and training from absent men. In the immediate postwar period and into the 1950s, in a society obsessed with normalizing daily life, men again returned to coaching and training, and women's sport became increasingly characterized by a remarkable emphasis on beauty, grace, femininity, and, for some, glamour.

The third turning point was the resurgence of feminist activity beginning in the late 1960s, which brought about the modern women's movement. It took some time for women's sport in Canada to become part of the feminist agenda, but eventually it did through, for example, legal challenges for the right of girls to play sports with boys, federal and provincial government gender equity policies and programs, and feminist advocacy organizations focused on women's sport and physical activity.

These three turning points – two world wars and the early women's movement – although important to the experiences of white Canadian women, are not essentially the benchmarks in time that should be used to construct histories of Aboriginal women in Canada (Forsyth 2005a, 76). Not only are they not the dominant historical events and movements of significance to Aboriginal women, but they also obscure how their identities have been simultaneously gendered and racialized throughout history. Much more important to the lives and experiences of Aboriginal women, especially over the past two hundred years, are their first encounters with Europeans, their role in fur-trade society, the Indian Act of 1876 and its various revisions, the establishment of reserves and forced residential schooling, and more recently, the confluence of sport and Aboriginal policies – very different benchmarks indeed.

The purpose of this chapter is to provide a historical framework around which the story of Aboriginal women's sport in Canada might be told, and at the same time tell the stories of several prominent Native women athletes whose lives have been influenced by the historical benchmarks mentioned above.

Traditional Games and Sports

Traditional Native societies were land-based cultures that had minimal contact with the invading Europeans. These cultures included the Iroquoian and Algonquian peoples in the east, the Plains Indians of the Prairies, several distinct tribes along the Pacific coast, the Dene of the Subarctic, and the Inuit in the Arctic. Aboriginal historians agree that although considerable differences existed within the various indigenous nations, their common values and practices prior to the arrival of the Europeans sustained Aboriginal womanhood (Anderson 2000, 57). Indigenous communities had a sense of women's power and their position within the community. The slow dismantling of Aboriginal womanhood took place along the path of colonization, a process beginning over five hundred years ago, when Europeans realized that in order to dominate the land and the people occupying it, they needed to disempower the women. As Kim Anderson adroitly points out, "Indigenous systems that allocated power to women were incompatible with the kind of colonial power dynamics that would be necessary to maintain colonial power" (ibid., 58). For example, she argued that where menstruation was a sign of the incredible power of the feminine, Judeo-Christian culture saw menstruation as a manifestation of female sin, contamination, and inferiority.

Sports, games, and physical activities in these traditional societies were a means to learning how to survive on the land and ensuring basic survival; they were also key sites for reinforcing the social, political, economic, and spiritual aspects of life (see, for example, Heine 1999, 2002). Some games were restricted to men, some to women, and in a few both sexes participated, sometimes against each other. Again, and as Audrey Giles examines in Chapter 6, menstruation played a role in how women could associate with men given that notions of power and pollution surrounding menstruation were often in conflict. Even today among the Dene there is controversy regarding the role of menstruating women in traditional games (see especially Giles 2004, 2005). It is important to realize that our picture of the role women played in these traditional games and sports has been shaped almost entirely by the early European explorers, traders, and painters who provided the record. Joseph Oxendine (1995) argues, for example, that it was almost impossible for non-Natives to observe Aboriginal games and ceremonies in their traditional form and significance because when they entered the Natives' midst, it was always as outsiders.

Shinny, a hockey-like ball game played on a field or on ice in winter, was often considered a women's game. The small, round ball made of wood or stuffed buckskin was hit along the ground (or ice) with a curved stick, the object being to get it through two posts or sticks at the ends of the field (Cheska 1982, 21). Double ball, a more difficult and faster version of shinny, was also primarily a women's game. Among the Cree, this game was called *tishevy's,* which means "a pair of stones" (testicles) – two stuffed leather balls attached together by a thong six to ten inches long and caught by means of sticks thirty or more inches in length (Thomas 1990, 15). The object of the game was to carry these balls or throw them through the opponent's goal (similar to lacrosse); goals could be as far as one mile apart.[2]

Bagaa'atowe (as the Anishinaabek called it) or lacrosse (as the Jesuits named it) was mainly a men's game, often with religious and ceremonial significance, or it was used as a training exercise for young warriors. Among some tribes, women would run onto the field during the pre-game preparations to bestow gifts of beads or other tokens on their favourite player. George Beers, a Montreal dentist who in the late nineteenth century modified and organized lacrosse for white players, considered this practice a wonderful incentive and wished that Canada's "fair daughters" would revive the fashion: "How it would put one on one's mettle to be a crack player!" (Beers 1869, 22). Some tribes permitted women to play provided it was away from male eyes, but in a few the two sexes played together with modifications to even the contest; for example, women used their hands while men played with sticks, or in some cases women were allowed five players for every male counterpart (Vennum 2008, 184).

Many physical activities contributed to the learning of skills necessary for survival. Among Plains Indians, boys and girls were able to ride a horse by an early age, usually around five. For safety, they were put in a woman's high-pommelled saddle with rawhide ropes tied around the front and rear pommels. Games were devised to teach the skills of warfare, such as the "overhang," whereby a rider hung under the neck of a galloping horse and shot at the enemy (Pakes 1990, 27-28). Although girls were not expected to undergo the exacting discipline experienced by boys, they were trained for the responsibilities they would assume, at a relatively young age, as wives and mothers:

> Dolls taught the child the culture to which she belonged – the beadwork designs, the cut of the clothing, and their meaning. A miniature cradleboard allowed the girl to practise the method by which the baby was safely contained by it. A model horse was in fact a scale model of the real thing given to her so that she could practise loading it correctly for transportation of the family goods, with miniature replicas of the parfleche bags and travois. (Ibid., 28)

Other games and activities, designed mostly for fun, made use of the terrain and seasons. The object of snowsnake, a game usually played by women, was to see how far they could throw long willow sticks, often tipped with the horns of buffalo calves, across the ice (Pakes 1990, 30). Winter also brought tobogganing on a sled constructed from buffalo ribs fastened together on willow crossbars, with a skin seat. A less complicated sled was a strip of basswood bark four feet long and six inches wide. Riders stood on one end, slippery side down, and held onto the other end while they coasted down long hills. Boys and girls often tobogganed together, with the "hunter" boys chasing the "buffalo" girls (ibid., 31).

Aboriginal women's traditional sports and games before colonialism, argues Jennifer Hargreaves (2000, 82), were numerous and flourishing features of indigenous history, integral to individual and group identities and to ideologies about harmony with nature and the environment. Colonialism, she argues further, reduced indigenous sports in general to residual status and in most cases rendered Aboriginal women's sports completely invisible.

Aboriginal Women in Fur-Trade Society

For many Native peoples, first contact and fur trade occurred at the same time.[3] Aboriginal traders greeted European explorers with furs, ready to make exchanges. Various trading companies, but specifically two powerful rivals, the Hudson's Bay Company and the North West Company, were responsible for the development of the fur trade in what is today western Canada. Historian Sylvia Van Kirk (1980, 83) argues that the coming of fur traders offered Aboriginal women the prospect of an alternative way of life, and it promised sufficient relief from life on the land to induce numerous Aboriginal women to choose a different way. Fundamental to the growth of fur-trade society was widespread intermarriage between Aboriginal women and the traders. Aboriginal women helped traders to survive in a new and hard life simply by sharing their traditional knowledge of trapping, sewing, building, and mending. They also helped the traders build alliances to facilitate their access to furs. On the other hand, they used these marriages to solidify their place as cultural mediators and to enhance the wealth and prestige of their kin (Sleeper-Smith 2006).

Native women often accompanied the traders in the fur brigades on their annual voyages by canoe and York boat to Hudson's Bay or Lake Superior and back. In fact, as Van Kirk (1980, 63) suggests, inland journeys that did not involve the women were often doomed to failure because it was Native women who set up camp, cooked the food, dried the meat, collected berries, dressed the skins, mended the snowshoes, and did myriad other tasks. They may even have shared in the paddling, though probably did not engage in the heavy work of canoeing, such as portaging and tracking (Gottfred 2000).

The combined European and Aboriginal elements of fur-trade society were symbolized through the emergence of an increasing number of mixed-blood children. The Native wife was slowly replaced by a mixed-blood wife, which led to widespread intermarriage among fur-trade families. Among successive generations of mixed-blood girls there was a noticeable tendency, especially on the part of Company officers, to wean their daughters away from their Aboriginal heritage and encourage them to emulate the style of European ladies (Van Kirk 1980, 5). We can speculate that their "Indian" ways were discouraged, including their participation in traditional Aboriginal sports and games to the extent that Victorian deportment became the norm. In other words, restricted by voluminous skirts and Victorian ideas about their physical and mental frailty, these young women were never welcome at the growing number of male-only sports clubs, nor could they form their own. Very limited forms of physical activity were available to Canadian women in the 1860s and 1870s, and those considered appropriate were individual or family recreations, and restricted mostly to those of wealth and leisure.

We can also speculate that, unlike several Native male runners and lacrosse teams that were part of touring shows for the entertainment of settlers, nineteenth-century Aboriginal women rarely participated in any form of white-organized sport. One exception appears to be water regattas, where Native women sometimes took part in canoeing events. For example, in 1867, at the annual summer regatta in Lachine, Quebec, just south of Montreal, an observer writing in the *Gazette* reported that two canoes "each manned, or rather *womanned*, by six or eight squaws came forth to battle for aqueous supremacy."[4] Among the sailing, outrigger, canoeing, and sculling races were a four-mile "Indian" canoe race for men and a two-mile race for women. The account in the *Gazette* was very unflattering and by today's standards both racist and sexist. The writer described the canoeists as "prosaic squaws, each weighing about two and a half hundred weight, each dressed in modest skirts and jacket of crimson, orange, or unassuming blue, each jabbering with female loquacity." They were unfavourably compared with the more acceptable "Indian maidens of romance, with gazelles' eyes, and forms like pine trees." After observing a boat rowed easily by a "lady with braids of glossy brown hair, shading a round cheek glowing with exercise, good health and good humour," the regatta reporter suggested that instead of lavishing a twenty-five-dollar prize on "fourteen wrinkled bedames, redolent of rum and onions," the organizers should double the stakes, invest in a bracelet prize, and let the "ladies" (one assumes white women) have a quarter-mile race.

These mid-nineteenth-century stereotypical images of Aboriginal women, especially the romanticized Indian princess and the primitive squaw, are part of a colonial heritage that perpetuated racism and sexism.[5] Native women paddlers also appeared to threaten male-held beliefs about female frailty and beauty, and their obvious athleticism was rendered irrelevant. Aboriginal women were a long way from benefiting from the growing movement among white women settlers, especially in urban centres, to escape the bonds of tradition and to experience at least a modicum of independence and adventure. In fact, Native girls' and women's lives were to become even more restrictive.

Increasing Government Control

Between 1850 and 1876, colonial authorities enacted several key pieces of legislation that increased government control over Indian lands, introduced measures to protect Indian reserves from encroachment by white settlers, assumed responsibility for deciding who was Aboriginal, and encouraged Natives to forgo their Indian status and be drawn into the larger colonial society as regular citizens (and, hence, become "civilized"). In 1876, the Government of Canada consolidated all prior federal legislation regarding Aboriginals through the Indian Act, adopting an explicit vision of assimilation in which Aboriginals would be encouraged to leave behind their Indian status and traditional cultural practices and become full members of the broader Canadian society. In this context, Aboriginals were viewed as children or wards of the state, for which the government claimed a paternalistic duty to protect and civilize.

Various amendments to the Indian Act, beginning in 1885, were implemented by the government to repress indigenous religious ceremonies among Aboriginal peoples, including potlatches and giveaways (redistribution of goods), and ceremonial dances like the sun dance. Missionaries and administrators considered these activities immoral and a detriment to the assimilation of Aboriginals into Euro-Canadian society. Any "endeavour to substitute reasonable amusements for this senseless drumming and dancing" was supported by Indian Agents, who took initiatives to replace indigenous ceremonies with Euro-Canadian versions of recreation such as exhibitions and sports days (Pettipas 1994, 160; Paraschak 1998). Again we can only speculate, but it is unlikely that Aboriginal women were encouraged, or even allowed, to participate in these recreational and sporting activities given the negative attitude among white Canadian males toward Victorian women taking up vigorous exercise.

Where it suited the commercial interests of entrepreneurs in developing tourism in western Canada, traditional indigenous activities and ceremonies were encouraged. The Banff Indian Days, for example, began in 1889 as a summer attraction to entertain guests at the new Banff Springs Hotel and by 1907 had become an annual event. Stoney Aboriginal peoples from the Morley reserve, just south of Banff, would set up a teepee camp and recreate aspects of their traditional culture through parades, ceremonies, dances, and sporting contests. Although Aboriginal women were involved in many aspects of the Banff Indian Days, their role in the sporting contests is unclear. One researcher suggested that both sexes competed equally in sporting events, but with separate contests for each – for example, a "squaw's" foot race for women and an archery competition for men (Meijer Drees 1993, 12). In the early days of the Banff Indian Days, women's sporting events consisted mainly of foot races, but also included horse races, in which the women competed for small monetary prizes (Mason 2010). These events were not consistent from year to year and over time became more rodeo-oriented; again, the role of Aboriginal women is unclear, though there is some evidence they may have competed in early rodeo contests.[6] Similarly, at an annual Calgary fall fair that began in 1886, Aboriginals performed social and war dances; had tug-of-war contests, races, and other athletic events; showed off their finery; and visited friends from other reserves (Dempsey 2008, 49). The first Calgary Exhibition and Stampede was held in 1912; over a six-day period, some eighteen hundred Natives attended, offering daily dances and parades, and performing in the grandstand show. Also on the stampede program were various rodeo events for "cowgirls," including fancy and trick riding, a relay race, fancy roping, and bronc riding (LeCompte 1993, 50). Aboriginal women do not appear to have taken part in these events, nor were they allowed to participate in the "Indian" relay race – that was open only to their male counterparts. The lives of Aboriginal girls and women were becoming increasingly more restricted within Canada's gendered and paternalistic society, and even more so as the residential school system took hold.

The Gendered Work of Residential Schools

The modern residential school system was created in the 1880s and lasted until the late 1960s, when government-sponsored schools were slowly phased out. Thousands of Aboriginal children and teenagers were forced to attend these residential schools, which were sometimes far away from their families. These institutions were located throughout Canada, but especially on the Prairies and in British Columbia. Some schools were eventually taken over by a Native administration. The last federally run residential school closed its doors in 1996 in Saskatchewan. Janice Forsyth's chapter in this book examines Native residential schools and the role of sports and games in these institutions. As well, Miller's comprehensive study (1996) on the history of Native residential schools in Canada provides a wealth of information. Consequently, I am brief here, except to emphasize the gendered nature of the physical activities offered at residential schools and the implications for Aboriginal women's sport.

As Miller (1996, 217-18) points out, "Notions of gender were so embedded in the attitudes of officials and missionaries as to be taken for granted," such that the "ways in which people perceived the aptitudes, roles, and destinies of females and males profoundly influenced the operation of these institutions." Although residential schools were mostly coeducational, boys and girls were segregated and there was a strict division of labour – girls worked in the kitchen and did laundry and other cleaning, while boys worked out of doors in the barns and stables, and chopped and hauled wood. According to Miller (ibid., 220), a regime of separate and unequal treatment was also noticeable in other aspects of school life, such as instruction, recreation, and provisions for leisure time. Boys were given the best recreational equipment, had more time to play outdoors, benefited from more clubs and sports teams, and in many ways were given more freedom. Miller quotes one female former resident who makes a poignant statement about the discrepancy between male and female activities at school, demonstrating that at least some female residents were highly dissatisfied with the differential treatment: "Boring, that's what play time was. Some play. We couldn't do nothing. Dolls, knitting, things like that but not playing, not like the boys. They had balls, bats, hockey sticks, everything. Sundays were the worst. I hated Sundays. We couldn't even work on Sundays. Just sat in the play room or went out on those awful walks" (ibid., 250).

The implication of a residential schooling experience for Aboriginal women in sport is at least twofold. First, many generations of Native girls were denied the opportunity to practise and enhance their skills in traditional sports and games because they were usually disallowed at the residential schools. Aboriginal girls were far less physically active at these schools than they would have been in their own environments because they were never allowed to swim, canoe, race, wrestle, test their strength, play shinny, or explore the outdoors. Second, they were also denied opportunities to participate in Euro-Canadian sports like cricket, baseball, soccer, and ice hockey, which were taught to the boys – although by the 1950s, basketball for girls was an exception (Miller 1996, 273). Many white Canadian girls and women were also discouraged from these sports, but they usually had a choice in the matter and many fought back by forming their own teams and demanding to play and compete. We know very little about how Aboriginal females responded, but their stories would certainly give us a richer picture of Aboriginal women as significant actors in Canadian sport history.

One example of the many Aboriginal women athletes in Canadian sport history whose story up until now has been unwritten and untold is Roseanne Allen. In 1959, her family (mother, stepfather, and eleven siblings) was relocated from Aklavik to nearby Inuvik in the Northwest Territories. Five years later, at age eight, she was sent to Grollier Hall, a Roman Catholic hostel that housed residential students, because her mother (who eventually had six more children) no longer had the financial means to keep her at home.[7] The decision dramatically altered Roseanne's life: "I was guaranteed three square meals a day. I was guaranteed parkas and mukluks for winter. Most important, my move to the hostel kept me on the right side of life. I had lots of friends in Inuvik who moved down a different track" (Manning 2006, 47). Roseanne started cross-country skiing in 1966 at age ten, and by age thirteen, in 1968, was the youngest winner ever at the Canadian Junior Championships. Roseanne's story is just one such story; several more are introduced below.

Emergence of Organized Sport for Women

The period from the end of the First World War through the 1920s and 1930s brought significant change to Canadian women's sport: the growth of teams and leagues, especially those sponsored by industrial concerns; the beginning of international competition, primarily in track and field; and the increasing control by women over the administrative affairs of their sports. Softball, basketball, hockey, track and field, swimming, and a host of new sports, such as bowling, badminton, alpine skiing, competitive cycling, and even cricket, saw unprecedented participation. During this period of consolidation in white women's sport in Canada, Aboriginal women (and men) were actively marginalized from the developing structure of Euro-Canadian sports and games.

One exception was softball, which was popular among Native women, in particular those who lived on reserves and in Métis settlements. The "Caledonia Indians," for instance, came mostly from the Six Nations reserve along the Grand River in Ontario, though there were also some white women on the team. Off the reserve they played exhibition games in southern Ontario, including with Toronto leagues. They were also highly competitive, and in 1931 were semifinalists in the Provincial Women's Softball Union championships. Dorothy Wilson, an Aboriginal woman from the Six Nations reserve, played on the team in the early 1930s and remembers, "We'd come home from school, do our homework, eat dinner, do the dishes, and practice until you couldn't see for the dark. I lived for ball. I started getting excited the day before the game" (Robinson 1997, 173). When her team went to Toronto to play, it was treated as an exciting novelty, as reflected in sportswriter Phyllis Griffiths's comment: "INDIANS ARE COMING: Beaches Girls Softball League fans have a real attraction arranged for them at Kew Gardens Saturday evening when the Caledonia Indians will play one of the Beaches teams. The Indians have several honest-to-goodness Indians in their line-up, and are a good team into the bargain" (Griffiths 1935, 23). By today's standards this was a racist remark, but it does illustrate how unusual it was for Aboriginal women to be seen playing sport in the 1930s. The Beachettes, whose Chinese pitcher was also noted, beat the Caledonia Indians that particular time.

Postwar Role Models

By the late 1940s and throughout the 1950s, women's sport in Canada was characterized by a remarkable emphasis on beauty, grace, femininity, and, for some athletes, glamour. Gone for the most part were debates about whether sport would masculinize women competitors, because the proof was there for all to see: so long as women participated in "beauty producing" sports like figure skating, synchronized swimming, or gymnastics, and so long as they looked feminine on the tennis and badminton courts, golf courses, and ski hills, they would not be criticized and they would be rewarded. This was the era of figure skater Barbara Ann Scott, who after a highly successful amateur career turned professional and toured with an ice show. Younger athletes like swimmer Marilyn Bell, golfer Marlene Stewart, and skiers Lucille Wheeler and Anne Heggtveit were also very popular. Each represented the girl-next-door with special talent, whom all of Canada was proud to claim, provided she was white and preferably from English Canada. There was no place in this idealized world for the "other," including women athletes of Aboriginal descent who chose to play sport. Again for some, softball was their preferred sport and one of the few activities that offered opportunities and alternatives.

Ruth Hill was known as Ruthie to her friends and teammates. As a teenager (then Ruth Van Every) in the late 1940s, she was well known for her softball pitching. The Ohsweken Mohawks, a team formed in 1945, was the major outlet for talented women ballplayers on the Six Nations reserve. Ruth joined the team in the early 1950s. With a deadly rising fastball, she pitched in many a tournament and usually struck out more than a dozen players each game. In 1964, after an outstanding season with the Mohawks, Ruth was asked by Toronto Carpetland, the Canadian champions, to join that team at the World Championships in Florida. The only game Toronto Carpetland won was the game Ruth pitched; she also batted in the winning run. Soon after, she lost a finger on her pitching hand in an accident, but she continued to pitch for many more years.

Phyllis "Yogi" Bomberry, whose nickname reflects her superb catching ability on the fastball and softball diamonds, was born in 1943, the second oldest in a family of four brothers and two sisters, members of the Cayuga tribe, Wolf Clan. Looking back on her childhood, she readily traces the reason for her early competitiveness and prowess in sports: "To be 'in' with the kids, you had to play with the guys," she remembers, which meant a steady rough-and-tumble diet of hockey, football, lacrosse, even hunting and shooting, and, of course, hardball (Koserski 1969, 45). She recalls catching ball for her father and brother, both amateur players who needed to practise their pitching skills. In school, she eagerly participated in basketball, badminton, gymnastics, and volleyball, and in house leagues both on and off the reserve, she played softball.

By the late 1950s, Phyllis was experienced enough to join the Ohsweken Mohawks, helping them win the Intermediate "B" Provincial Women's Softball Union Championships in 1960 and 1962. She played with the team until

1963, when she moved to Brantford to attend high school. The Toronto Carpetland team, which played in the Ontario senior women's league, saw in Phyllis an obvious talent and helped her to obtain employment on the assembly line at a communications factory in Toronto so she could attend regularly scheduled practices. The team won the Senior Canadian Women's Softball Championships in 1967 and again in 1968, with Phyllis being named top batter the first year and all-star catcher in both years. She was also a member of the Ontario senior women's championship team in 1967 and 1968, and played with that team when it won the gold medal at the Canada Games in 1969. Phyllis herself won the Canadian all-star catcher and most valuable player awards at these Games.

While playing for the Carpetlands team, Phyllis had to deal with racial slurs hurled from spectators; as the team's catcher, she was often within earshot of these remarks. There was little Phyllis could do, since she was playing and competing in an environment that implicitly supported racial discrimination by not taking action when it surfaced. No one on the team stood up for her when insults occurred, nor did the coaches or umpires deal with these situations in any official way. Phyllis had to endure this form of racism if she wanted to continue playing on an integrated team, which was the only opportunity she had to compete at the national level in the mainstream sport system (Forsyth 2005b, 194-95).[8]

Bev Beaver (née Henhawk) is a Mohawk also from the Six Nations reserve. Born in 1947, she honed her athletic skills playing hockey, softball, and soccer with boys. At thirteen she was a star forward on a boys' bantam hockey team but could play only in exhibition games because girls were not allowed to play in regular league or championship games. She became an outstanding athlete in three sports (fastball, ice hockey, and bowling), participating on both Native and non-Native teams.

Summers were spent on the fastball diamond pitching for the Ohsweken Mohawks, which at that time competed with mostly non-Native teams in the Niagara and District Fastball League in southern Ontario. Bev won numerous top pitcher and most valuable player awards in her more than thirty years (1961-94) of competitive fastball. In 1979, for example, she was named best pitcher, top batter, and most valuable player at the Canadian Native Championship in Kelowna, as well as all-star pitcher at the North American Native Ladies Championship in Saskatoon. In 1980, the Ohsweken Mohawks were tournament champions at the National Indian Activities Association tournament in Anadarko, Oklahoma, and Bev was again named top batter and most valuable player. "She's got that sixth sense you can't teach," observed one of her coaches (Paikin 1980, 18). During the 1980s, the Ohsweken Mohawks were perpetual winners of the Canadian Native Ladies Fastball Championships. Throughout her softball career, Bev chose not to play for any non-Native teams; although she too was recruited by the Toronto Carpetland team, she did not accept its offer. Bev was proud that the Ohsweken Mohawks never recruited "outside" players when she was on the team because they did not need anyone from outside the community to help them be competitive (Forsyth 2005b, 195).

In winter, Bev switched to her favourite sport, ice hockey, which she played competitively for nearly thirty years. She began playing in 1963 with the Six Nations Indian Girls Hockey Club, and in 1967 joined the Burlington Gazettes of the Central Ontario Women's Hockey League, one of the top teams in Canada. Bev played centre and over the years accumulated many top scorer and most valuable player awards. She tried to retire several times, but each time came back to play again for love of the sport. Her last team was the Brantford Lady Blues – in 1990, at age forty-two, she played with her twenty-four-year-old daughter when the team won the Southern Ontario Ladies Hockey League Championships. She finally retired from the game in 1992.[9]

It is important not to generalize from the experience of athletes like Ruth Hill, Phyllis Bomberry, Bev Beaver, and others from the Six Nations reserve to all girls and women on reserves in the past and now. Six Nations is one of the better-serviced Native communities, in part because of its independent political status, large population base, and close proximity to urban centres in southern Ontario (Forsyth 2005b, 30n27). It also has a long and rich history of women's sport participation, which makes it unique among reserves in Canada (see Paraschak 2005).

Old Crow, home to the Vuntut Gwitch'in First Nation, is about eight hundred kilometres northwest of Whitehorse, in Yukon. Martha Benjamin, born in 1935, grew up in this tiny traditional Native community, where hunting and trapping sustained the village. She married young and had five children by the time she was twenty-five. Always athletic, but with little opportunity to play sports, Martha took up cross-country skiing under the guidance of Father Jean-Marie Mouchet, an Oblate priest who had served with the French ski troops during the Second World War. In the late 1950s, he recognized the potential for encouraging and producing top-level skiers in the Mackenzie Delta and, on his own, set up a training program for those interested.

Given the isolated location of Old Crow, it was difficult for Father Mouchet's skiers to compete except among themselves, though he got them to a competition in Fairbanks, Alaska, where they had "no trouble cleaning the field" (*Whitehorse Star*, January 28, 1963, 1). In January 1963, he managed to bring several men and women (including Martha) to Whitehorse so they could train for the Canadian Cross-Country Ski Championships (Western Division) in Revelstoke, British Columbia, with a view to putting several Old Crow skiers on the Olympic team. Whitehorse businesses and residents responded generously, and in the end some $3,000 was raised to aid the skiers. Martha, along with Ben Charlie, flew to Ottawa to train and compete in the US nationals in Franconia, New Hampshire; the North American Ski championships in Crested Butte, Colorado; and finally the Canadian championships in Midland, Ontario. Father Mouchet predicted: "Martha is steel, straight steel. She could go on forever" (*Whitehorse Star*, February 7, 1963, 1).

Aside from races in Alaska, this was the first time Martha had competed against top North American skiers. In the early 1960s, there was little interest among Canadian and American women in cross-country ski racing, and those who did compete had mostly Finnish or Norwegian backgrounds. Sometimes there were no other women competing at all, as was the case at the US Nationals in New Hampshire, where Martha placed twenty-sixth in a field of sixty-nine men. She had new boots, skis, and correct fittings, supplied through the Department of Indian Affairs. At the Canadian championships in Midland, and racing against women, Martha won the ten-kilometre event with a time of 43:29. She crossed the finish line nearly a minute and a half ahead of more experienced skiers and was declared the official 1963 Canadian women's Nordic champion.

Returning to Old Crow, Martha continued to train, hoping to make the Canadian Olympic team. Unfortunately, there was no money and little interest on the part of the Canadian Olympic Committee to send her to the 1964 Winter Olympics in Innsbruck, Austria.[10] Although women's cross-country ski (now called Nordic) events had been part of the Olympic program since 1952, it was not until 1972 at the Sapporo Winter Olympics in Japan that Canada (and the United States) sent a women's team.

The Confluence of Sport and Aboriginal Policies

When Pierre Trudeau and his Liberal government came to power in 1968, he established a task force to examine Canada's poor performance on the international sporting stage, especially in ice hockey. The *Report of the Task Force on Sport for Canadians* recommended a more interventionist approach by the federal government to amateur sport in general. Throughout the 1970s and 1980s, Canadian governments at the federal, provincial, and territorial levels put more effort and resources into the improvement of Canadian performance in international competition and the development of elite athletes, as well as the encouragement of mass participation for fitness and enjoyment.

The Territorial Experimental Ski Training (TEST) program, established in Inuvik, Northwest Territories (NWT), in 1965, was initially supported by funds from the federal government and later through the NWT government. Like Father Mouchet's earlier project of training skiers in the Mackenzie Delta, the original purpose of TEST was not skiing as such; the basic premise was that Native youth could be motivated to achieve as students and citizens through participation in competitive athletics. The northern environment meant that cross-country skiing was the sport in which they would most likely excel at national and international levels, and those who were successful might become role models for their peers. Norwegian Bjorger Pettersen was hired by the Canadian Amateur Ski Association to work with the TEST program and find the best skiers. At its peak, TEST involved more than five hundred skiers, divided into twelve squads, all based in Inuvik.[11]

Identical twins Sharon and Shirley Firth emerged from this program to become Canada's top female cross-country skiers in the 1970s and early 1980s. Their mother was a status Indian of Gwich'in (meaning "people of the caribou") descent who lost her status when she married her husband, a Loucheux Métis of Scottish heritage. With ten siblings, the Firth sisters grew up in a traditional Native family, living off the land, first in Aklavik and then in Inuvik, where they relocated in 1959. Introduced to skiing as young teenagers by Father Mouchet, they soon became members of Bjorger Pettersen's elite team, travelling to both national and international competitions.

The Firth sisters, along with Roseanne Allen from Inuvik and Helen Sander from Ontario, competed in the cross-country events in the 1972 Winter Olympics in Japan – the first Canadians to do so. Moreover, Allen and the Firths were the first-known Canadian Aboriginal women ever to compete in an Olympic Games. Lacking the experience of the Nordic and other European skiers, Sharon did very well to finish twenty-sixth in the five-kilometre event and twenty-fourth in the ten-kilometre. Unfortunately, Shirley had just recovered from a severe bout of hepatitis and was not in her usual form. Still, in the three-by-five-kilometre relay event, the Firths with anchor Allen came tenth, less than five minutes behind the winning Soviets.

Over careers that lasted almost twenty years, Sharon and Shirley Firth competed in four consecutive Winter Olympic Games and together won seventy-nine national medals, forty-eight of which were gold, twenty-four silver, and seven bronze. As well, they competed in three World Championships.[12] Yet their accomplishments did not come without hardship, prejudice, and, above all, a sense of worthlessness after their competitive careers ended. Rather than being positioned as empowering, pioneering female athletes with remarkable careers, the Firths were sometimes treated by the media as northern "primitives" who were out of their element yet privileged through their involvement in elite sport (O'Bonsawin 2002, 105-6). When Sharon retired from competition, expecting to reap the benefits of an illustrious career, she struggled for years to find suitable employment:

> We were guinea pigs, experimental human beings, at that time we didn't think about it, as we were so young. But now it is terrible, horrible, although we got to travel, we did work hard, train hard with little financial support. We competed from 1968-1985, and left the sport penniless. When we retired it was like we never existed. There was no support in place to help us find other careers, no support for education, the only formal education we received was high school. I was really frightened and scared, didn't know where to turn for help and guidance, in fact it took me years to find employment with the Government of the North-west Territories. (Quoted in ibid., 94)

Although the TEST program gave many of its participants the confidence, strength, and courage they needed for later success, there is no question that others, especially among the elite skiers, had difficulty finding their way once their skiing days were over. Roseanne Allen, for example, tried college and failed; then she went to secretarial school and quit. After working in a local bar, she finally settled into secretarial work in Inuvik and then Yellowknife. In other words, the TEST program, whose underlying purpose was to encourage Native youth to achieve and be successful, failed to teach or provide any post-retirement survival skills. It did not recognize that its participants would have basic needs – such as an education – beyond competitive sport; it also failed to grasp that its participants would be exposed to the racist attitudes of white society beyond the borders of Inuvik and the North.

Aboriginal women have experienced sport and recreation differently from Aboriginal men and certainly other Canadian women, and yet we have so little knowledge, and consequently an inadequate understanding, of these realities and how they ought to be addressed through policies and practice (Paraschak and Forsyth 2011).

A Collective Sense of Self

The paradox of cultural repression, residential schooling, and derision and exclusion, argues Janice Forsyth (2005b, 59), is that they led to the reaffirmation of Aboriginal cultural institutions and identities through powwows and traditional gatherings, the emergence of all-Native sporting competitions, and the elevation of Aboriginal athletes to the status of role models for Native people. Contrary to long-standing state intentions of assimilation, opportunities to participate in Euro-Canadian sports have helped to construct and reinforce Native identities, and perhaps have contributed to ideas about self-determination.

Other authors in this book (for example, Victoria Paraschak) discuss the origin, development, and current status of Canadian Aboriginal sport policy, and how Native and mainstream sport systems articulate. It is important to point out that, for more than thirty years, Aboriginal sport leaders have been building a Native sport system and, at the same time, providing opportunities for Aboriginal athletes to integrate into and receive benefits from the mainstream sport system. The Aboriginal Sport Circle, for instance, is a national organization dedicated to Native sport and recreation development in Canada. Equally important are opportunities for athletes to acknowledge and enhance their Aboriginal cultural identities through events such as the North American Indigenous Games, a major sport and cultural festival held approximately every three years (Forsyth 2005b, 146-47).

The mainstream sport system privileges the values and traditions of white Euro-Canadians who dominate it and hold the most power; in other words, systemic racism persists. All sport systems are gendered, though the Canadian sport system has made significant strides over the last forty years to become more inclusive of women. Well-known Native athletes are overwhelmingly male, mainly because of the opportunities available to them to become professional athletes. There has also been a gender imbalance in the recognition of the accomplishments of Aboriginal male and female athletes in Canada. When the Tom Longboat Award, which had different categories of awards, was established in 1951, there were few opportunities for Native females to demonstrate their athletic prowess and therefore less opportunity to compete for these awards at both the regional and national levels. The initial criteria did not specify if the awards were open to both males and females, instead simply calling for Native athletes who had made a significant contribution to Canadian amateur sport. Formal exclusion from these awards was not necessary, since most Native females did not have access to organized competitive sport. From 1951 to 1972, a total of 149 Tom Longboat Awards were awarded to regional and national recipients. Of that number, only thirteen women (less than 1 percent) were named regional award winners. Only one woman, Phyllis Bomberry, was named a national recipient during that time (in 1968). Between 1973 and 1998, eleven of fifty-two recipients were women, six of whom received the national award. From 1999 onward, with the transfer of the awards to the Aboriginal Sport Circle, there has been a better attempt at gender equity (Forsyth 2005b).

The recognition of Aboriginal athletes within mainstream Canadian sport is not always easy. Some athletes discuss their heritage openly, making a point of emphasizing their Native heritage, and are proud to be singled out as role models for Native youth, but others do not. Recognizing Aboriginal peoples, especially for surveys, research, awards, job hiring, and the like, is often dependent on them self-identifying. As a result, we are not always aware of the accomplishments of Aboriginal women athletes who have chosen to participate in the mainstream sport system. Nevertheless, Aboriginal athletes can be found in a tremendous variety of sports, and just like everyone else, their individual stories differ.

Athletes Roseanne Allen, Martha Benjamin, Ruth Hill, Phyllis Bomberry, Bev Beaver, and Sharon and Shirley Firth have been mentioned already. Another early athlete was Beverly Stranger, a blind woman from the Timiskaming Band of Notre Dame du Nord, in Quebec. In 1976, when just thirteen years old, she competed in the Torontolympiad (Olympics for the physically disabled, a forerunner of the modern Paralympics), where she won a gold medal in the high jump and two silver medals, one in the pentathlon and another in the javelin. The same year she was named one of two national winners, and only the second female, of the Tom Longboat Award.

Very few Aboriginal women athletes have been named to a Canadian Olympic or national team. As mentioned, Roseanne Allen and the Firth sisters were the first Canadian Native women to compete in an Olympics when they did so in 1972 in Sapporo, Japan. It was not until 1988 that another Aboriginal female athlete competed for Canada at the Olympics. Angela Chalmers, born in 1963 in Brandon, Manitoba, to a Scottish father and Sioux mother, is a member of the Birdtail Dakota Nation and was one of this country's greatest middle distance runners. After graduating from high school, Angela attended Northern Arizona University on an athletic scholarship; there she was an eight-time all-American in track and cross-country running. She had her first taste of international success in 1984, winning a bronze in the 3,000 metres at the World University Games in Kobe, Japan. She won silver in the same event at the Pan American Games in 1987, and was a double gold medallist (1,500 metres and 3,000 metres) at the Commonwealth Games in Auckland, New Zealand, becoming the first woman ever to win both events. In 1992, at the Summer Olympic Games in Barcelona, she won the bronze medal in the 3,000 metres. By popular choice, Angela was the Canadian flag-bearer at the opening ceremonies of the Commonwealth Games in Victoria in 1994. Whether or not this was intentional, she became a symbol for inclusiveness, togetherness, and oneness, allowing Canada as the host country to communicate to the rest of the world that Native peoples have equal opportunities to reach the highest levels of achievement (Hargreaves 2000, 95). This symbolism was further consolidated when Chalmers again won the gold medal in the 3,000-metre event, breaking both the Canadian and Commonwealth records.[13]

Another Olympian is Waneek Horn-Miller, a Mohawk born in Kahnawake, Quebec, and one of four daughters of long-time Native activist Kahntineta Horn. In the summer of 1990, at age fourteen, she accompanied her mother to the Mohawk community of Kanesatake, also known as Oka, about thirty miles north of Montreal. The Oka Crisis erupted when the Mohawks tried to stop golf-course development from encroaching on their ancestral burial grounds, leading to a bloody confrontation between Natives, Quebec's provincial police, and the Canadian army. As Waneek tried to leave the scene with her four-year-old sister, a soldier stabbed her in the chest with his bayonet, leaving physical and emotional scars. "I grew up during the crisis," she observed; "I just realized how important being Native was and how important our culture is" (Wong 1996, 16).

Always keenly athletic, Waneek began swimming competitively at age seven, eventually winning some twenty gold medals at the North American Indigenous Games. In 1989, she was an Ontario age group champion, the same year she began playing water polo on her high school team in Hull, Quebec. In 1993, she made the national junior team, helping it finish fifth at the Junior World Championships that year in Quebec City. After graduating from high school, she attended Carleton University in Ottawa, where she played on the women's water polo team and was named female athlete of the year three years in a row. Promoted to the senior national team in 1995, she helped Canada win a gold medal at the 1999 Pan American Games. The team earned a berth at the 2000 Summer Olympics in Sydney, where women's water polo was on the program for the first time. With Waneek as co-captain, the team came in fifth out of six nations. As the first Canadian woman of Mohawk heritage to compete in the Olympic Games, she proudly adorned the cover of *Time* magazine, appearing naked except for a water-polo ball concealing her breasts. She wanted to show other Aboriginal young women a healthy and beautiful body primed to achieve the best in her sport and at the same time change stereotypical beliefs about Native women by showing herself to be strong and dominant, as opposed to weak and sexually submissive (Henrie 1999).

After nine years, Waneek was removed from the national team – a decision she fought, accusing Water Polo Canada of racism. Through mediation, she came to accept that her removal was not because of racism but, rather, differing "cultural perspectives" and miscommunication. As a result, Water Polo Canada agreed to work with the Aboriginal Sport Circle with a view to opening lines of communication to discuss cross-cultural issues in sport.[14] Waneek has continued to speak out courageously against racism in Canadian sport and to encourage Aboriginal youth to see sport and higher education as a means to a better life. She is the coordinator of First Peoples' House at McGill University, a centre for Aboriginal students on campus, as well as an activist, speaker, and television personality.

Pentathlete Monica Pinette, a Métis from Langley, British Columbia, was the lone Canadian Aboriginal, male or female, at the 2004 Summer Olympics in Athens, and also in Beijing in 2008. The modern pentathlon is a demanding event requiring skills important long ago in the military: épée fencing, pistol shooting, swimming, equestrian show jumping, and cross-country running. She placed thirteenth in Athens but fell to twenty-seventh in Beijing. Monica has only recently embraced her Aboriginal heritage – her father is Métis and her Kenyan mother is white – prompted by her discovery that there were no other Aboriginal competitors on the Canadian team. At the closing ceremonies in Athens, she proudly wore a colourful Métis sash around her waist, something she was prevented from doing in Beijing because of strict rules against political statements of any kind (Mickleburgh 2008).

Despite a strong Aboriginal cultural presence at the 2010 Winter Olympics in Vancouver, the two-hundred-member Canadian team was again lacking representation from athletes of Aboriginal heritage. One member was

Caroline Calve, a snowboarder from Lachine, Quebec, who claims an Aboriginal background of Algonquin heritage; she competed in the women's parallel giant slalom, placing twentieth overall. Caroline is also part of the First Nations Snowboard Team, a group promoting Aboriginal involvement and success in sport.

Several other Native athletes have achieved international success in their sport. Doris Jones, a Métis from Selkirk, Manitoba, is a world-class archer who proudly wears a Métis sash, using it as a belt for her arrow quiver. Lara Mussell Savage, an international ultimate Frisbee competitor, is a member of the Skwah First Nation of Chilliwack, British Columbia. In 2004, she was named Aboriginal female athlete of the year, winning the national Tom Longboat Award. Ringette player Shelly Hruska, a Métis from Winnipeg, played a key role in Canada's gold medal at the 2004 World Ringette Championships. She is now a teacher and coach contributing both to the sport of ringette and to the well-being of children in her community. Tara Hedican is an Anishinaabe from Ontario whose wrestling career led her to be named an alternate to the 2004 Olympic team. In 2001, she received a Tom Longboat Award as the country's top female Aboriginal athlete.

Other athletes have made a name for themselves at the national level: Chelsie Mitchell, a snowboarder, grew up on a reserve in Moricetown, British Columbia, and dreams of making the Canadian national team; Brooke Pighin, a Métis from Port Alberni, British Columbia, is a Western Canada Games gold medalist and has been on a track scholarship (javelin is her speciality) at both Fresno State and the University of Washington; and Faith McDonald, a Cree from Nelson House, Manitoba, was the first Aboriginal athlete to join the Olympic Oval High Performance Female Hockey Program in Calgary. In addition to these are the many athletes who have achieved success at the North American Indigenous Games and the Arctic Winter Games, or who have won a regional or national Tom Longboat Award for their athletic prowess.

Aboriginal women coaches, officials, and sport administrators have always played an important role in Native sports and recreation, as well in the mainstream amateur sport system. Influential and devoted Aboriginal coaches are now being recognized through the National Aboriginal Coaching Awards, sponsored by the Aboriginal Sport Circle. Women are certainly among those receiving recognition, but they are also under-represented, as are women in general in Canadian sport leadership. Moreover, very few Aboriginal women have made inroads into the higher levels of coaching and sports administration in mainstream sport in Canada. Similarly, only a few exceptional women have infiltrated the top administrative levels in the Aboriginal and mainstream Canadian sport system.[15]

Conclusion

Writing the story of Aboriginal women in Canadian sport has not been an easy task, and this chapter is only a beginning – hence the word "toward" in the title. First of all, we lack basic research. For example, many anthropological studies on Aboriginal traditional games are gender-biased because, for the most part, they were undertaken before "gender" as a category of analysis became important. We also know very little about the patterns of Native female involvement in sport on specific reserve settings, both in the past and present. Paraschak's research (2005) on the Six Nations Reserve in Ontario is an exemplar of what can be done; it needs to be replicated on many other reserves and in Métis settlements throughout the country. Similarly, we know something about how gender impacted the lives of Aboriginal children and youth in residential schools, but there is more to be done with regard to their participation (or lack of it) in games, sports, and other recreational activities.

We also need to hear more from Aboriginal sportswomen both current and former; in other words, we need to provide opportunities for them to tell their own stories. In sum, we need to engage in much more oral history. Studies like those by Christine O'Bonsawin (2002) on the Olympian Firth sisters and by Janice Forsyth (2005b) on Tom Longboat Award winners, both researchers having made extensive use of interviews with the athletes themselves, are exceptional examples. Sally Manning's well-researched account (2006) of the Arctic cross-country skiers who challenged the world is very valuable, and we need more books like it. Jennifer Hargreaves's scholarly analysis (2000) gives ample space to Aboriginal women to share their lived experiences, identities, and cultures.

Not only do we need more studies documenting the experience of Aboriginal females in sport but we also need to utilize more sophisticated analyses of how race, class, and gender intersect and shape their experiences. For example, the lack of visibility of Native women in both written histories and award structures (e.g., sports halls of fame and museums) reinforces the myth that Aboriginal women do not participate in sport, and that if they do, they are not worthy of recognition (Forsyth 2005b). This chapter shows that many Native women have made a name for themselves in Native or non-Native sport – and some in both – and still they have not received the recognition they so richly deserve. Beyond stating the obvious, it is important to analyze why this is the case.

Finally, the notion of role model, especially as it applies to Aboriginal women athletes, requires some rethinking. It seems obvious that Aboriginal women athletes who achieve success, especially in mainstream Canadian sport, would see themselves as positive role models to inspire more Native females to participate and compete in sport. Indeed, most research studies and sport policy statements emphasize the need for more Native athletic role models. Some scholars, however, point to the racialized discourse embedded in role model terminology. For instance, Kenneth Shropshire (2002, 136, emphasis in original), argues that the term "role model" can be viewed as an updated version of the old adage "You must be *a credit to your race*" and thus reinforces racist notions about white cultural superiority. Certainly, successful white women athletes become role models and some make a living as motivational speakers, but the important point here is that successful Aboriginal athletes are frequently labelled role models only for *Native* youth. They still must learn to negotiate their Native identities in relation to non-Native athletes in mainstream sport (Forsyth 2005b). For example, no Aboriginal female athlete has ever been awarded either the Bobbie Rosenfeld Award or the Velma Springstead Trophy. Since 1933, the former has been given annually to Canada's best female athlete as voted upon by members of the Canadian Press. The Springstead trophy, also known as the "Rose Bowl," was first awarded by the Women's Amateur Athletic Federation in 1934 to Canada's outstanding female athlete; it is now managed by the True Sport Foundation. Yet, no Aboriginal athlete, male or female, has ever won the Lou Marsh Trophy, awarded annually since 1936 by a panel of sports journalists in recognition of Canada's top professional or amateur athlete. Researchers could enhance our understanding of this problem by examining the social and historical relationship of symbolic systems like the Lou Marsh Trophy, the Bobbie Rosenfeld Award, and the Velma Springstead Trophy, asking why Aboriginal athletes, despite their obvious success in sports, have not yet won any of these awards. Aboriginal athletes, especially female athletes, still must negotiate their involvement in sport from a position of marginality.

NOTES

1 Readers wishing to learn more about Aboriginal women's history in Canada will find an extensive bibliography in Kelm and Townsend (2006, 407-18).

2 There are very few representations of women playing double ball, and most accounts are based on this slim evidence. One is by the early-nineteenth-century painter and author George Catlin, who described and sketched a game played by Sioux women, which he witnessed at Prairie du Chien on the Mississippi River in the southern United States (see Catlin 1841, 144-47). Also, painter Seth Eastman recorded a similar scene in 1829 among the Menominee in the vicinity of Fort Crawford, Wisconsin.

3 For an understanding of gender (and in particular women) in Canadian fur-trade society from the late seventeenth to the late nineteenth century, see the early work of feminist historian Sylvia Van Kirk (1980) and anthropologist Jennifer Brown (1980). More recent analyses include chapters by Susan Sleeper-Smith and Bruce M. White in Kelm and Townsend (2006).

4 This account can be found on the second page of the *Montreal Gazette,* August 5, 1867, under the title "The Lachine Regatta."

5 For useful discussions about these stereotypes and how they have continued to perpetuate racism and sexism, see Acoose (1995), Burgess and Valaskakis (1992), and Francis (1992).

6 In addition to the article by Laurie Meijer Drees (1993), see also her master's thesis (1991). For additional critical analysis of the Banff Indian Days, see Mason (2008, 2010), and for a more popular history, see Parker (1990). See also Kelm (2011) for a history of rodeo in western Canada, and especially her discussion of competitions in which contestants vied within their own gendered and racialized categories.

7 Grollier Hall was one of two residences of the Aklavik Catholic Indian Residential School (later Inuvik Indian Residential School) that housed hundreds of Dene, Métis, and Inuit children from all over the western Arctic. This school opened in 1925, closed in 1952, reopened in 1959, and closed finally in 1985. Four former employees of Grollier Hall were later convicted of sexual assault and given jail sentences.

8 Information about Phyllis Bomberry comes from an interview I conducted with her in 2002, as well as from an interview by Janice Forsyth in 2004 for her doctoral dissertation. Phyllis is now retired and lives on the Six Nations reserve in Ontario. An injured left knee and other health problems have prevented her from actively playing and competing in sport for many years. Instead, she enjoys watching almost all sports on television, especially football, and pursuing a long-time interest in Native artwork and crafts.

9 Information about Bev Beaver comes from interviews I conducted with both her and her husband in 2002. I am grateful to George Beaver for providing newspaper clippings, articles, and other information about his wife's accomplishments. Additional information came from an interview conducted in 2004 by Janice Forsyth for her doctoral dissertation. Today, Bev and her husband live on the Six Nation reserve.

10 I interviewed Martha Benjamin in May 2002, and she is mentioned in Manning (2006). Today, she is a lively, active woman with thirteen grandchildren. She has her own dog team and loves to spend time at her cabin in the bush. She still skis and helps maintain the trails around Old Crow. She is a member of the Canadian Rangers, part-time reservists who provide a military presence in remote, isolated, and coastal Canadian communities, and in 2001, she received the Governor General's Caring

Canadian Award. In 1989, she was inducted into the Sport Yukon Hall of Fame for her accomplishments in cross-country skiing.

11 For more information on TEST, see O'Bonsawin (2002) and Manning (2006).

12 Much more information about the Firth sisters, including their many accomplishments, can be found in O'Bonsawin (2002) and Manning (2006). Today, they both reside in Yellowknife, where Sharon Firth is a youth adviser with the Government of the NWT. Shirley Firth-Larsson, a teacher, lived in France for more than twenty years with her husband and three daughters; the family has now returned to Canada. Among their many honours, Shirley and her sister have both received the Order of Canada and a National Aboriginal Achievement Award.

13 There is an interesting television program about Angela Chalmers in the *Chiefs and Champions* series, available (as a DVD) through Moving Images Distribution of Vancouver. Today, she is the mother of two children and lives in Queensland, Australia. In 1994, she received a National Aboriginal Achievement Award. Also available in the *Chiefs and Champions* series are programs about Sharon and Shirley Firth, and also Waneek Horn-Miller.

14 This information comes from a press release issued by Water Polo Canada on January 19, 2004. See http://www.sirc.ca/news_service.cfm.

15 For an excellent discussion of the many issues concerning Aboriginal women's involvement in sport and recreation leadership, see Forsyth and Paraschak (2008).

REFERENCES

Acoose, J. 1995. *Neither Indian Princesses nor Easy Squaws*. Toronto: Women's Press.

Anderson, K. 2000. *Recognition of Being: Reconstructing Native Womanhood*. Toronto: Sumach Press.

Beers, W.G. 1869. *Lacrosse*. Montreal: Dawson Bros.

Brown, J.S.H. 1980. *Strangers in Blood: Fur Trade Company Families in Indian Country*. Vancouver: UBC Press.

Burgess, M., and G.G. Valaskakis. 1992. *Indian Princesses and Cowgirls: Stereotypes from the Frontier*. Montreal: Orboro.

Catlin, G. 1841. *Letters and Notes on the Manners, Customs, and Conditions of the North American Indians*. Vol. 2. London, UK: G. Catlin.

Cheska, A. 1982. Ball game participation of North American Indian women. In R. Howell, ed., *Her Story in Sports: A Historical Anthology of Women in Sports* (19-34). West Point, NY: Leisure Press.

Dempsey, H.A. 2008. The Indians and the Stampede. In M. Foran, ed., *Icon, Brand, Myth: The Calgary Stampede* (47-72). Edmonton: Athabasca University Press.

Forsyth, J. 2005a. After the fur trade: First Nations women in Canadian history, 1850-1950. *Atlantis: A Women's Studies Journal* 29(2): 69-78.

–. 2005b. The power to define: A history of the Tom Longboat Awards, 1951-2001. PhD diss., University of Western Ontario.

–. 2007. To my sisters in the field. *Pimatisiwin: A Journal of Indigenous and Aboriginal and Community Health* 5(1): 155-68.

Forsyth, J., and V. Paraschak. 2008. *Moving Forward: A National Roundtable on Aboriginal Women in Sport February 22-24, 2008 Final Report*. Ottawa:

Canadian Association for the Advancement of Women and Sport and Physical Activity. http://www.caaws.ca/.

Francis, D. 1992. *The Imaginary Indian: The Image of the Indian in Canadian Culture*. Vancouver: Arsenal Pulp Press.

Giles, A.R. 2004. Kevlar®, Crisco®, and menstruation: "Tradition" and Dene games. *Sociology of Sport Journal* 21(1): 18-35.

–. 2005. A Foucaultian approach to menstrual practices in the Dehcho Region, Northwest Territories, Canada. *Arctic Anthropology* 42(2): 9-21.

Gottfred, A. 2000. On the question of female voyageurs. *Northwest Journal* 7: 40-43. http://www.northwestjournal.ca/VII6.htm.

Griffiths, P. 1935. The girl and the game. *Toronto Telegram,* June 4, p. 23.

Hall, M.A. 2002. *The Girl and the Game: A History of Women's Sport in Canada.* Peterborough, ON: Broadview.

Hargreaves, J. 2000. Aboriginal sportswomen: Heroines of difference or objects of assimilation? In *Heroines of Sport: The Politics of Difference and Identity* (78-128). New York: Routledge.

Heine, M. 1999. *Dene Games: A Cultural and Resource Manual.* Yellowknife: Sport North Federation.

–. 2002. *Arctic Sports: A Training and Resource Manual.* Yellowknife: Sport North Federation.

Henrie, K.A. 1999. Naked Waneek Horn-Miller: Incredible performances call for reinterpretation. MA thesis, University of Ottawa.

Kelm, M. 2011. *A Wilder West: Rodeo in Western Canada.* Vancouver: UBC Press.

Kelm, M., and L. Townsend, eds. 2006. *In the Days of Our Grandmothers: A Reader in Aboriginal Women's History in Canada.* Toronto: University of Toronto Press.

Koserski, L. 1969. Indians triumph. *Hamilton Spectator,* June 6, p. 45.

LeCompte, M.L. 1993. *Cowgirls of the Rodeo: Pioneer Professional Athletes.* Champaign: University of Illinois Press.

Manning, S. 2006. *Guts and Glory: The Arctic Skiers Who Changed the World.* Yellowknife: Up Here Publishing.

Mason, C.W. 2008. The construction of Banff as a "natural" environment: Sporting festivals, tourism, and representations of Aboriginal people. *Journal of Sport History* 25(2): 401-16.

–. 2010. "All of our secrets are in these mountains": Problematizing colonial power relations, tourism productions and histories of the cultural and physical practices of Nakoda peoples in the Banff-Bow valley, 1870-1980. PhD diss., University of Alberta.

Meijer Drees, L. 1991. Making Banff a wild west: Norman Luxton, Indians and Banff tourism, 1902-1945. MA thesis, University of Calgary.

–. 1993. "Indians' bygone past": The Banff Indian Days, 1902-1945. *Past Imperfect* 2: 7-28.

Mickleburgh, R. 2008. Politics unravels Aboriginal athlete's plan to wear traditional garb. *Globe and Mail,* August 19, p. A9.

Miller, J.R. 1996. *Shingwauk's Vision: A History of Native Residential Schools.* Toronto: University of Toronto Press.

O'Bonsawin, C.M. 2002. Failed TEST: Aboriginal sport policy and the Olympian Firth sisters. MA thesis, University of Western Ontario.

Oxendine, J.B. 1995. *American Indian Sports Heritage.* Lincoln: University of Nebraska Press.

Paikin, S. 1980. The team in dark uniforms aroused a love of sports. *Hamilton Spectator*, August 2, p. 18.

Pakes, F. 1990. "Skill to do comes in the doing": Purpose in traditional Indian winter games and pastimes. In E. Corbet and A. Rasporich, eds., *Winter Sports in the West* (26-37). Calgary: Historical Society of Alberta.

Paraschak, V. 1998. Reasonable amusements: Connecting strands of physical culture in Native lives. *Sport History Review* 29(1): 121-31.

–. 2005. An examination of sport for Aboriginal females on the Six Nations Reserve, 1968-1980. In C.R. King, ed., *Native Athletes in Sport and Society* (170-88). Lincoln: University of Nebraska Press.

Paraschak, V., and J. Forsyth. 2011. Invisible but not absent: Aboriginal women, knowledge production and the restructuring of Canadian sport. In D. Adair and S. Pope, eds., *Sport, "Race" and Ethnicity: Narratives of Diversity and Difference* (219-34). Morgantown, WV: Fitness Information Technology.

Parker, P. 1990. *The Feather and the Drum: The History of the Banff Indian Days 1889-1978.* Calgary: Consolidated Communications.

Pettipas, K. 1994. *Severing the Ties That Bind: Government Repression of Indigenous Religious Ceremonies on the Prairies.* Winnipeg: University of Manitoba Press.

Robinson, L. 1997. *She Shoots, She Scores: Canadian Perspectives on Women in Sport.* Toronto: Thompson Educational.

Shropshire, K. 2002. Race, youth, athletes, and role models. In M. Gatz, M. Messner, and S. Ball-Rokeach, eds., *Paradoxes of Youth and Sport* (135-40). Albany: State University of New York Press.

Sleeper-Smith, S. 2006. Women, kin, and Catholicism: New perspectives on the fur trade. In M. Kelm and L. Townsend, eds., *In the Days of Our Grandmothers* (26-55). Toronto: University of Toronto Press.

Thomas, G. 1990. Sports and leisure in the nineteenth century fur trade. In E. Corbet and A. Rasporich, eds., *Winter Sports in the West* (13-25). Calgary: Historical Society of Alberta.

Van Kirk, S. 1980. *Many Tender Ties: Women in Fur-Trade Society, 1670-1870.* Winnipeg: Watson and Dwyer.

Vennum, T. 2008. *American Indian Lacrosse: Little Brother of War.* Baltimore: Johns Hopkins University Press. First published 1994 by the Smithsonian Institution Press.

White, B.M. 2006. The woman who married a beaver: Trade patterns and gender roles in the Ojibwa fur trade. In M. Kelm and L. Townsend, eds., *In the Days of Our Grandmothers* (56-92). Toronto: University of Toronto Press.

Wong, C. 1996. Oka vet water polo national. *Windspeaker* 14(1): 16.

PART 2

CONTEMPORARY ISSUES

Aboriginal Peoples and the Construction of Canadian Sport Policy

VICTORIA PARASCHAK

In 2005, the federal government released *Sport Canada's Policy on Aboriginal Peoples' Participation in Sport* (the Aboriginal sport policy). In this chapter, I examine the ways the policy described in this document contributes to the ongoing development and institutionalization of Aboriginal sport in Canada, as well as the significance of the policy to the Canadian sport system. I do this through three interconnected themes related to the Aboriginal sport policy. Using the model of the double helix, I explain the ways that the sport structure for Aboriginal peoples in Canada provides a racialized, a racializing, and at times a racist sporting space for Aboriginal peoples. For each of these three themes, I first explain it and discuss the ways it works, then explore how Aboriginal feedback in the policy process, as well as the final policy released by Sport Canada, did or did not address each theme or provide relevant recommendations. These themes, taken together, suggest that (1) the Aboriginal sport policy has formalized a federal presence in Aboriginal sport development that contributes to a legalistic but potentially inclusive racialized structure for Aboriginal participants, (2) the Aboriginal sport policy acknowledges the positive racializing contributions made by the Aboriginal sport system through events such as the North American Indigenous Games (NAIG), and by Aboriginal role models who can help to promote a uniquely Aboriginal vision of sport, and (3) the Aboriginal sport policy does not adequately address racist problems in the mainstream sport system or the unequal power relations that continue to undercut the legitimation of an Aboriginal vision of sport in favour of one that privileges the mainstream sport system, and thus falls short of its goal of fostering a more values-based Canadian sport system.

Aboriginal Racialized Sporting Spaces: The Double Helix

> *We are what we are not.*
>
> – *Jean-Paul Sartre,* Being and Nothingness[1]

The double helix is a concept used by the national Aboriginal Sport Circle to describe the sport structure for Aboriginal peoples in Canada.[2] One strand of the double helix is the Aboriginal sport system, the second strand is the mainstream sport system. The Aboriginal and the mainstream sport systems shape and are shaped by racialized, racializing, and at times racist practices that both strengthen Aboriginal identities and problematize them.[3] Rungs that join these two systems indicate points of connection between them, offering the possibility that participants in the Aboriginal sport system can benefit through insights from the mainstream sport system, and non-Aboriginal participants can benefit from Aboriginal approaches to sport. The Aboriginal sport policy is potentially one such rung, enabling Sport Canada to enhance services for Aboriginal participants in both the Aboriginal sport system and the mainstream system, while addressing under-representation and racism in the mainstream sport system. The degree that the Aboriginal sport policy contributes to this possibility is the focus of the following analysis.

Framework for Analysis

This discussion, centred on the double helix model for Aboriginal sport, is premised on the theoretical assumptions underlying (1) duality of structure, (2) unequal power relations, and (3) a strengths perspective. In keeping with duality of structure, it is assumed that both Aboriginal and mainstream sport systems are constantly being (re)created through the actions of individuals who are operating within the boundaries they can imagine for sporting spaces – and that, through their actions, these individuals continue to reinforce, or at times challenge, the structures that already exist (Giddens 1984; Paraschak 2000). Particular individuals (e.g., organizers, administrators) hold the authority to make the rules that govern behaviour within sport – they can thus create and reinforce (e.g., through the control and provision of desired resources) the type of sport system that they prefer. Consequently, those individuals who create the rules or are more able to access available resources are privileged over others in a sport system. The underlying unequal power relations, which privilege some individuals while marginalizing others, facilitate the creation of particular understandings about socially constructed personal characteristics such as gender, age, physical ability, and race. In keeping with this framework, identifying who makes the rules and who has greater access to the resources is necessary to clarify who is privileged versus subordinated within each sport system (Paraschak and Tirone 2008). Lastly, this analysis incorporates a strengths perspective (Saleebey 2009). The strengths perspective assumes that in any situation there are already strengths being demonstrated, including by members living within marginalized or disadvantaged conditions. Existing strengths are identified by individuals within a group or community, who are then encouraged to build upon what they already do well, while simultaneously identifying and addressing challenges to those strengths. This perspective differs from a deficit perspective, wherein individuals begin by identifying barriers they face to successfully operate within the mainstream system – what they "need" to change so that they can "fit" into it (Baikie 2003). In keeping with these academic frameworks of duality of structure, unequal power relations, and the strengths perspective, I assume in this chapter that Aboriginal participants and organizers should be empowered in both Aboriginal and mainstream sport systems to reproduce their strengths and address challenges to those strengths. Accordingly, the Aboriginal sport policy would ideally make a contribution to the ongoing development of Aboriginal sport in Canada by facilitating existing strengths in the system and reducing unequal power relations.

Racialized, Racializing, and Racist Spaces

"Space" is a socially constructed resource. It comes into existence as a desired, defined item, bounded and accessible to some more so than others, as determined by privileged decision makers in positions of power. Sporting events occur within and are themselves socially constructed "spaces" – that is, opportunities with defined boundaries. Embedded in the structuring of those spaces are hierarchies of acceptable practices, as defined by various social determinants, including gender, class, age, physical ability, sexual orientation, race, and ethnicity. For example, Coakley and Donnelly (2004, 241) have identified professional sport as a masculine space, underpinned by a gender logic whereby those who participate and those who spectate view the "doing" of societally dominant or "hegemonic" masculinity, described as "virility, power, and toughness," as the preferred and celebrated social practice. In effect, an operational hierarchy by gender is reinforced and facilitates the privileging of particular notions of gender over others.[4] These notions shape and are shaped by broader unequal gender relations in North American society.

The dominant sport system in Canada is likewise underpinned by "race logic." Cosentino (1998), for example, argues that concepts of amateurism were grounded in race discrimination in North America, as opposed to the class discrimination underlying amateurism in Britain. In an earlier work (Paraschak 1996, 9), I explore the concept of racialized spaces in relation to Aboriginal peoples with a focus on the powwow, observing that "space acts as a resource potentially available to all people, but is in reality too often defined and controlled by those in positions of privilege. Racialized spaces thus become social spaces defined, often by 'the other,' in terms of Aboriginal access or non-access. Such spaces are constructed within the context of unequal societal race relations, and subsequently tend to reproduce those relations over time." More recently, racialized spaces were discussed in terms of "whitestream sport," as applied to the mainstream sport system. Paraschak and Tirone (2008, 90-91) noted,

> Claude Denis (1997) uses the term *whitestream society* "to indicate that Canadian society, while principally structured on the basis of the European, 'white', experience, is far from being simply 'white' in socio-demographic, economic and cultural terms" (p. 13). Extending his term, the rules of mainstream or "whitestream" sport have been primarily shaped by individuals of white European heritage in ways that privilege their traditions, practices, meanings, and sport structures. This is an example of "institutionalized racism," since the structure of the system, if followed, will always produce outcomes that discriminate against those who are not white – it will privilege Caucasians of European heritage over others.

In this analysis, I continue to build on the idea of racialized spaces, but I am also paying attention to potential outcomes of that racial structuring for the participants. Specifically, I look at sport as a racializing space and, at times, a racist space. A racializing space is created when the "doing" of an operational race hierarchy facilitates the (re)creation of racialized identities. For example, individuals may participate in a local Aboriginal sporting competition (e.g., hockey, basketball, bowling) involving only Aboriginal participants and organizers, and leave that event with no shifts in or reflections on their racial identity. They are, of course, "doing race," but it remains at the level of their practical consciousness[5] – they continue to naturalize a particular understanding of their racial identity, but it remains unexamined. The same Aboriginal participants may, however, compete at the NAIG, surrounded by Aboriginal cultural performers from different nations across North America, and leave with an enhanced sense of his or her Aboriginal identity because the racial structuring of that sporting space facilitated a heightened awareness of a particular interpretation(s) of Aboriginality. A Caucasian spectator may likewise come away, after watching the Aboriginal participants at these games, with a heightened sense of his or her Caucasian (i.e., non-Aboriginal) racial identity. In both cases, their racial identity has come to the forefront through a sporting experience; this sporting event has thus become an overtly racializing space.

A racist space is (re)constructed when participants or spectators are treated as the racialized "other" within a sporting space; the operational race hierarchy thus constrained and devalued them, by race, within that environment. However, the longer-term consequences of that racist experience differ. When those who are privileged in the broader society leave what was for them a racist sporting space, the race hierarchy wherein they are privileged returns and the experience of being a racialized "other" is ended. For groups that are marginalized in the broader society, however, the experiencing of a racist sporting space further reinforces the unequal race relations – and their sense of being a racialized "other" – within the broader society.[6]

As mentioned, the Aboriginal Sport Circle has adopted the double helix model as its model for Aboriginal sport. Stylized loosely on a genetic DNA strand, this model recognizes that for Aboriginal sport participants there are two separate sport systems – the Aboriginal sport system and the mainstream sport system – which can connect to each other at various points. This model recognizes the legitimacy of sporting competitions organized by Aboriginal administrators for Aboriginal participants as existing alongside and being equal to the mainstream sport system. In both systems, events range from grassroots, community-level sport through to regional, national, and international competitions. Both sport systems have national, provincial or territorial, and local administrative sport organizations overseeing sporting opportunities. As racialized spaces, however, they are somewhat different. The Aboriginal sport system is overtly structured along racial lines;[7] participants are regulated in some manner in keeping with Aboriginal heritage, privileging Aboriginal over non-Aboriginal participants. The mainstream sport system is officially open equally to all Canadians, regardless of race. In keeping with whitestream sport, however, the structure of the system is covertly aligned with Euro-Canadian notions of sport and thus constrains Aboriginal participation relative to Caucasian participants. Both of these systems can operate as racializing spaces or as racist spaces, though the longer-term consequences of racist spaces vary. For example, the broader power relations in sport and in Canadian society will privilege Caucasians over Aboriginal peoples in general. Below I discuss each of these three characteristics (racialized, racializing, and racist sporting spaces) of the double helix, addressing the strengths and accompanying challenges implicit in each, and the degree to which the Aboriginal sport policy helps to optimize Aboriginal involvement in sport in terms of that characteristic.

Racialized Sporting Spaces

Defining participants based on their Aboriginal heritage is a central feature of the Aboriginal sport system, which makes it an overtly racialized sporting space. Determining who is allowed to participate in sport varies, depending on the event. For example, the "Little NHL" is the longest-running inter-reserve First Nations hockey tournament in Ontario. The first hockey tournament was held in 1971 in Little Current, hosted by the Whitefish River, Sucker Creek, and West Bay First Nations, and involved seventeen teams (Greater Sudbury Department of Growth and Development 2005). The thirty-sixth Little NHL, held March 11-16, 2007, in Sudbury, welcomed "more than 2,000 young aboriginal [male and female] players, from Tyke to Midget, along with up to three thousand coaches, officials and family members" (Greater Sudbury Department of Growth and Development 2006). To be eligible, participants were required, among other things, to provide evidence of Aboriginal heritage, as outlined in the 2011 player eligibility criteria:

> a) Players must have a valid "Certificate of Indian Status" indicating an Ontario First Nation;
>
> OR
>
> b) Players, without status cards from Ontario, must have at least one biological parent who has a "Certificate of Indian Status" card from an Ontario First Nation. Any player using their parents' status card MUST provide a "Statement of Live Birth" long form or B.C.R. from their Parents' First Nation which verifies that the parent is a member

> of that Ontario First Nation. Document MUST be received by the Host First Nation by the final deadline date. (Little Native Hockey League 2011, 2)

Eligibility was further determined by the size of the community, with rules on team composition varying for communities of five thousand or more, versus smaller communities (Little Native Hockey League 2011, 3). The eligibility criterion based on community size thus provided for greater inclusivity among "legitimate" Ontario First Nations participants, recognizing the different conditions faced by potential athletes.

The national chief of the Assembly of First Nations and the Grand Council chief of the Union of Ontario Indians attended the 2006 Little NHL opening ceremonies. They were accompanied by the deputy mayor of Greater Sudbury, who noted, "The Little NHL is much more than a hockey tournament; it is one of the foremost cultural gatherings in our country and a unique opportunity for us to embrace the Aboriginal culture that is a critical part of our community" (Anishinaabe Blog 2006). Through this statement, he identified the Little NHL as a unique Aboriginal cultural event, and Aboriginal peoples as a unique group within the community. In doing so, he alerted both Aboriginal and non-Aboriginal peoples to the racialized nature of this event – in contrast to sporting events that remain undeclared in terms of their racial structuring. The Little NHL example illustrates one of many ways that Aboriginal sporting events can be racialized.

Another example of a racialized sporting space is the NAIG. Held for the first time in Edmonton in 1990, the NAIG has its own set of rules governing Aboriginal participants. The 2008 eligibility rules noted:

> All athletes competing in the NAIG must be born of North American Indigenous ancestry. All participants must make proof of ancestry available. The following will be accepted as proof of ancestry:
>
> Canada: Treaty/Status Card, First Nations Card, Inuit and Inuvialuit identification or Provincial Metis Card.
>
> United States: Tribal Card or Declaration of Ancestry.
>
> (North American Indigenous Games Council 2008, section 2.1)

If none of the above applied (e.g., non-status Indians), a Declaration of Indigenous Ancestry had to be completed by the athlete, submitted to the team, and endorsed by the team chef de mission. If a protest was lodged against such a participant, the declaration accompanied by all relevant proof of ancestry (birth certificate, tribal/band letters, and all other pertinent documents) had to be presented by the team on behalf of the athlete, as proof of ancestry.

These examples demonstrate the complex, legalistic approach to defining "legitimate" Aboriginal participants at events within the Aboriginal sport system. A strength of these sporting events is that it is Aboriginal organizers who create the rules that structure the events' racialized nature. Thus, Aboriginal individuals are in control of defining the rules for access to the events in a manner that is not possible within the mainstream sport system. The Little NHL's decision to acknowledge differences created by size of community, or to allow for a Declaration of Indigenous Ancestry for the NAIG, follows from organizers' awareness of varying factors they believe have an impact on potential participants. An accompanying challenge to this strength, then, is that defining who counts as an Aboriginal can be divisive among Aboriginal peoples; this does not happen in the mainstream sport system, since participants from all heritages are theoretically eligible to compete. The determination of who "counts" as Aboriginal, and thus who qualifies for the accompanying resources, has had a long and contentious history in Canada.

Various resources are connected to the federal government's awarding of Indian status, as defined in the Indian Act. In 1985, the criteria for determining Indian status were amended through Bill C-31. Up until then, status Indian women who married non-Aboriginal men lost their status and treaty rights, as did their children. After Bill C-31 was passed, the women could regain their rights and Indian status, including the option to move back to their reserves to reside, if they wished; however, if their child was to marry a non-Aboriginal spouse and then have a child who also married a non-Aboriginal spouse, that grandchild would lose his or her Indian status (Aboriginal Affairs and Northern Development Canada 2012). This government-regulated process for defining Indian status is contentious among Aboriginal peoples; the use of government-derived definitions within the Aboriginal sport system extends that controversy into the sporting realm. In this way, sport has an ability to be divisive (rather than to foster inclusion) among potential Aboriginal participants. As a next step, then, it is important that the rules defining "legitimate" Aboriginal participants be examined in light of the broader goals of the Aboriginal sport system. If inclusion is a goal of that system, then organizers could consider broadening their definition to include participants who have any Aboriginal ancestors, regardless of the government's assessment of their official Aboriginal status.

The same situation arises in the Aboriginal sport policy concerning who exactly is being addressed by this policy promoting "Aboriginal" peoples' participation in sport. Aboriginal peoples are defined in Appendix A of the policy as follows: "The term Aboriginal Peoples in a constitutional context, the Constitution Act, 1982, defines the Aboriginal Peoples of Canada as including Indians, Inuit and Métis" (Canadian Heritage 2005, 9). The policy does not further clarify who can or cannot benefit from the resources available through it, but the definition implies a legalistic approach to Aboriginal status, drawing upon government-constructed definitions of Aboriginal peoples and so adopting the problems embedded within those definitions. The Aboriginal sport policy thus potentially reproduces the narrow definition of "who counts" as an Aboriginal participant, rather than facilitating the broadening of it to be more inclusive.

On the other hand, the policy does identify barriers that relate to differences in conditions among Aboriginal peoples – by economic circumstance, by distance, by jurisdiction, and by sport infrastructure (Canadian Heritage 2005, 4-5). The barrier of distance is reflected in a comment made by the Ontario delegates, who noted during the consultation process on the development of the Aboriginal sport policy that "geographical realities [need to] be explicitly identified in the policy framework. While the new ... policy may not have a dramatic impact ... on small or isolated communities, overlooking the fact that these inequities [e.g., increased competition travel costs due to greater isolation from other communities] exist will distort the overall effectiveness of the policy and further marginalize those communities" (Sport Canada 2003, 12).[8] This issue was in turn addressed in the Aboriginal sport policy. It was mentioned as one of the guiding principles – "Aboriginal Peoples in Canada live in a complex environment and geography. Challenges exist in transportation and provision of competition and training opportunities for Aboriginal Peoples living in remote locations" (Canadian Heritage 2005, 5) – and in Appendix A, definitions of key terms, in the definition of equitable access: "There may still exist discrepancies in sport services for individuals living in geographically remote areas or in economically disadvantaged situations" (ibid., 9).

The Policy Statements section for Enhanced Participation states that "programs, services and resources must recognize the unique need of all Aboriginal populations, including youth, girls and women, and persons with a disability" (Canadian Heritage 2005, 6). This Sport Canada position, aimed in part at significantly increasing Aboriginal participation in quality sport activities, along with the aforementioned guiding principle and addressing the identified barriers outlined above, could facilitate a broader, more inclusive interpretation of "Aboriginal participants." Such an understanding would align with current eligibility criteria in the Aboriginal sport system, which recognizes different conditions facing participants and incorporates this understanding into the criteria that defines a "legitimate" participant in an event.

Appendix D of the Aboriginal sport policy, titled "Demographic Information," provides a largely grim picture of the lives of Aboriginal peoples in Canada. The appendix could have served a very different purpose if the statistics had been complemented by a recounting of the many ways Aboriginal peoples have actively worked to create cultural practices linked to sport, as broadly understood by them. Such information would highlight their efforts in and commitment to incorporating physical activity into their lives, and their many strengths and skills; instead, the appendix consists only of statistics that reinforce a victimized construction of indigenous lives in Canada – a deficit versus strengths perspective. The strengths perspective approach can be seen in the Maskwachees Declaration (Appendix B of the policy), which outlines Aboriginal peoples' commitment to "improving the health, wellness, cultural survival and quality of life of Aboriginal/Indigenous Peoples, through physical activity, physical education, sport and recreation" (Canadian Heritage 2005, 10). As part of the declaration, delegates outlined the strengths that support Aboriginal peoples, followed by the issues that challenge them as they attempt to meet this commitment.

Racializing Sporting Spaces

As stated earlier, a racializing space is created when the "doing" of an operational race hierarchy facilitates the (re)creation of racialized identities. The North American Indigenous Games are an excellent example of a racializing space in the Aboriginal sport system. This international multi-sport event, created and administered by Aboriginal organizers, began in 1990 in Edmonton. The Games are held approximately every three years, with the location alternating between Canada and the United States. Sporting events at the NAIG are largely modelled on mainstream Olympic sports; for example, in the 1990 Games, the fifteen sporting competitions were archery, basketball, boxing, box lacrosse, canoeing, golf, marathon, rifle shooting, rodeo, soccer, softball, swimming, track and field, volleyball, and wrestling

(Living Traditions, n.d.). These sports competitions are complemented by an equally extensive cultural program highlighting the wide variety of indigenous arts and performative traditions in North America. As mentioned, athletes must be of Aboriginal heritage to participate. As such, this multisport event is a racialized sporting space. Even though the sports competitions align with mainstream sporting practices, several elements of the event mark it as Aboriginal, thus identifying it as an overtly racializing sporting space. For example, at the Games' 1990 opening ceremonies, Alwyn Morris, 1984 Olympic gold medallist in pairs kayaking, referred to their purpose and spirit:

> Through the fire of our will we look to the future. Through the spirit of warrior in our hearts we have great vision of tomorrow. We struggle through prayers and sacrifices to achieve our goals, a moment of victory, a moment of glory, like that of athletes of old. Like the first peoples of this great land, we have to overcome all obstacles to achieve harmony within ourselves. (Living Traditions, n.d.)

Further, explicitly Aboriginal aspects of the structuring of the NAIG include the Sacred Run rather than a torch relay, and the NAIG logo, which emphasizes several features of Aboriginal philosophy in its design. A strength of this racializing sporting competition is that Aboriginal youth from across North America have access to an international sporting opportunity where pride in their Aboriginal identity is fostered – an outcome unattainable for many Aboriginal athletes in mainstream sport. Two elders involved in the NAIG explained their aspirations for the Games this way:

> For the future, I envision the North American Indigenous Games to continue. Certainly at the regional level, there is a need for participation; and perhaps at the provincial level, to compete at the provincial level with mainstream sports; and at the national level, say in Canada here, that we see more brown faces in competition, in national competition. (Charles Wood, quoted in Living Traditions, n.d.)

> For young people to come and witness, to get a sense of the North American Indigenous Games, to get a feel for the power of sport and the power of culture. And it does allow you, as young people to come and explore what is awaiting you in this world. Then for you to find this forum to help express and empower you to say: "I am who I am and I deserve to be heard; I deserve

> to be seen; I deserve to be felt." I guess that's the opportunity the Indigenous Games offers. (Alex Nelson, quoted in ibid.)

Although Aboriginal pride through athletic competition is fostered at the Games, one challenge to this strength is the place of traditional sports/games there. To date, all games with an Aboriginal origin and where the participants remain primarily Aboriginal – such as Arctic (Inuit) Sports and Dene Games – have been located in the cultural program rather than being included as a sporting event.[9] Meanwhile, other traditional games that have been widely taken up by non-Aboriginal participants, such as canoe racing, cross-country running, and field lacrosse, are located among the sports competitions at the NAIG. This approach reinforces the assumption that traditional games are different from sport, a position often promoted by mainstream sports officials who then refuse to fund traditional games under their sport portfolio.[10] Unfortunately, this has often resulted in a lack of resources for traditional games events. A next step might be for NAIG organizers to reflect on their objectives, including what might be gained – and lost – if they were to reframe traditional games as a sporting event, as broadly understood from an Aboriginal perspective, and resituate them within the sporting program. Post-event evaluation of each NAIG would help ensure that the Games are effectively achieving the desired objectives.

The significance of the NAIG is acknowledged in the Aboriginal sport policy, first briefly under the heading of "Enhanced Participation" and then more extensively in Appendix C, which provides a historical overview of federal involvement in Aboriginal peoples' participation in sport. In this overview, the federal government recognizes its support for increased equity for Aboriginal participants in the Canadian sport system through funding of the Aboriginal Sport Circle, the Arctic Winter Games, and the NAIG. The racializing nature of the Games is also acknowledged:

> The NAIG provide Aboriginal youth from Canada and the United States of America (USA) an opportunity to showcase their heritage, history and culture through a variety of sport and cultural events. "This two-week celebration demonstrates unity among Indigenous Peoples from all regions and cultures across Canada and the USA through friendly competition in sport and cultural events and helps to promote the holistic concepts of physical, mental, cultural, and spiritual growth of individuals [www.2002naig.ca]." (Canadian Heritage 2005, 13)

This description of the NAIG documents its positive racializing role for Aboriginal participants, further legitimating this strength within the Aboriginal sport system.

The importance of cultural retention for Aboriginal peoples through traditional games is acknowledged in the Aboriginal sport policy in various places. In the historical account in Appendix C, the stated purpose of federal support for the Arctic Winter Games is in part to "preserve native traditions in sport and culture ... recogniz[ing] Arctic Sports and Dene Games as traditional games" (Canadian Heritage 2005, 14). An increasing interest in traditional knowledge is mentioned in Appendix D, which provides demographic information, with traditional games being identified as one aspect of traditional knowledge (ibid., 15). The "traditional" view of sport within Aboriginal communities as holistic was also acknowledged. For example, the Aboriginal Sport Circle is described as promoting increased sport participation through "the development and delivery of holistic, culturally based programs" (ibid., 13). The delegates at the gathering where the Maskwachees Declaration, endorsed by the Aboriginal sport policy, was created affirmed that "the holistic concepts of Aboriginal cultures, given by the Creator and taught by the Elders, promote balance through the integration of the physical, mental, emotional and spiritual growth of the individual" (ibid., 10). One rationale in the declaration refers to delegates' belief in the importance of traditional lifestyles and active living, further highlighting the racializing nature of traditional games and physical activities, since they "provide opportunities for developing a spiritual foundation of the individual, incorporating traditional values" (ibid., 11).

Honouring Aboriginal peoples' unique approach to sport was presented as a rationale for the Aboriginal sport policy, since a "renewed relationship with Aboriginal Peoples can only be built upon a realization of the uniqueness of Aboriginal cultures and a recognition and awareness of the contribution of Aboriginal Peoples in Canada" (Canadian Heritage 2005, 3). Thus, the policy must "reflect a holistic approach, advance sport as a vehicle for social change, and respect the diversity of Canada's Aboriginal Peoples" (ibid., 5). The guiding principles include references to traditional knowledge and cultural teachings, as well as to Aboriginal protocol, which is to be respected "when consulting or promoting federal sport policies and program developments to Aboriginal Peoples" (ibid.).

The abovementioned guiding principles acknowledge and potentially further legitimate the racializing characteristics promoted through the

Aboriginal sport system. When these principles are used to formulate policy statements – for example, of enhanced participation – events such as the NAIG and the Arctic Winter Games are linked to an Aboriginally contextualized (i.e., racializing) concept of competition that "provide competitive opportunities for Aboriginal athletes in an environment that reflects Aboriginal cultures, values and lifestyles. They offer Aboriginal Peoples an opportunity to share their cultural values with the broader Canadian public and internationally" (Canadian Heritage 2005, 6). This statement once again acknowledges, and in doing so legitimates, the important racializing role of such activities for both Aboriginal and non-Aboriginal peoples.

Aboriginal role models provide another opportunity for sport to act as a racializing space. Role models, from a duality of structure perspective, can be understood as mentors who illustrate various paths or choices. Role models' life stories suggest to others, especially youth, different possible boundaries within which actions can be taken. The Tom Longboat Award, awarded annually since 1951 in Canada to outstanding Aboriginal athletes in Canada (Aboriginal Sport Circle 2004),[11] contributes to a racialized sporting space in that select athletes, by heritage, are eligible for the award. The criteria state that to be eligible, individuals "must be of Aboriginal descent" (Who Is Eligible section). It also contributes to the creation of a racializing sporting space; the brochure about the award notes that it serves "as a proud national symbol for all Aboriginal peoples in Canada" (para. 3). As part of the application process, a supporting narrative written by the nominator (self-nominations are permitted) must be provided for all nominees. Desired qualities of an Aboriginal role model become evident in the categories outlined for this narrative: personal commitment to athletic development; positive image reflecting the principles of fair play and sportsmanship; concern for holistic development, including a balanced physical, mental, emotional, cultural, and spiritual outlook; and personal achievements in athletics (Nominations section). A strength of this sporting excellence award is that the award winners provide examples of "good" lifestyle choices and foster pride in Aboriginal heritage through their success stories. A challenge connected to this strength, however, is the pressure put on these role models to provide only a "positive" story, leaving out the more challenging, confusing, or dark aspects of their lives (Forsyth 2005).

Tom Longboat Award winners consistently demonstrate success in the mainstream sport system, but, as mentioned, the Aboriginal sport system is a second and equally legitimate sport system within the double helix model of Aboriginal sport. The next steps that could broaden the kinds of role models considered legitimate for the Tom Longboat and other athletic awards would be to ensure that people of both sexes and of different ages and athletic backgrounds (i.e., from the both mainstream and Aboriginal sport systems) are recognized. As well, the process whereby these award winners are selected needs to be made more transparent, and better aligned with the various paths that can be taken to be successful in Aboriginal sport. The National Aboriginal Role Model Program is promising in that it encourages youth involvement, including youth nominating youth. Each year, twelve youth role models who are chosen by a selection committee made up of the role models from the previous year visit Aboriginal communities and speak to their peers about making healthy and positive life choices (National Aboriginal Health Organization n.d., para. 1). This program clearly focuses on the process of selection, the qualities desired, and the outcomes expected of the role models who, it is hoped, will broaden the boundaries considered by Aboriginal youth when making life choices.

The Aboriginal sport policy also refers to the development of potential Aboriginal role models. The importance of working in partnership with Aboriginal sport leaders to increase Aboriginal participation in sport is highlighted as a guiding principle (Canadian Heritage 2005, 5). This, as a result, further legitimates the role of Aboriginal sport leaders as key administrators – and role models – in the double helix model. The importance of role models is noted in the Maskwachees Declaration in terms of the challenges delegates face in wishing to use elders in Sport Canada program design and delivery, specifically, "the need for more leaders and positive role models" and "the need to recognize success and celebrate participation" (ibid., 11). The policy statement for enhanced excellence could also help produce role models, since it suggests creating more high-performance Aboriginal athletes, coaches, and officials through "access to, and support for, quality and meaningful training, developmental and competitive opportunities" (ibid., 7). Further development of role models is specifically identified in the Enhanced Capacity section: "There is a need to increase the number and the capacity of Aboriginal leaders (i.e., coaches, officials, administrators, and volunteers) to strengthen sport within Aboriginal communities and to provide athletes and sport leaders as role models for youth" (ibid.). There therefore seems to be an acknowledgment in the Aboriginal sport policy of the importance of generating role models, which have a positive racializing role for Aboriginal participants in sport.

Racist Sporting Spaces

A racist space is (re)constructed for participants or spectators when they experience treatment as a racialized "other" in sport. When this racist experience aligns with the unequal race relations of the broader society, it reinforces the person's awareness that he or she is operating in a system that allows people to be treated differently because of race, and in keeping with formal and informal rules and the unequal distribution of resources along racial lines. Whitestream sport in Canada, which, as noted earlier, is a sport system that has been shaped primarily by individuals of white European heritage, is one example of institutionalized racism. As such, Aboriginal participants in the mainstream Canadian sport system recognize that Caucasians of European heritage are privileged because their understanding of sport "fits" with the system. Individual acts of racism can also occur, whereby a person from a more privileged group, by race, treats someone in a derogatory fashion based on a negative racial stereotype. Through these racist experiences, sport becomes a space where the unequal race relations in the broader society are reinforced.

Substantial attention has been directed by scholars and activists to the ways Indian mascots in North American whitestream sport have (re)constructed sport as a racialized and a racist space.[12] Staurowsky (2000), for example, discusses aspects of professional baseball that identify it as a racialized and racist space. Franchise rules governing Progressive Field (formerly Jacobs Field), home of the Cleveland Indians baseball team, prohibit the display of banners that contain obscene, political, or commercial messages, as well as any anti-social conduct considered offensive to others. During a playoff game in 1997, Cleveland Indian supporters were able to harass and heckle two people who carried a banner reading "People – Not Mascots" and with the Chief Wahoo logo crossed out, whereas the two Aboriginal protesters were detained in holding cells under the stadium for several hours. The stadium thus became a place where non-Aboriginal people who valued the mascot were privileged over Aboriginal people and their allies who protested against it.[13]

The presence of Indian mascots in whitestream sport makes sports fields and stadiums both racializing and racist. The mascots are constructed to represent a stereotypical Indian. As the mascot and non-Aboriginal spectators "act Indian," they temporarily take on, in a stereotypical fashion, a racial identity that is not their own. By painting their faces in supposed war paint, by doing the "tomahawk chop," and by chanting to a stereotypical drum beat, they can pretend to be the "other" – an Indian – without fear of reprisal. Their ability to do so reinforces Caucasian racial privilege while at the same time reinforcing the subordination of Aboriginal people who might be offended by such images. Aboriginal people's subordination here is indicated by the fact that even though an image linked to their own culture is at issue, they lack the resources to construct it in preferred ways (including its elimination altogether). The practices associated with Indian mascots are also racist because sports fields and stadiums facilitate non-Aboriginal peoples, who are privileged in the broader society, to extend that privilege into sport as they (re)construct Indian images in keeping with their stereotypes without consequence.

A strength that Aboriginal people share is their ability, over time, to facilitate the limiting, changing, or elimination of Indian mascots even though they are in a minority position in decision-making processes. An article in *Sports Illustrated* notes that, since 1969, over 600 nicknames considered offensive by Native American groups were dropped from school teams and professional minor sports teams (Price 2002). The National Collegiate Athletic Association (NCAA) took action in 2005 to limit post-season displays of "hostile and abusive racial/ethnic/national origin mascots, nicknames or imagery at any of the 88 NCAA championships" (NCAA.org 2005). Its policy guidelines have led to a further elimination of Indian mascots for university sports teams, even at places such as the University of Illinois, which has fought to keep Chief Illiniwek as its mascot despite ongoing public pressure from anti-mascot activists. There are several offensive Indian mascots still in existence in sport (including with professional teams – the Cleveland Indians, the Atlanta Braves, and the Washington Redskins, to name but three); nevertheless, activists from various organizations have been successful in eliminating many inappropriate Indian mascots over the past four decades.

An associated challenge faced by Aboriginal peoples and their allies as they attempt to change or eliminate Indian mascots stems from the attachment non-Aboriginal people claim toward "their" Indian mascots, identifying them, for example, as a part of their tradition. An example of this occurred at the University of North Dakota in relation to its mascot, the Fighting Sioux. Alumnus Ralph Engelstad, a Las Vegas casino owner, had promised the university $100 million, largely to build a new hockey arena that would bear his name. When several students and faculty at the university sought to eliminate the Fighting Sioux name as the umbrella name for the varsity athletics teams because they saw it as demeaning, he threatened to abandon the half-completed project if the university dropped the name. A decision was immediately made by the university president to retain it (Brownstein 2001; Dohrmann 2001), which demonstrates Engelstad's privileged position, in light of his ability to provide – or withdraw – desired financial resources, relative to that of the protesters. Through this action, a racist sporting space was likewise retained.

Continued research and pressure are both next steps that will help to eliminate or reshape Indian mascots. Anti-mascot activists are using the court system to challenge the legitimacy of Indian mascots, and researchers are also carefully deconstructing these mascots to challenge claims that the mascots honour Aboriginal peoples (e.g., Staurowsky 2001). So, although Indian sports mascots create a racist space, sport is also one of the places where many non-Aboriginal activists have been willing to join in with Aboriginal activists to eliminate them.

What is evident in the discussion on Indian mascots is that unacceptable racist practices, and the underlying unequal power relations that disadvantage Aboriginal peoples, can and have been identified and altered through significant effort by Aboriginal peoples and their allies. In a similar manner, several barriers faced by Aboriginal peoples that contribute to a racist sport system in Canada were identified in the Aboriginal sport policy – specifically, cultural insensitivity in programs and activities; limited numbers of coaches who are sensitive to Aboriginal cultures; and racism, which is "an ongoing problem in Canadian society manifesting itself in sport practice as it does in all socio-cultural practices. Racism is a socially constructed idea that alienates many Aboriginal People by causing fear, anxiety and distrust, ultimately serving as a barrier to their full participation in Canadian society, including sport" (Canadian Heritage 2005, 5).

In the Aboriginal sport policy, the federal government through Canadian Heritage (Sport Canada) explains that over the past decade it has "consistently moved towards a value-based approach to sport including support for Aboriginal Peoples" (Canadian Heritage 2005, 1). It advocates for "the full and fair participation of all persons in sport ... [and for facilitating] the participation of under-represented groups in the Canadian sport system" (ibid.). It also recognizes in the Aboriginal sport policy "that enhancing the sport experience for Aboriginal Peoples will only strengthen the value base of Canada's sport system and the quality of life of all people in Canada" (ibid., 1-2). These comments would all seem to reinforce Sport Canada's position that there are problems in the mainstream sport system, and that it is ready to address them for the betterment of Aboriginal participants and the overall sport system.

However, several statements and omissions in the Aboriginal sport policy suggest otherwise. Although the Aboriginal sport system is recognized in the guiding principles, which notes that "an Aboriginal sport delivery system exists and it is important to work with the ASC [Aboriginal Sport Circle], its national body, to identify and address the areas of priority to advance Aboriginal Peoples' participation in sport" (Canadian Heritage 2005, 6), the Aboriginal sport system is characterized as being less legitimate than the mainstream sport system, the latter defined in Appendix A as the one in which "sports [are] played by people of all nationalities and which have recognized sport organizations that guide them" (ibid., 9). This is a pattern often used in sport to mask privilege and to reproduce a naturalized understanding of "legitimate" participants. For example, you might hear in a news report about both the NCAA basketball championships and the women's NCAA basketball championships. The omission of "male" in the first instance reinforces men's basketball as the "normal" and women's basketball as the gendered "other" sporting event. The same can be said for the use of the terms "Aboriginal sport system" and "sport system" in the Aboriginal sport policy.

The adoption of mainstream notions of sport and traditional games also continues to privilege whitestream concepts of the Canadian sport system. For example, the idea of traditional activities is itself problematic. The term, through its naturalized use, tends to promote a static, invariant understanding of physical cultural activities linked to an Aboriginal heritage, rather than the ongoing development of such activities so that they provide relevant meaning to Aboriginal participants. It also naturalizes mainstream activities as the legitimate face of sport in Canada by focusing on the exotic otherness of so-called traditional activities. An example of this can be seen in the media coverage of the Arctic Winter Games. Although most of the activities in the Arctic Winter Games are considered to be mainstream – speed skating, cross-country skiing, hockey, basketball, and gymnastics – media coverage overwhelmingly attends to the "unique" Aboriginal events – Arctic Sports and Dene Games. Most people reading about the Games or watching them on television gather that these Games are legitimated through federal funding because they include traditional activities. Indeed, to some extent, the inclusion of traditional activities and the associated media coverage has likely helped protect these international games from losing their funding.

Traditional activities do provide an opportunity for Aboriginal peoples to generate cultural pride and a unique identity, but they are given resources only if they formalize and become invariant. A static concept of traditional sports is then reinforced, leading to the privileging of mainstream activities and their structural approach as being the legitimate cultural way to do physical activities. Traditional physical activities tied to Aboriginal heritage are thus legitimated only when they reproduce an invariant exotic otherness linked to Aboriginal peoples and their traditional activities. In contrast to this, the promise inherent in recognizing the validity of living, changing traditional activities includes the chance for traditional physical cultural practices to flourish and promote cultural pride. This promise was pointed out by the Yukon delegates in their feedback on one of the Aboriginal sport policy drafts. They encouraged the integration of traditional Arctic (Inuit) Sports into school curricula, which would naturalize participating in such games alongside other "traditional" sports and thus allow them to be continued and to flourish, noting, "In the Yukon, the school system could be used as a tool to bring Arctic Sports to children and youth. Youth need to see the opportunities for participation and competition in Arctic Sport and not just as a demonstration event. The excellent job NWT has done in promoting participation in Arctic Sports [is] noted" (Sport Canada 2003, 25).

This perception of traditional activities as different from sport can be seen as well in the NAIG, where "traditional games" are put into the cultural part of the program rather than included as sporting events. The Aboriginal sport policy and the NAIG hence both reinforce this dichotomy, further naturalizing sport and traditional games as being fundamentally different rather than being on a continuum of meaningful ways to express movement.

Another complicated term in this policy is "sport," raising the question, what gets legitimated as sport for the purposes of the policy? Sport Canada financially supports elite athletes through a hierarchy in which Olympic sportspersons are the most deserving of resources, and potential medallists the most deserving of all. This naturalizes a sport system driven by international understandings of what sport is, rather than legitimating the broad range of physical cultural practices incorporated within an Aboriginal understanding of the term. As humans, we all come to know ourselves, in part, through our bodies and how they move. Put another way, we write our cultures on and through our bodies. Importantly, then, who gets to define what counts as sport really does matter greatly because over time that definition will legitimate certain forms of movement and marginalize others.

Aboriginal peoples experienced this through government restrictions on their movements in the late 1800s – for many, sun dances, potlatches, and even free movement off reserves or entry into a pool hall became illegal acts. This historical precedent reminds us of a potential limitation of the Aboriginal sport policy, for nowhere in this policy is "sport" defined, although in more than one place there is a recognition that

> games, play – and more recently, sport – have always played an important role in Aboriginal cultures, as traditional Aboriginal lifestyles were very physically active ... [these activities were] centred on important principles within their belief systems and cultural values. The holistic approach of Aboriginal Peoples emphasizes the development of the whole person, balancing the physical, mental, emotional, cultural, and spiritual aspects of life ... [this] perspective does not distinguish between sport, recreation, and physical activity; all of these activities are intertwined and integral to personal and community well-being. (Canadian Heritage 2005, 3)

Since sport is not formally defined in the policy, it will likely get operationalized by Sport Canada staff in keeping with their mainstream understandings. If this were to happen, barriers faced by Aboriginal participants who wish to participate in activities and qualify for resources in keeping with their cultural understanding of sport will remain unaddressed, which will reinforce and naturalize unequal power relations. Unique aspects of an Aboriginal sport approach will therefore remain undeveloped because the funds required to develop them will not be provided until they are legitimated.

This concern could be seen in the feedback from the NWT delegates during the consultation on the policy. They stressed that mainstream sport should include traditional Aboriginal activities, noting, "For Aboriginal athletes to be part of the mainstream system a level playing field is needed. The inclusion of Aboriginal events at the Canada Games would be an excellent opportunity to expose other provinces to these events. At the Arctic Winter Games both Aboriginal and non-Aboriginal athletes compete in traditional games" (Sport Canada 2003, 21).

Regardless of how narrowly sport is defined, the possibilities stemming from the Aboriginal sport policy are exciting. They include increased Aboriginal participation, which will lead to increased exposure to the benefits of sport, in turn leading to increased individual and community health through physical activity. A broad definition of sport, one that makes sport culturally relevant to Aboriginal peoples, is needed for these exciting possibilities to be realized. This is pointed out in different ways in the policy statements for enhanced capacity: policies and programs need to be developed in consultation with the Aboriginal sport community; facilities, resources, and culturally appropriate sport programs are needed in communities; and "all levels of program delivery must be culturally sensitive, flexible and adaptive to the diverse needs of Aboriginal populations" (Canadian Heritage 2005, 7). Including a definition of sport in Appendix A that recognizes the Aboriginal vision of sport already outlined in the body of the policy would have greatly strengthened the Aboriginal sport policy's ability to reshape unequal power relations in sport so that Aboriginal peoples are the definers of the way they wish to (re)construct "sport."

The brief history of federal government involvement in Aboriginal sport making up Appendix C held promise as a record documenting Aboriginal struggles to shape their sporting practices but ends up being problematic in several ways. The policy makers used two scholarly articles (Paraschak 1995, 2003) on the history of Aboriginal-government relations in sport but ignored the points being made: that Aboriginal peoples were actively creating sport opportunities in keeping with their view of sport, and that unequal power relations continued to allow government agents to legitimate only those aspects of Aboriginal sport that fit within a mainstream purview. This Sport Canada policy history thus provided a one-sided, government point of view about appropriate Aboriginal sport, meaning those sport practices that fit within the Canadian or mainstream sport system. Accordingly, the implied Aboriginal "problem" is Aboriginal peoples' inability to integrate into the mainstream sport system. There is no recognition of the unique nation-to-nation relationship the federal government has with Aboriginal peoples in Canada, which could justify a unique form of support for Aboriginal sport. There is no evidence of the ongoing struggle between Sport Canada and Aboriginal peoples over who gets to define what counts as sport, what the legitimate sport structure looks like, and how resources are allocated. And there is no detailing of the institutionalized and individual racism present in mainstream sport that continues to make it an uncomfortable and racist place for Aboriginal participants. Unequal power relations remain the greatest barrier for Aboriginal peoples in sport, in part because those inequalities are written out of histories about federal government involvement in Aboriginal sport. As the federal government's story is told and legitimated through policy, Aboriginal peoples' stories about their own past disappear; their history is "un-made" yet again.

The idea of contested histories is not new. Linda Tuhiwai Smith (1999), the Maori author of *Decolonizing Methodologies*, speaks to the importance of histories for indigenous peoples, challenging the idea that once "the truth comes out," the system will be corrected and justice will occur. She writes:

> History is also about power. In fact history is mostly about power. It is the story of the powerful and how they became powerful, and then how they use their power to keep them in positions in which they can continue to dominate others ... Much of what I have read has said that we do not exist, that if we do exist it is in terms which I cannot recognize, that we are no good and that what we think is not valid. (Ibid., 34-35)

The final version of the historical overview in Appendix C of the Aboriginal sport policy fits with this analysis. The federal version of Sport Canada's involvement in Aboriginal sport tells the story of how the organization has helped to enhance Aboriginal sport, yet it fails to share the ways that it undercut Aboriginal attempts to reshape Aboriginal sport in a preferred, Aboriginal fashion. As such, this historical overview erases any account of Aboriginal efforts to oppose the version of Aboriginal sport preferred by the federal government; the power to define Aboriginal sport consequently remains with the government.

Smith (1999) also talks about the "indigenous problem" as a recurrent theme when westerners (e.g., Euro-Canadians) deal with indigenous peoples, highlighting the problem this creates for indigenous peoples: "For indigenous communities the issue is not just that they are blamed for their own failures but that it is also communicated to them, explicitly or implicitly, that they themselves have no solutions to their own problems" (ibid., 92). Her comment fits well with the Aboriginal sport policy's Appendix D, "Demographic Information." As stated earlier, this information outlines the various problems faced by Aboriginal peoples while omitting their many strengths. Reading this appendix, both Aboriginal and non-Aboriginal people are left focusing only on the "failures" facing Aboriginal peoples that supposedly will be addressed by this policy with the help of Sport Canada, as opposed to Aboriginal peoples – or else why include it in the Aboriginal sport policy?

Conclusion

When *Sport Canada's Policy on Aboriginal Peoples' Participation in Sport* was released in May 2005, it marked an important milestone in Aboriginal sport–mainstream sport relations. Through this policy, Sport Canada officials acknowledged the legitimacy of Aboriginal sporting spaces, such as the NAIG and the Arctic Winter Games. They also acknowledged the federal government's desire to enhance relations with Aboriginal peoples in order to make the Canadian sport system more values-based, more inclusive, and equitable for Aboriginal participants.

The policy has several strengths. It legitimates, through policy, the existence of the Aboriginal sport system. The policy also creates an avenue for receiving government resources, for example, through its recognition of the NAIG. There was some consultation with Aboriginal peoples in its formation (although the ultimate decisions about it remained with the federal government) – perhaps an appendix listing those who were consulted in the policy development process, as was included in the recent *Actively Engaged: A Policy on Sport for Women and Girls* (Canadian Heritage 2009a), would have been insightful. Select existing research on the history of Aboriginal peoples–government relations in sport was incorporated into a history included as an appendix to provide background for those uninformed about it, which had the potential to be a strength if it had acknowledged Aboriginal efforts as fully as it acknowledged government efforts. In this policy, Sport Canada also committed to an ongoing relationship with Aboriginal people by agreeing to establish an action plan aligned with the objectives of the 2002 Canadian Sport Policy – a promise it has, unfortunately, yet to keep, even though action plans have been released for subsequent Sport Canada policies dealing with persons with disabilities (Canadian Heritage 2006), and with women and girls (Canadian Heritage 2009b).

Challenges have the potential, however, to undercut these strengths. For example, the policy acknowledges the intertwined ways that Aboriginal peoples view sport, recreation, and physical activity, yet government officials fail to provide a definition of sport in the policy and thus maintained, by omission, their right to define it. The mainstream notion adopted by Sport Canada is evident in its definition of a sport system. As such, unequal power relations are maintained, since the right to define sport – so central to the meaning of this policy – is retained by Sport Canada officials rather than negotiated with, or defined by, Aboriginal peoples. Further, the choice to not attach financial resources, linked to an action plan that could be used to evaluate progress, means that federal resources can be shifted, reduced, or eliminated as government perspectives on Aboriginal peoples, and on sport specifically, change. Useful next steps include ongoing research and monitoring of the policy and its implementation (e.g., development of an action plan linked to actual resources being provided to Aboriginal sport), as well as the development of a communication strategy so that communities become aware of the policy. These steps will help to ensure that the many strengths embedded in the creation of the policy become reality, thus enhancing sporting opportunities for Aboriginal participants.

Aboriginal peoples in Canada have the right to determine their own cultural practices, including sport. Aboriginal concerns about the Aboriginal sport policy can be understood in light of unequal power relations. Sport Canada can actively work to reduce these unequal power relations by facilitating Aboriginal control over the shaping of sport forms and meanings, and by increasing resources needed for Aboriginal sport to flourish. If *Sport Canada's Policy on Aboriginal Peoples' Participation in Sport* was created to achieve this vision, then the invisible barrier that exists within Aboriginal sport – unequal power relations – would be addressed in a way that would really make sport, and all its benefits, more accessible to Aboriginal peoples across Canada. It is only by institutionalizing, through policy, an altered relationship of power so that Aboriginal peoples ultimately get to decide what Aboriginal sport in Canada will look like that a new, more inclusive, structure of sport in Canada will be facilitated. If this were done in the Aboriginal sport policy, then the last point made in the Policy Statements section, under Enhanced Interaction, could truly be realized: "Supporting the full participation of Aboriginal Peoples in sport demonstrates Canada's values, celebrates Canadian culture, and exhibits to the world our commitment to human rights" (Canadian Heritage 2005, 8).

NOTES

1 With apologies to Jean-Paul Sartre (1956, 575), I paraphrase him to identify that underlying the analysis in this chapter is my belief that we come to know ourselves not by how we are similar to others but rather by "what we are not"; that is, our difference from the "other." Thus, when we are operating within a racialized space, which has embedded within it certain understandings of race, if those understandings do not cause us to see ourselves as different from the "other," then our racial identity remains unexamined. It is when we become aware of our differentness from the "other" that we consciously reflect on and (re)construct our own racial identity. At this point, the racialized space becomes a racializing space – one that heightens our awareness of our racial identity relative to the "other."

2 The term "double helix" was initially coined by Alex Nelson, an elder with the Aboriginal Sport Circle (Paraschak, Forsyth, and Heine 2005).
3 I would like to acknowledge a conflation between concepts of racial and cultural difference. I am not analytically separating the construction of an identity that is race-specific, and one that is attached to a particular cultural group wherein race may (or may not) be considered as one identifying characteristic. For example, when someone looks at an Aboriginal individual wearing eagle feathers and traditional dress, and identifies that person as an "Indian," I am not sure whether that label is limited to a racial concept of Indian, or a cultural concept of Indian, or a cultural concept of Indian that includes a racial construction as part of the understanding. These differences are important and worthy of further analysis and clarity, but will not be tackled in this chapter.
4 For a discussion on gender hierarchies and Aboriginal sport, see Paraschak (2007).
5 Giddens (1984, xxiii) describes practical consciousness as "consist[ing] of all the things which actors know tacitly about how to 'go on' in the contexts of social life without being able to give them direct discursive expression."
6 This approach aligns with section 15(2) of the 1982 Canadian Charter of Rights and Freedoms, on equality rights, which notes that differential treatment is appropriate for those who have been marginalized, to ameliorate the "conditions of disadvantaged individuals or groups including those that are disadvantaged because of race, national or ethnic origin, colour, religion, sex, age or mental or physical disability" (Paraschak and Tirone 2008, 90).
7 Race is a socially constructed category whereby distinctions are based on genetic heritage and marked by skin colour and physical features. There are many cultural practices among Aboriginal peoples, and differing ways of defining who is "Aboriginal." The same, of course, is true for Caucasians.
8 As part of the creation of the Aboriginal sport policy, there was a meeting with Provincial/Territorial Aboriginal Sport Body representatives to review the draft policy framework. The comments attributed to delegates are taken from the 2003 Sport Canada summary of this consultation meeting. The eighth draft of the Aboriginal sport policy was provided to Aboriginal delegates representing the various provinces and territories across Canada. Some of their comments on that draft were captured in the accompanying report.
9 This approach differs from the Arctic Winter Games, another international, biennial sporting competition begun in 1970, where Arctic Sports and Dene Games are two of the sporting events alongside mainstream sports such as cross-country skiing, basketball, and hockey.
10 For an extended discussion of this point, see Paraschak (1997).
11 For an extensive history of this award, see Forsyth (2005).
12 For an extensive discussion on "playing Indian," see Deloria (1998) and Francis (1992). For excellent works addressing various mascot issues, see King and Springwood (2001) and King et al. (2006).
13 For an extended explanation of "allies," see Bishop (2002).

REFERENCES

Aboriginal Affairs and Northern Development Canada. 2012. Loss and restoration of Indian status. http://www.aadnc-aandc.gc.ca/.

Aboriginal Sport Circle. Tom Longboat Awards application brochure. 2004. http://www.owha.on.ca/.

Anishinaabe Blog. 2006. "Little NHL will return to Sudbury in 2007," blog entry by Bob Goulais, March 20. http://www.anishinaabe.ca/.

Baikie, S. 2003. "The bright side of the road": The strengths perspective in Nain, Labrador. In V. Paraschak and J. Forsyth, eds., *North American Indigenous Games Research Symposium Proceedings* (70-76). Winnipeg: University of Manitoba.

Bishop, A. 2002. *Becoming an Ally: Breaking the Cycle of Oppression in People.* 2nd ed. Halifax: Fernwood.

Brownstein, A. 2001. A battle over a name in the land of the Sioux. *Chronicle of Higher Education,* February 23. http://chronicle.com/article.

Canadian Heritage. 2005. *Sport Canada's Policy on Aboriginal Peoples' Participation in Sport.* Ottawa: Minister of Public Works and Government Services Canada.

–. 2006. *Policy on Sport for Persons with a Disability.* Ottawa: Her Majesty the Queen in Right of Canada.

–. 2009a. *Actively Engaged: A Policy on Sport for Women and Girls.* Ottawa: Her Majesty the Queen in Right of Canada.

–. 2009b. *Actively Engaged: A Policy on Sport for Women and Girls; Action Plan, 2009-2012.* Ottawa: Her Majesty the Queen in Right of Canada.

Coakley, J., and P. Donnelly. 2004. *Sports in Society: Issues and Controversies.* 1st Cdn ed. Toronto: McGraw-Hill Ryerson.

Cosentino, F. 1998. *Afros, Aboriginals and Amateur Sport in Pre World War One Canada.* Canada's Ethnic Group Series, booklet no. 26. Ottawa: Canadian Historical Society.

Deloria, P. 1998. *Playing Indian.* New Haven, CT: Yale University Press.

Dohrmann, G. 2001. Face-off. *Sports Illustrated,* October 8, 95(14): 44-49.

Forsyth, J. 2005. The power to define: A history of the Tom Longboat Awards, 1951-2001. PhD diss., University of Western Ontario.

Francis, D. 1992. *The Imaginary Indian: The Image of the Indian in Canadian Culture.* Vancouver: Arsenal Pulp Press.

Giddens, A. 1984. *The Constitution of Society: Outline of the Theory of Structuration.* Berkeley: University of California Press.

Greater Sudbury Department of Growth and Development. 2005. Little NHL hockey tournament returns to Greater Sudbury in March 2006. City of Greater Sudbury news release, October 11. http://www.city.greatersudbury.on.ca/.

–. 2006. Little NHL will return to Greater Sudbury in 2007. City of Greater Sudbury news release, March 14. http://www.city.greatersudbury.on.ca/.

King, C.R., and C.F. Springwood, eds. 2001. *Team Spirits: The Native American Mascots Controversy.* Lincoln: University of Nebraska Press.

King, C.R., E. Staurowsky, L. Davis-Delano, and L. Baca. 2006. Sports mascots and the media. In A. Raney and J. Bryant, eds., *Handbook of Sports and Media* (559-75). Mahwah, NJ: Lawrence Erlbaum Associates.

Little Native Hockey League. 2011. *Little Native Hockey League Rules and Regulations.* http://www.lnhl.ca/Forms/Rules_2011.pdf.

Living Traditions. n.d. The Dream for the NAIG. http://www.virtualmuseum.ca/.

National Aboriginal Health Organization. n.d. National Aboriginal Role Model Program. http://www.naho.ca/rolemodel/.

NCAA.org. 2005. NCAA Executive Committee issues guidelines for use of Native American mascots at championship events. August 5. http://fs.ncaa.org/Docs/PressArchive/2005/.

North American Indigenous Games Council. 2008. NAIG governing rules. http://www.teamsask.fsin.com/.

Paraschak, V. 1995. The Native sport and recreation program, 1972-1981: Patterns of resistance, patterns of reproduction. *Canadian Journal of History of Sport* 26(2): 1-18.

–. 1996. Racialized spaces: Cultural regulation, Aboriginal agency and powwows. *Avante* 2(1): 7-18.

–. 1997. Variations in race relations: Sporting events for Native peoples in Canada. *Sociology of Sport Journal* 14(1): 1-21.

–. 2000. Knowing ourselves through the "other": Indigenous peoples in sport in Canada. In R. Jones and K. Armour, eds., *Sociology of Sport: Theory and Practice* (153-66). Essex, UK: Longman.

–. 2003. "Get into the mainstream": Aboriginal sport in Canada, 1967-2002. In V. Paraschak and J. Forsyth, eds., *North American Indigenous Games Research Symposium Proceedings* (23-30). Winnipeg: University of Manitoba.

–. 2007. Doing race, doing gender: First Nations, "sport," and gender relations. In K. Young and P. White, eds., *Sport and Gender in Canada,* 2nd ed. (137-54). Don Mills, ON: Oxford University Press.

Paraschak, V., J. Forsyth, and M. Heine. 2005. Aboriginal sport in Canada: The double helix. Workshop held at the Management Issues, North American Society for Sport Management Centennial Symposium, Regina, June 2-3, 2005.

Paraschak, V., and S. Tirone. 2008. Race and ethnicity in Canadian sport. In J. Crossman, ed., *Canadian Sport Sociology* (79-98). Scarborough, ON: Nelson Thompson Learning.

Price, S.L. 2002. The Indian wars. *Sports Illustrated* 96(10): 66-72. http://sports illustrated.cnn.com/.

Saleebey, D. 2009. Introduction: Power in the people. In D. Saleebey, ed., *The Strengths Perspective in Social Work Practice,* 5th ed. (1-23). Boston: Pearson Education.

Sartre, J.-P. 1956. *Being and Nothingness: An Essay on Phenomenological Ontology.* New York: Philosophical Library.

Sport Canada. 2003. *Sport Canada Aboriginal Sport Policy: Report on Consultations with Provincial/Territorial Aboriginal Sport Bodies on the Draft Policy Framework.* Ottawa: Sport Canada.

Staurowsky, E. 2000. The Cleveland Indians: A case study in cultural dispossession. *Sociology of Sport Journal* 17(4): 307-30.

–. 2001. Sockalexis and the making of the myth at the core of Cleveland's "Indian" image. In C.R. King and C.F. Springwood, eds., *Team Spirits: The Native American Mascots Controversy* (82-106). Lincoln: University of Nebraska Press.

Tuhiwai Smith, L. 1999. *Decolonizing Methodologies: Research and Indigenous Peoples*. Dunedin, NZ: University of Otago Press.

Canadian Elite Aboriginal Athletes, Their Challenges, and the Adaptation Process

ROBERT J. SCHINKE, DUKE PELTIER, AND HOPE YUNGBLUT

Sport psychology is a domain in its infancy (Cox 2006; Weinberg and Gould 2003). With knowledge founded upon a history of less than one hundred years, mostly of white scholars, those practising sport psychology tend to inadvertently apply a narrow set of cultural norms, values, and beliefs to their work (Martens, Mobley, and Size 2000). Sport psychology consultants are culturally educated, formally speaking, and the basis of their knowledge is often white, mainstream, and Eurocentric (i.e., of European origin) (Reba and Wright 2005). Although consultants sometimes misguidedly believe that sport psychology is culture-free and relevant to all clients, through the use of the same tools, one need only consider the terms "self-determination," "self-confidence," "self-empowerment," and "self-esteem" to gain a better understanding of how the values belying such frameworks intersect with mental training (Kashima et al. 1995). All of these terms are culture-bound and reflect an emphasis on (and the priority of) the individual's needs over those of the collective (Schinke, Harahan, and Cantina 2009). When a client is motivated by an individualist orientation where one's self is primary and at the centre, mental training skills steeped in theories of the self, such as self-affirmations (Rollick 2000), intuitively make sense. That being said, the intent of sport psychology is to address the needs of clients, which means its provisions should align with the standpoints of each client and not just those with a preference for mainstream practices (Butryn 2002; Hill 1993). When sport psychologists proceed naively into the field, unaware that their clients sometime have unfamiliar or dissimilar cultural standpoints, such as a group versus self-interest perspective, they are not only providing insensitive services but they are also unintentionally silencing and subverting the views and preferences of those they are meant to be supporting (Fisher, Butryn, and Roper 2003). People from marginalized cultures are deeply affected by this silencing, since it contributes to the ongoing devaluation of their perspectives in everyday life (Schinke, Blodgett, et al. 2009). Exacerbating the potential negative consequences that can result from employing a mainstream approach in sport psychology is the problem whereby clients from marginalized cultures are asked (and sometimes told) by those in the mainstream to adopt mainstream cultural practices. Such assimilative demands extend beyond the more common adaptation challenges experienced by most every athlete who progresses to the elite level and must adjust to the practicalities of relocation, increased technical demands, a new coaching staff, and mounting performance pressures (Schinke, Gauthier, et al. 2007). More extensive adaptation challenges tend to further marginalize some athletes by discounting the cultural identity of minority athletes as they seek sporting excellence and by perpetuating sport environments that favour white athletes, and those who are able and willing to assimilate into white mainstream sport culture. Sometimes, aspiring athletes faced with the challenges associated with cultural adaptation beyond the cross-cultural (common to all cultures) demands of sport choose to deselect out of sport on account of the discomfort they feel within those environments and return to their cultural communities instead of pursuing their goals in mainstream sport (Schinke, Michel, et al. 2006). Losing these athletes has significant implications for sport that extend well beyond what the athletes lose personally in terms of hopes, dreams, and opportunities. Losses are also felt by the athletes' cultural communities (local and national) in terms of role models and, though often unacknowledged, there is a loss to mainstream athletes, who might have benefited from increased exposure to a culturally diverse sport context wherein they are provided with a wider variety of life experiences and perspectives.

Canadian Aboriginal athletes often experience the abovementioned adaptation challenges that have exemplified the need for a culturally sensitive and relevant motivational approach to sport psychology practice (termed a cultural sport psychology or CSP). CSP services in some cases can be provided or facilitated by mainstream sport psychology consultants, either when athletes are acculturated (see Kontos and Breland-Noble 2002 for a review) or when mainstream services are sought out by the athlete

(Schinke, Hanrahan, et al. 2007). However, motivational support for Aboriginal athletes can (and often times should) come from cultural means, offered by resources within Aboriginal communities, such as from elders, medicine people, and family members, as well as from local and national Aboriginal sport service providers (Schinke, Eys, et al. 2006). In fact, it was not long ago that Waneek Horn-Miller, a Mohawk from Kahnawake, Quebec, and co-captain of the Canadian women's water polo team that competed in the 2000 Summer Olympic Games in Sydney, Australia, indicated her wish for a "sports psychology and a sport psychologist that will understand you, coming from that community, coming from your reality ... that would be my dream" (North American Indigenous Games Sport Research Panel 2003, 67). The benefit of drawing from cultural resources within Aboriginal communities, be they traditional or mainstream resources, is that they can serve to reaffirm the athlete's identity in relation to his or her culture, while also enhancing the potency of a CSP through relevant strategies by culturally informed providers (see Thomason 1991). The development of a culturally driven approach to Canadian Aboriginal sport psychology (see also Hanrahan 2004; Schinke, Blodgett, et al. 2009) is the focal point of this chapter, the authors of which are from both Aboriginal and Euro-Canadian backgrounds.

Within this chapter we consider the topic of CSP in relation to Canada's Aboriginal peoples. We start by providing an overview of the experiences of the first two authors (one mainstream, one Canadian Aboriginal) with Canadian elite Aboriginal athletes through applied sport psychology service. These stories are illustrative of why Eurocentric approaches are problematic. Transitioning from our personal experiences to the experiences of Canadian elite Aboriginal athletes who have participated in our research, we then offer strategies that these athletes have reported using in order to adapt to high-level Eurocentric sport. These strategies comprised personal adaptation strategies and social support resources facilitative of athlete adaptation, which can be employed during an athlete's daily training and also throughout competition. Finally, recommendations for practice are considered, along with final conclusions.

Early Experiences That Informed Our Research

The lead authors' experiences informed the inception of a CSP that aligns with the wishes of Canadian Aboriginal athletes. Rob's reflect the vantage of a mainstream white sport psychology consultant whose research interests initially did not meet the needs and standpoints of elite Aboriginal athletes and who subsequently had to make adaptations. Duke was an elite ice hockey player with junior and varsity experience. His views, representing the vantage of one Aboriginal community (Wikwemikong, Ontario), coincide with Rob's consulting experiences and reaffirm the adaptation challenges that may be encountered by aspiring elite Aboriginal athletes who are placed within unfamiliar mainstream sport settings.

Rob's Sport Psychology Experiences

Applied sport psychology is at least as much a matter of context (with clients at the centre and service providers at the periphery) as it is a matter of theoretical knowledge. I learned this valuable lesson when first working with the Canadian national boxing team more than a decade ago. Boxing is a multicultural sport context with a wide variety of recently immigrated Canadians as well as more established Canadians from francophone, white anglophone, and Aboriginal descent (Schinke 2007). From 1997 to 1999, the first three years I worked with international amateur boxers, there was at least one Aboriginal athlete on the team each year, though never the same athlete for two consecutive years. In 1997, reflecting limited applied consulting experience, my goal was to approach and subsequently work with all athletes the same way: a race-blind strategy according to Butryn (2002). Race blindness is an approach to practice whereby every athlete is met individually, and similar discussions, reflecting a similar motivational approach, ensue. All of the athletes are met based on the terms and strategies of the mainstream consultant, who assumes that every athlete should be met on the same terms, employing, for example, the same language, level of eye contact, and use of personal space (Schinke, Hanrahan, and Catina 2009). During my early consulting, generic discussions often pertained to the athletes' previous experiences; as relationships were built, topics extended to competition planning and athlete onsite management for international tournaments.

When I worked for the first time with an Aboriginal elite athlete, the exchange felt somewhat stilted – the result of my generic approach to sport psychology practice. There is an important distinction between treating athletes the same (i.e., providing cross-cultural strategies) and providing athletes with equitable treatment (i.e., providing culturally relevant strategies for each client from the client's perspective – a CSP approach). I recall asking too many questions and always filling any silences during the encounter. I struggled to connect with the athlete, who often gave a one-word response, frequently avoided eye contact, and sat farther away from me than was usual in my meetings. Something was wrong with the exchange. The athlete was uncomfortable with my approach, my designated role within the team, or his location within the hierarchical structure of the sport organization, where he was compelled to meet with a sport psychology consultant – or, most likely, all of these things. I had only one exchange with the athlete, after which he discontinued my services and then left the national team. From that first experience, I realized that I failed in my attempt to become a supportive resource. It also became clear to me that my colleagues on the team's coaching staff were committing the same critical race-blind mistakes, founded, as with me, upon their ignorance as mono-cultural (i.e., Eurocentric) service providers.

Over the next two years, there were more opportunities to work with Aboriginal national team athletes before and during international tournaments. Each time, I noticed that the athletes incorporated aspects of their traditional cultural backgrounds into their sporting lives. Some used sacred medicines and bundles, or integrated healers, elders, sweat lodges, and sun dances in their preparation for training and competition (Schinke et al. 2009). In an attempt to better meet the sport psychology needs of Aboriginal athletes, mostly with those who incorporated traditional practices into their daily routines, I began the exchanges with the invitation to meet and discuss their performance, and as part of the invitation, I asked the athletes whether they wanted someone to accompany them to the meeting. Underlying the shift in approach was my adaptation to the bicultural relationship by taking into account the collective nature of my Aboriginal clients and also their unfamiliarity and potential discomfort with the mainstream practice of sport psychology. The athletes also adapted by agreeing to receive sport psychology services in a slightly adjusted format – a small group setting. Thanks to our negotiation to experience one another's customs, I was exposed early on in my consulting career to the use of (and invited to try) a few sacred medicines (primarily sweetgrass and tobacco). Through discussions about eagle feathers and other parts of the athletes' bundles, I also learned about the reciprocal importance of athletes to their community and the inherent value of the community's support for each athlete.

The relevance of a CSP grounded in Aboriginal culture was reaffirmed each time I travelled with the athletes to international tournaments (the 1998 Pan American Championships and 1999 Pan American Games, both held in Canada). During each of these events, members from the athletes' communities arrived by the busload to support the athletes in their pursuits.

On one occasion, a venue that remained empty of spectators for almost a week of competition filled with some five thousand Aboriginal supporters when our Aboriginal team member was scheduled as part of the evening's competition. Nevertheless, the athletes would persist for one season only, leaving the coaching staff to wonder why the Aboriginal boxers did not attend selection trials the following year. Were the athletes disinterested in pursuing elite sport because they had reached their objectives? Or were the athletes drawn to their communities so much that continuing as a national team member was less important to them than being in their communities? Another possibility, and the one I feared most, was that the athletes found their single year on the national team so distasteful that they opted to deselect.

Duke's Adaptation Challenges within Mainstream Sport

When Rob and I first met, as Wikwemikong's lead representative for a funded project about the culturally informed motivational practices of Canadian Aboriginal elite athletes, I immediately became interested in the development of an Aboriginal CSP. As a former elite athlete, and the current director of sport and recreation in Wikwemikong, I recalled the challenges associated with relocation; I moved several times within Ontario to pursue ice hockey at the junior level before heading to Saskatchewan and then the United States to compete in university sport. Initially, the challenges I encountered at the junior level included loneliness; I missed not only my family but also my community. That loneliness grew when I was assigned to teams that were based far from my home community of Wikwemikong. In addition, my coaches' general approach often emphasized structured practice and technical drills rather than scrimmages. The shift from playing opportunities through scrimmages to mundane technical drills felt like a shift in focus away from learning through fun and toward repetitive isolated tasks. Off the ice, the approach to coaching sometimes manifested in top-down confrontations. I am accustomed to the consensus decision-making process of a sharing circle, whereby members of the team (including athletes) collectively discuss and strategize how to resolve the issues at hand. Instead, in my new surroundings, the coaching staff often criticized one athlete in front of the group – an approach I regarded as a form of shaming. It seemed that shame was used to motivate athletes, but I could not comprehend why the coaches chose to shame rather than show a sense of pride and enjoyment, or foster a cooperative sense of community.

When Rob and I related our experiences to each other, we had preliminary suspicions as to why many Aboriginal athletes did not pursue their careers on national teams beyond one year, instead returning to their families and communities. One of the possibilities I put forward was loneliness for family, friends, cultural community, and missing what I regard as an Aboriginal approach to sport (i.e., learning through fun). Rob suggested that another possible reason was the coaching staff's insensitive approach to meeting athletes' sport psychology needs. Thus, although the adaptation challenges the athletes experienced offered them opportunities to develop personally and athletically, these opportunities were offset by unfamiliar and sometimes confusing ways of life.

Our Unified Ambition

With a shared interest in Aboriginal people answering our questions, we developed a partnership that included researchers from Laurentian University and community members of Wikwemikong. This partnership continues at the time of publication, though our focus has recently shifted to a community sport imperative (youth sport involvement at the developmental level) and away from the elite sport strategies that serve as the focal point of this chapter. Below, we outline our research findings on Aboriginal elite athletes' sport-related adaptation strategies.

Research Limitations

Our goal was to develop a relevant CSP practice intended for Canadian Aboriginal athletes, yet we were faced with a scarcity of culture-specific sport psychology research. Instead, the majority of sport psychology practices reflected the values of white North Americans and continental Europeans (Ryba and Wright 2005; see also Riggs 2004 in relation to psychology proper). The information that does exist is generally the work of mainstream researchers who believe they are engaged in cultural research when they elicit information from someone whose cultural background is different from theirs (Schinke, Peltier, et al. 2009). What is gleaned from such work often reflects mainstream strategies, be they quantitative questionnaires distributed in an attempt to identify cross-cultural similarities in relation to universal characteristics such as self-evaluation (Peters and Williams 2006) or to identify cultural uniqueness, albeit through mainstream questions and methods (e.g., work such as what we focus on in this chapter). Indeed, with the research that informs this chapter, incidents of cultural insensitivity occurred, an overarching error that our team addressed and continues to address in the research relationship (Peltier et al. 2006; Schinke, Peltier, et al. 2009). For example, Rob initially conceived the project, and only once the grant was drafted did he seek support from the people of Wikwemikong. Furthermore, once the project was underway, during the initial phase of data collection, we relied primarily on semi-structured individual interviews (see Appendix 5.1) and made limited use of talking circles to explore athletes' experiences (Running Wolf and Rickard 2003). With historical roots in Native American culture, talking circles are a traditional way of bringing people together to share knowledge, experiences, feelings, and values while promoting respect for diversity and effective listening (ibid.). The circle formation symbolizes the interconnectedness of all life and the collectivist nature of the people – sacred themes in many Native cultures. In addition, our work reflected a general grouping strategy (see Andersen 1993) whereby we considered patterns across Canadian Aboriginal athletes, as opposed to identifying cultural nuances that are inherent among every community of indigenous peoples (see Smith 1999). It is with these early missteps that we offer a glimpse into a CSP practice intended for Canadian Aboriginal athletes. What follows is intended only as a starting point for a more general line of inquiry, one that other researchers are encouraged to pursue with specific Aboriginal groups – and other groups of Canadians – in locations throughout Canada so as to create a more robust and constructive field for sport psychology.

The Athletes/Participants

Twenty-three elite Canadian Aboriginal athletes were invited to participate in the research that informs this chapter. We used three criteria for participant eligibility. First, all of the athletes had to have a minimum of national amateur sport experience at the university level. Second, the participants required at least one Aboriginal parent, and in keeping with guidelines from Indian and Northern Affairs Canada (2003), the federal department that determines Aboriginal status, also needed to self-identify as Aboriginal. Third, Duke and some vested community members with a background in elite sport and youth proposed or vetted all participants who were willing to share their sport experiences and provided suggestions for how to recruit and retain athletes from Aboriginal cultures for sport.

The participants were from three provinces: sixteen athletes were from Ontario, four from Manitoba, and three from Saskatchewan. The participants represented seven sport disciplines: ice hockey (seven male, two female), lacrosse (one male, one female), boxing (six male, one female), track and field (one male), soccer (one female), tae kwon do (one male), and cross-country running (two female). Sixteen of the participants were males and seven were females. The athletes averaged 7.22 years of elite athletic experience (a range of 1 to 18 years), and their mean age was 28.09 years (a range of 17 to 42 years).

Personal Adaptation Strategies

There are many adaptation factors to consider when working with aspiring Canadian Aboriginal athletes. These factors are informed by the extent to which athletes retain traditional aspects of their culture or assimilate within mainstream culture (Thomason 1991). To be sure, some Aboriginal athletes represent (and are represented by) communities where traditional Aboriginal cultural practices are prevalent in daily life. For example, during his encounters with athletes from remote communities in Manitoba and Saskatchewan, Rob noticed that some of the athletes smudged each day, used bundles, and sought the advice of elders and medicine people when they experienced motivational challenges in training and onsite at competitions (Schinke, Hanrahan, et al. 2007). These athletes talked about the predicaments they faced when trying to deal with the many unfamiliar cultural practices they encountered in mainstream sport, such as working with formally trained coaches who employed a structured approach to sport and who relied heavily on technical drills for training. In contrast, Aboriginal athletes from large urban centres (those portrayed herein as acculturated) were usually very familiar with mainstream cultural practices. As well, they typically came from households where the first language was typically French or English and whose practising religion was a form of Christianity: these athletes experienced fewer challenges in adapting to mainstream sport. Thus, it seems that the extent to which Canadian Aboriginal athletes have been socialized to traditional cultural norms influences the time and effort they spend adapting to many of the cultural practices found within Canadian mainstream society (e.g., extended eye contact, an event-based concept of time, varying dietary practices such as consuming processed food and commercially butchered meat, a focus on individual pursuits in sport, and individual criticism). Consequently, the adaptation strategies that follow can be used as guidelines to help Aboriginal athletes adjust to mainstream competitive sport environments; the degree to which they are followed will depend in part on the cultural characteristics of the athlete's community of origin (e.g., more extensive implementation of strategies may be suitable for those athletes from a community that retains indigenous cultural practices).

Aspects of Adaptation

Athletes across all cultures experience adaptation challenges, including getting used to new coaches and team members, potential relocation, and increased demands for excellence and outputs in sport – the more elite the competition, the greater the demand (Schinke, Gauthier, et al. 2007). Among Canadian Aboriginal athletes, we found the challenges that exist also include, to varying degrees: (1) making the commitment to pursue and persist in sport, (2) learning about mainstream sport's organizational structure, (3) gaining acceptance with and in turn accepting teammates and coaching staff within the mainstream sport context, and (4) resisting aspects of mainstream sport practices (among athletes who choose to persist in elite sport on their own terms as Aboriginal athletes) (Schinke, Michel, et al. 2006). The four abovementioned challenges listed were followed by the four adaptation strategies outlined below, which are integral to Canadian Aboriginal athletes' pursuit of excellence at the elite level.

Making the Commitment

One of the key questions that guided our research was why some Aboriginal athletes pursued elite sport for one year and then opted to deselect from national teams and return to their home communities. Elite athletes often need to relocate in order to access a higher level of coaching (Canadian Heritage 2005). The Aboriginal athletes from remote areas whom we interviewed indicated that the commitment level required of them was much higher than that for athletes from mainstream culture. Beyond the challenges associated with pursuing sport in a new location there is the necessity to live within another's culture, where many of the daily activities reflect unfamiliar customs. Among the new practices the athletes encountered were a hierarchical sport structure where the athletes were not consulted on decision that affected them, insensitive coaching practices (e.g., confrontation in front of peers), and unfamiliar diets (e.g., processed foods in place of more land-based, wholesome local foods such as wild rice, wild game, and fish). In addition, the expansive social support network athletes often benefited from in their home communities did not exist or was significantly altered in their new urban locations. For instance, once having relocated in order to play with a mainstream sport team, these athletes' home community involvement was limited to phone calls (i.e., relations from a physical distance); gone was the daily onsite support, and the physical support typically experienced when the athletes competed. The loss of daily community and social support is undoubtedly a challenge for every relocated athlete across cultures. However, among Aboriginal athletes who have moved far from home and are facing a life change, the challenge is compounded given the strong value placed on community (i.e., the connection to their home and people).

Learning about Mainstream Sport's Organizational Structure

Within mainstream sport, there is often an emphasis on technical drills as an integral part of training. Not only is training structure culturally informed but so is the approach to coaching. For example, some of the athletes we met considered mainstream coaching to be a top-down practice, with the coaches providing directives and the athletes responding accordingly (Schinke, Ryba, et al. 2007). In providing feedback to athletes during team meetings, coaches often voice critiques of each athlete's performance in front of the group, in a manner sometimes regarded as shaming. The Aboriginal athletes who expressed a concern about shaming want to build positive relations through sport but prefer to do so while keeping a heightened value of the group at the centre, with the individual's desires – including the coach's – considered as part of the group, as opposed to its centre.

A common characteristic of training structure in Aboriginal communities is an emphasis on playing scrimmages rather than doing technical drills (i.e., learning through doing, and having fun while doing). Consequently, we identified the need for increased awareness within Aboriginal communities of what aspiring athletes might experience prior to their engagement in elite sport (Schinke, Michel, et al. 2006). For example, an effective coping strategy might be for the athlete or someone representing the athlete to apprise coaching staff of the athlete's cultural sport background and where Aboriginal sport practices might diverge from mainstream sport practices. We see tremendous potential in developing a coaching leadership strategy whereby sport staff, in light of this knowledge, discuss with new recruits how to adjust to unfamiliar sport practices, such as those based on a hierarchical leadership model (versus a circular one), as they enter a mainstream context.

Gaining and Offering Acceptance

There is a transition period when joining a new team – the formation of bonds between coaches and athletes, as well as among athletes, is not instantaneous. Athletes must be accepted by and also offer acceptance to those with whom they train. When cultural differences add to the complexity of fostering these relationships, at least initially in bicultural relations (Canadian Aboriginal, Canadian mainstream), it seems to take more effort on the part of both cultures for full acceptance and cultural understanding to develop. For Canadian Aboriginal athletes, relations were initially challenged by the unfamiliarity of mainstream environments and also their shyness during encounters in athletic and daily life (Schinke, Michel, et al. 2006). Given what seemed, among the athletes we learned from, to be a practice of listening before speaking, in contrast to the mainstream practice of being heard over all others (Schinke, Hanrahan, and Catina 2009), and also an initial lack of confidence in mainstream sport contexts, many of the athletes struggled with their shyness immediately after relocating to pursue sport. With shyness regarded as the barrier to overcome, there was a consistent pattern across the athletes of gradually sharing knowledge of their experiences in sport, their life histories, and their local cultural practices with those in the mainstream. By merging their cultural identities with their athletic identities and sharing their life experiences with others, the athletes were actively addressing their shyness in sport while also enriching their sport contexts and creating a place for two cultural standpoints where initially there might have been only one.

Resisting Aspects of Mainstream Sport Culture

It is not unheard of for athletes who are facing adaptation challenges to go through a period of resistance. Resistance is often a matter of understanding the contextual demands posed by the new sport context and then directing one's efforts to work effectively within its parameters (Schinke, Michel, et al. 2006; Schinke, Gauthier, et al. 2007). Problems surface, however, when this resistance is interpreted negatively. Indeed, the Aboriginal athletes who resisted their new environments believed their actions were construed by coaching staff and other athletes as defiance rather than as a matter of cultural preference. Sometimes, when athletes are not provided with the support to adapt to their new environments, and this disconnect is felt throughout the course of a season, the consequence appears to be the personal decision (as opposed to a social-structural issue) to deselect and return home. Although Schinke, Michel, et al. (2006) identified compromise as the most common resolution to setbacks caused by resistance, we propose that the solution rests more generally in any course of action that is facilitative of multicultural understanding. Within such actions, sport staff, including coaches, might consider how to communicate in a manner that reaches the athletes through norms (e.g., appropriate eye contact, physical space, listening practices) and values (e.g., hierarchical or consensus-oriented) with which they are aligned.

Social Support Facilitators of Athlete Adaptation

The Aboriginal athletes identified an extensive social support network as an important factor in their success. Given the athletes' collective orientation, it is no surprise that their social support system would be well developed, with each resource offering unique aspects of support. The network generally consisted of (1) family, (2) role models, (3) medicine people and elders, and (4) the national Aboriginal community (Schinke, Eys, et al. 2006). Aboriginal athletes who relocated from their communities to pursue elite-level sport opportunities had less immediate access to community resources and thus sought them from a distance.

Family

A web of family resources provided the athletes with a form of support that sport scientists seldom take seriously (Schinke, Eys, et al. 2006). For instance, parents often encouraged a healthy and active lifestyle and provided transportation to sport activities, guidance when it came to sport challenges, and financial aid. They also typically encouraged sport participation from an early age and guided the aspiring athletes into sports programs. The athletes' family support systems included grandparents, aunts and uncles, siblings, and cousins; this extended family often travelled great distances to encourage and support the athletic activities. And although parents may have catalyzed sport engagement, we heard many stories of grandparents driving the athletes to competitions and also relaying their pride in the athletes' accomplishments in sport. In addition, some of the athletes talked about how their aunts and uncles were previously successful athletes who shared with them stories of struggle and accomplishment through sport. Siblings and cousins assumed their parts in the process, typically playing in sport with the athletes early on and consequently contributing to the athletes' becoming hooked on sport. As the athletes reflected upon their elite sport experiences, they restated that, without their family's extensive ongoing support, it would have been a real challenge to continue in sport and to adapt to mainstream sport demands.

Role Models

Role models provided a significant source of social support for athletes throughout the various stages of their athletic careers (Danielson et al. 2006). From an early age, the athletes reported being inspired by their role models' persistence and success. By listening to and sometimes reading about the stories passed from one generation of athletes to the next, the Aboriginal athletes became aware of cultural assimilation challenges and effective adaptation strategies (i.e., pathways that have already led to sport success on the national and international stage). The athletes generally likened these stories to walking a path in life (a life journey through sport) and used the stories as motivational strategies to pursue their goals for sport. The athletes identified family members, community members, past and present established athletes both within and outside the community, and current teammates as role models. These role models exemplified hard work, self-improvement, and personal achievement, as well as demonstrating sport-related skills and accomplishments (Blodgett et al. 2008). From what we have learned thus far anecdotally, Canadian Aboriginal athletes' experiences need to be deliberately promoted, as they are a potent source of motivation among Aboriginal youth.

Medicine People and Elders

Spirituality is an important part of many Aboriginal cultures. Historically and today, sacred medicine plays a significant role in maintaining health and spirituality. Even in sport it is not uncommon for Aboriginal athletes to offer prayers to the Creator by smudging (burning tobacco, sage, or sweetgrass) at the beginning and end of each day (Schinke, Hanrahan, et al. 2007). We found that when enculturated Aboriginal athletes encountered a challenge in training or competition, and the challenge could not be overcome through personal strategies, they often sought the assistance of medicine people or elders to help them work past the challenge. Medicine people and elders were not always available in a mainstream sporting context, though some professional athletes with more extensive financial resources were able to integrate these resources as part of their repertoire, especially during the week before competition. Community elders were sought for their perspective and their inspirational stories, whereas medicine people provided information about the effective use of sacred medicines and traditional herbs. In combination, these culture-specific resources can be aptly compared with today's sport science resources (e.g., sport doctors and sport psychologists, respectively) commonly used in mainstream sport settings. The knowledge that elders and medicine people have acquired appears to supersede mainstream sport psychology such that generations of hands-on learning and refining appears to be valued more than the knowledge gleaned from highly structured, institutionalized settings. When considering both cultural resources (Aboriginal and mainstream), it becomes apparent why Aboriginal athletes sometimes regard mainstream sport science as inappropriate, oppressive, and marginalizing. Consequently, sport scientists need to better understand that their roles as service providers are culture-bound, and that their tactics for sport development might be regarded as foreign and perhaps even inapplicable when working with Aboriginal athletes. On the other hand, Aboriginal athletes might wish to consider what traditional Aboriginal and mainstream practices they want or need to integrate into their performance plans to help them succeed in sport.

National Aboriginal Community

The Aboriginal athletes we interviewed generally regarded the national Aboriginal community as an important resource that could help them to succeed in elite-level mainstream sports. In Canada, Aboriginal peoples and their allies have established a strong support network to help Aboriginal athletes gain access to and stay involved in elite-level sport. Resources that were identified from our early work include the Aboriginal Sport Circle, the national representative organization for Aboriginal sport and recreation development in Canada; and exposure to athlete role models through Aboriginal media outlets such as the Aboriginal Peoples Television Network. Finally, there are national- and international-level competitions for Aboriginal athletes. These environments foster and promote Aboriginal cultural traditions and pride, and include a variety of venues, from sport-specific events such as the Little Native Hockey League (LNHL), an Ontario-based event that encourages personal effort and fair play among First Nation youth hockey teams, to major multi-sport events like the North American Indigenous Games (NAIG) and the Arctic Winter Games. Whereas the NAIG are open to Aboriginal athletes of all ages from Canada and the United States and usually take place every three years, the Arctic Winter Games are a biannual sport and cultural event for athletes living in the circumpolar region of the globe. Although the Arctic Winter Games feature many mainstream events, they also include traditional Dene and Inuit sports. Common to all three events (the LNHL, NAIG, and Arctic Winter Games) is acknowledgment that sport plays an important role in Aboriginal communities by bringing people together through a shared sense of pride and accomplishment.

Practical Recommendations

Although CSP is still in its infancy, our research findings suggest that several practical recommendations might offer some tentative steps in fostering a form of sport psychology that better meets a wider variety of clients' needs. Here, we offer three key recommendations. Elite-level athletes face many challenges as they progress to higher levels of sport, moving away from family and community, adapting to new environments, and encountering pressures to succeed. Added to the cross-cultural adaptation challenges encountered by most athletes are culture-specific challenges. The accumulated adaptation challenges can (and we argue should) be approached through mutual understanding of one's culture and the effective integration of culturally relevant motivational strategies in the daily lives of elite Aboriginal athletes. The use of such strategies should depend upon the extent to which the athletes retain their cultural traditions.

Challenges such as new sporting customs, unfamiliar coaching styles, and feelings of displacement and loneliness can contribute to shortened athletic careers and, in some cases, premature deselection from sport teams. The solution to the aforementioned can be found in the integration of Aboriginal practices and national resources from both within and beyond one's cultural community.

Cultural adaptation is a bidirectional process, with mainstream members (i.e., coaches, teammates, sport scientists, managers, sponsors, owners) who need to develop an appreciation for a culturally sensitive approach that aligns with the standpoints of those presently outside the mainstream. Sport psychology itself is culture-bound in terms of who provides the knowledge (e.g., an academic who might be less than thirty years of age), where such knowledge is gleaned (often from books and sometimes from academics with limited experience in the applied field), and also what is prioritized (e.g., the mainstream athlete at the centre). By gaining an appreciation of the ways in which all aspects of sport are steeped in culture, we will be better able to reflect on and challenge those values, beliefs, and practices that marginalize people, so as to create a more inclusive and welcoming space in sport for all.

Conclusion

Aboriginal cultural sport psychology (one example of CSP) is an attempt by sport psychologists to better understand and effectively support athletes in relation to their culture(s) (Schinke, Blodgett, et al. 2009). Until recently, applied consulting was represented by a mono-cultural approach in the field (Ryba and Wright 2005). Athletes were assisted by sport psychologists whose techniques were developed and reinforced in the mainstream through formal learning, which thus contributed to the legitimization of that knowledge and its accompanying practices as the most valid and valuable, worthy of emulation, repetition, and resourcing. Although mainstream athletes, similar to mainstream sport psychology consultants, might not be aware that the profession is culture-bound, sport psychology as a domain is steeped in the values and customs of one culture (white, Eurocentric, mainstream). Because one culture's strategies are identified as the most important ones, many other strategies have been relegated to the margins. The one-size-fits-all approach to sport psychology has resulted in a discounting of many athletes' needs, which, at the very least, has contributed to extensive adaptation struggles when non-mainstream athletes (in this case, Canadian Aboriginal athletes) have been asked to acclimate to the dominant culture.

We propose that the development of a CSP that is attuned to cultural nuances and fosters an understanding of athletes' experiences in relation to their culture of origin and history will not be easy, but that it will contribute to a healthier sport environment, where athletes from every culture are supported and encouraged equally.

REFERENCES

Andersen, M.B. 1993. Questionable sensitivity: A comment on Lee and Rotella. *Sport Psychologist* 7(1): 1-3.

Blodgett, A., R.J. Schinke, L. Fisher, C. Wassengeso-George, D. Peltier, S. Ritchie, and P. Pickard. 2008. From practice to praxis: Community-based strategies for Aboriginal youth sport. *Journal of Sport and Social Issues* 32(4): 393-414.

Butryn, T.M. 2002. Critically examining white racial identity and privilege in sport psychology consulting. *Sport Psychologist* 16(3): 316-36.

Canadian Heritage. 2005. *Sport Canada's Policy on Aboriginal Peoples' Participation in Sport.* Ottawa: Ministry of Public Works and Government Services.

Cox, R.H. 2006. *Sport Psychology: Concepts and Applications.* Boston: McGraw-Hill.

Danielson, R., R.J. Schinke, D. Peltier, and T.V. Dubé. 2006. Role modeling sources and activities of elite Canadian Aboriginal athletes. Paper presented at the North American Indigenous Games Educational Symposium, Denver, June 30.

Fisher, L.A., T.M. Butryn, and E.A. Roper. 2003. Diversifying (and politicizing) sport psychology through cultural studies: A promising perspective. *Sport Psychologist* 17(4): 391-405.

Hanrahan, S.J. 2004. Sport psychology and indigenous performing arts. *Sport Psychologist* 18(1): 60-74.

Hill, T.L. 1993. Sport psychology and the collegiate athlete: One size does not fit all. *Counseling Psychologist* 21(3): 436-40.

Kashima, Y., S. Yamaguchi, U. Kim, S.C. Choi, M.J. Gelfand, and M. Yuki. 1995. Culture, gender, and self: A perspective from individualism-collectivism research. *Journal of Personality and Social Psychology* 69(5): 925-37.

Kontos, A.P., and A.M. Breland-Noble. 2002. Racial/ethnic diversity in applied sport psychology: A multicultural introduction to working with athletes of color. *Sport Psychologist* 16(3): 296-315.

Martens, M.P., M. Mobley, and S.J. Zizzi. 2000. Multicultural training in applied sport psychology. *Sport Psychologist* 14(1): 81-97.

North American Indigenous Games Sport Research Panel 2003. In V. Paraschak and J. Forsyth, eds., *2002 North American Indigenous Games Conference Proceedings* (67-70). Winnipeg: University of Manitoba.

Orlick, T. 2000. *In Pursuit of Excellence*. Champaign, IL: Human Kinetics.

Peltier, D., R. Danielson, R.J. Schinke, G. Michel, and T.V. Dube. 2006. Cultural sport psychology: The Wikwemikong perspective. Paper presented at the North American Indigenous Games Educational Symposium, Denver, June 30.

Peters, H.J., and J.M. Williams. 2006. Moving cultural background to the foreground: An investigation of self-talk, performance, and persistence following feedback. *Journal of Applied Sport Psychology* 18(3): 240-53.

Riggs, D.W. 2004. Challenging the monoculturalism of psychology: Towards a more socially accountable pedagogy and practice. *Australian Psychologist* 39(2): 118-26.

Running Wolf, P., and J.A. Rickard. 2003. Talking circles: A Native American approach to experiential learning. *Multicultural Counselling and Development* 31(1): 39-43.

Ryba, T.V., and H.K. Wright. 2005. From mental game to cultural praxis: A cultural studies model's implications for the future of sport psychology. *Quest* 57(2): 192-212.

Schinke, R.J. 2007. A four-year chronology with national team boxing in Canada. *Journal of Sport Science and Medicine* 6 (Combat Sports Special Issue – 2): 1-5.

Schinke, R.J., A. Blodgett, C. Ritchie, P. Pickard, G. Michel, D. Peltier, L. Enosse, et al. 2009. Entering the community of Canadian indigenous athletes. In R.J. Schinke and S.J. Hanrahan, eds., *Cultural Sport Psychology: From Theory to Practice* (91-102). Champaign, IL: Human Kinetics.

Schinke, R.J., M.A. Eys, G. Michel, R. Danielson, D. Peltier, C. Pheasant, L. Enosse, et al. 2006. Cultural social support for Canadian Aboriginal elite athletes during their sport development. *International Journal of Sport Psychology* 37(4): 1-19.

Schinke, R.J., A. Gauthier, N.G. Dubuc, and T. Crowder. 2007. Understanding adaptation in professional hockey through an archival source. *Sport Psychologist* 21(3): 277-87.

Schinke, R.J., S.J. Hanrahan, and P. Catina. 2009. Introduction to cultural sport psychology. In R.J. Schinke and S.J. Hanrahan, eds., *Cultural Sport Psychology: From Theory to Practice* (1-12). Champaign, IL: Human Kinetics.

Schinke, R.J., S.J. Hanrahan, D. Peltier, G. Michel, R. Danielson, P. Pickard, C. Pheasant, et al. 2007. The pre-competition and competition practices of Canadian Aboriginal elite athletes. *Journal of Clinical Sport Psychology* 1(2): 147-65.

Schinke, R.J., G. Michel, A. Gauthier, P. Pickard, R. Danielson, D. Peltier, C. Pheasant, et al. 2006. Adaptation to the mainstream in elite sport: A Canadian Aboriginal perspective. *Sport Psychologist* 20(4): 435-48.

Schinke, R.J., D. Peltier, S.J. Hanrahan, M.A. Eys, D. Recollet-Saikonnen, H. Yungblut, S. Ritchie, et al. 2009. The progressive integration of Canadian indigenous culture within a sport psychology bicultural research team. *International Journal of Sport and Exercise Psychology* 7(3): 309-22.

Schinke, R.J., T.V. Ryba, R. Danielson, G. Michel, P. Pickard, D. Peltier, L. Enosse, et al. 2007. Canadian Aboriginal elite athletes: The experiences of being coached in mainstream culture. *International Journal of Sport and Exercise Psychology* 4(2): 123-41.

Smith, L.T. 1999. *Decolonizing Methodologies: Research and Indigenous Peoples.* London: Zed Books.

Thomason, T.C. 1991. Counseling Native Americans: An introduction for non-Native American counselors. *Journal of Counseling and Development* 69(4): 321-27.

Weinberg, R.S., and D. Gould. 2003. *Foundations of Sport and Exercise Psychology.* 3rd ed. Champaign, IL: Human Kinetics.

◄ APPENDIX 5.1

Semi-structured athlete interview guide

Part A: Early Sport

1. Tell me about your sport background as an elite athlete.
2. What were your initial dreams starting off? Where did they come from?
3. What were your first sport experiences like?
4. What role did your family play during your earliest sport experiences?
5. Did you have any role models in your community?
6. Did you have any role models outside your community?
7. Were there any friends or family who encouraged you to stay where you were location-wise at this time? How did you respond?

Part B: Getting Serious

8. When did you realize that you were getting serious about your sport pursuits? Was there a specific incident that contributed to the realization?
9. Did there come a point in your sport development where you had to leave home? If so, what was that experience like?
10. Where did you get your encouragement from? Were there sources that were less encouraging (friends, elders, others)?
11. What sorts of daily support did you experience from family during this time?
12. What sorts of family support did you experience during earlier important competitions?
13. How did you manage in a mainstream (i.e., white) training environment? Tell me a little about your daily experiences with coaches, teammates, and structure.
14. What sort of coaches did you have during this time in your life? Tell me a little bit about what they were like.
15. What sorts of things facilitated and undermined your relationship with your coaches (wisdom, respect, their link with family, cultural sensitivity)?
16. Did you have any forms of support (spiritual, emotional, financial) from your First Nations community, or any other First Nations community for that matter?
17. What sorts of relationships did you form with other athletes as you immersed into a more serious training environment?
18. Were there any athletes who you looked up to within or outside your sport?
19. Did you have any setbacks or moments during your initial serious sporting experiences when you wanted to throw in the towel? Tell me a little bit about those experiences, and how you persisted.

►

◄ APPENDIX 5.1

Part C: Daily Consolidated Performance

20. Were/are there any athletes who've shared their success strategies at the highest level?
21. Do/did you integrate any spiritual practices within your day-to-day training routine (examples: smudging, sun dances, eagle feathers, visits with elders, and stories)? If so, can you tell me a little bit about each one?
22. Were/are there any other day-to-day (non-traditional) motivational practices that you integrated? Please tell me a little bit about those practices.
23. Did your coaches use any First Nations practices while helping you pursue your sport? Was this important to you?
24. What were the things you did the week before each competition to prepare and feel ready?
25. What sorts of things did you do the day of competition in order to feel prepared? Please provide specific tactics.
26. Tell me a bit about the people who would/do come to support you during competitions.
27. What is the role of your coach, family, friends, and community during competitions?
28. Have you ever competed in Aboriginal competitions? If so, what was that experience like for you?
29. Do you find there to be any cultural uniqueness factored into your communication exchanges when working alongside non-Native sport people (e.g., eye contact, being singled out, friendly expression?
30. Do you find that your view of winning and losing is the same as your competitors' and teammates'? Please give some examples of how you view each.

Part D: The Broader Perspective

31. If you have stopped competing, what were your last experiences like as an elite athlete?
32. What is/was important to you about being an elite First Nations athlete? Do you find your pursuits to be important to other First Nations people?
33. Do you work at all with young First Nations athletes? If so, what sorts of things do you emphasize when training/supporting them in their pursuits?
34. Do you have any suggestions for the parents and other family members of aspiring First Nations youth?
35. Are there any community-level strategies that might benefit aspiring First Nations athletes? What are they?

6 Women's and Girls' Participation in Dene Games in the Northwest Territories

AUDREY R. GILES

The advent of major international competitions in Aboriginal sports and games, such as the World Indigenous Games, and the inclusion of traditional sports and games in national and international competitions, such as the Arctic Winter Games (AWG) and the North American Indigenous Games, show the ways in which Aboriginal physical practices are gaining prominence in Canada and around the world. In this chapter I examine Dene games (i.e., games played by the Dene),[1] focusing in particular on women's and girls' participation in these games. Using data gathered during thirteen months of ethnographic research in three South Slavey Dene communities in the Northwest Territories (Sambaa K'e/Trout Lake, Thek'ehdeli/Jean Marie River, and Liidlii Kue/Fort Simpson), I outline the ways in which understandings of tradition and menstrual practices shape beliefs about how Dene games should be played and who should play them, as well as the challenges these issues pose to policy makers and programmers.

A History of Dene Games

The Dene are the First Nations people who inhabit a region they refer to as Denendeh, an expansive territory that stretches across the Canadian western Subarctic. Although this area covers portions of the Northwest Territories, as well as the northern part of the western Canadian provinces, for the purpose of this chapter I focus on the Dene and the games that they play north of the sixtieth parallel: in the Northwest Territories.

According to *Dene Games: A Culture and Resource Manual* (Heine 1999, 1.6), "There is a basic unity of Dene culture, and it is expressed by the way the people were connected to and survived on the land. What just about all groups of the Dene had in common was that surviving on the land meant travelling on the land. It was through their travels that the people most closely connected with the land." Heine notes that Dene games were heavily influenced by the connection between travel and life on the land. Strength, endurance, speed, and accuracy were necessary for survival, and these much-needed skills were often practised by playing traditional games. Furthermore, "The close link between games and the traditional way of life is also shown by the kinds of equipment used in most games, that is, very little to none. On the trail, people relied mainly on their own strength. They were able to pack heavy loads, but not everything could be taken along ... People generally knew how to make their own equipment for playing traditional games" (ibid., 1.37).

Dene games have become regional events. According to Paraschak (1983), the first regional Dene Games took place in Rae-Edzo (now BehchoK'o) in 1977. This multi-community sport and cultural festival was organized by the Dene-U Celebration Committee with the help of a grant from the Government of the NWT's (GNWT's) Recreation Division. This first Dene Games revolved around a softball tournament, which drew participants from communities close to Rae-Edzo. The next two Games, in 1978 and 1979, followed this format. Although there were no Games in 1980, the Dene Games Association, which consisted of the same people who sat on the Dene-U Celebration Committee, held an organizational meeting, funded by the GNWT. The result of this meeting was the 1981 Summer Dene Games, which were also held in Rae-Edzo and once again focused on a softball tournament but also included several traditional games (ibid.). The Dene Games then became established as an annual multi-community sport festival that rotated among communities. Although the activities differed from year to year, there were several that appeared at many of the Summer Dene Games: axe throw, bannock making, bow and arrow shoot, coin toss, canoe races, Dene baseball, dryfish making, fish filleting and frying, log splitting, spear throw, tea boiling, and tug-of-war. In 1999, funding for regional Dene Games was no longer available, and each community involved in the Games was encouraged to themselves develop Dene games by holding workshops. In 2002, the Dene Games were once again held as an intercommunity sport festival, an event that continued annually for the remainder of the decade.

Dene games are also played at the AWG, a multi-sport competition and cultural festival for the circumpolar region. The AWG began in 1970 with mostly European-derived games (e.g., badminton, curling, gymnastics, figure skating, and basketball); the Dene games component was not added until 1990. The games that were selected as Dene games events at the AWG differed from the events at the regional Summer Dene Games: finger pull, stick pull, snowsnake, pole push, and hand games (like gymnastics and track and field, Dene games involve various events). Unlike the mixed-sex categories at regional Dene Games, the AWG offered categories for men only. A category of Senior Men has been available since the inception of the Dene games category at the AWG; a category of Junior Men was added at the 2002 AWG.

In early 2000, several AWG contingents moved to create Dene games categories for girls and women at the AWG. The proposal to add a Junior Girls category clearly aligned the Arctic Winter Games International Committee (AWGIC) with gender equity policies as well as with groups that had lobbied for women's involvement in the Dene games portion of the AWG (e.g., the Mackenzie Recreation Association, which helps to administer sport and recreation in approximately half of the Northwest Territories). The addition of the Junior Girls category, however, also placed the AWGIC in conflict with the Denendeh Traditional Games Association (DTGA), a group of Dene men who argued that, based on tradition, Dene games should remain a male preserve. Despite the DTGA's strong objections, the AWGIC added the Junior Girls category to the 2004 AWG, which took place in the Wood Buffalo Region of northern Alberta.

To better understand why some people felt that women and girls should not participate in Dene games, I conducted ethnographic research in three Dene communities in the Northwest Territories and at the 2004 AWG, where the Junior Girls category was first introduced. In total, I spent thirteen months in the North, where I interviewed eighty-eight children, youth, adults, and elders, and conducted participant observation. Despite the strong familial and cultural ties that bind the residents of Sambaa K'e/Trout Lake (population 65), Thek'ehdeli/Jean Marie River (population 52), and Liidlii Kue/Fort Simpson (population 1,200), my research revealed that understandings of tradition and menstrual practices and residents' beliefs concerning women's and girls' participation in Dene games varied greatly between and within communities.

Tradition and Dene Games

In the past, Dene games were played almost exclusively by men (Helm and

Lurie 1966; Heine 1999; Giles 2004, 2005a, 2008, 2010). Although there are a few published examples of women's participation (e.g., Giles 2008), women's and girls' past involvement in Dene games, and particularly in a form of stick gambling, where opponents need to guess in which hand a token is hidden, known as hand games, which as I discuss are linked to Dene menstrual practices, appears to have been rare. Women's and girls' involvement continues to be quite limited in some communities and regions in the Northwest Territories. Thus, in some areas, some people might assert that women's and girls' involvement in Dene games, especially hand games, is untraditional. In contrast, females of various ages play hand games in other areas, for instance, Yukon.

Anthropologists have long struggled with understanding tradition. Debates often revolve around whether traditions can change, and if yes, what changes mean to the old ways. If a change occurs, is it still the same tradition, or does it become something new? Furthermore, what broader societal changes have led to the transition? What are the implications for the people to whom this tradition belongs? As Handler and Linnekin (1984, 288) point out, one of the major paradoxes that result in representations of traditions being contested is "that attempts at cultural preservation inevitably alter, reconstruct, or invent the traditions that they are intended to fix." Such is clearly the case with Dene games. As Giles (2004) notes, elders in the Dehcho Region remember Dene games of the past as being significantly different in both form and content from those currently played at regional and international events. Many of the changes are due to efforts to standardize events for intercommunity competitions, while others are because of modernization (i.e., the invention of new materials and substances). For example, the stick used in the game stick pull is now greased with Crisco© at the AWG (as per the rules in the AWG's technical manual), rather than fat directly off an animal (ibid.). Also, canoes used in canoe races at regional Dene Games are now typically made of Kevlar© rather than materials from the land (wood, bark). Thus, some aspects of these traditional games have been modernized to fit contemporary sporting demands for efficiency and performance. Handler and Linnekin (1984, 273) point out that "all cultures change ceaselessly"; we should expect traditions to also change to adapt to new social and material circumstances (Riphenburg 1997).

Not all changes, however, are accepted with ease. People who view tradition in a static way often believe that it is only by capturing "the way it was" that we can achieve authenticity and maintain tradition. In this view, Dene games that were played on the land in "the old days" are traditional and authentic; hence, to maintain the tradition and authenticity of such games, subscribers to this point of view see as crucial the reproduction of rules that were likely used in the past. Such is the case with the DTGA.

According to Kay (2002, B19), the DTGA said "it [is] important for people to understand they are forming a traditional association which will follow the ways the [Dene] games were played in the past." Notably, a key characteristic of "the ways the games were played in the past" was the typical non-participation of girls and women. Michael Vandel, the president of the DTGA, stated, "We should focus on the traditional way of [playing] it. It's respect for our elders. If ... [women] don't understand that, then we don't have room for them" (B4, B19). The DTGA, which was to be the Territorial Sport Organization for Dene games (the government-authorized regional representative body), then took the position that it would ban girls and women from participating in all Dene games activities that it organized. After the DTGA announced this position, the GNWT revoked the DTGA's funding. As Ian Legaree, the director of sport, recreation, youth, and volunteerism, put it: "[The DTGA] said no women, so no women means no support from the Government [of the NWT]" (Pers. comm., January 29, 2004). Following shortly after the revocation of its funding, the DTGA collapsed. But why did the DTGA's members feel so strongly opposed to women's and girls' participation?

Menstruation

All of the interviewees in my research reported that the reason girls and women did not typically participate in many traditional games, especially hand games, which involves a moosehide drum that many consider to be sacred, has to do with menstrual traditions and notions of purity and power – although this is rarely discussed openly. Menstrual practices and beliefs among the Dene have been documented by numerous authors (Abel 1993; Goulet 1998; Helm 2000; Giles 2004, 2008, 2010). In the past, Dene girls went through rites of passage when they had their first menses. Fort Simpson resident Suza Tsetso explained:

> As soon as they get their cycle ... they get a stick and they hit the tree and they make noise ... [and] the grandmother or auntie or mother knows that noise. They go to where she's at, build a little hut, a shelter around her, and they leave her there and she doesn't leave that spot, and that's where she'll stay for up to a year ... So what happens is that she stays there and the teachers come ... and this woman is created, her skills are created from all

> the elders and the people who have these skills, and they leave. When she's ready to come into the community, it's a whole celebration where she comes and there's gathering, there's a prayer offering and a prayer song, and she's brought back into the community where she does a dance once around the circle, and that's where she's starting her life. And the whole community celebrates that. (Pers. comm., February 14, 2004)

Menstrual practices continued into women's adult lives. When menstruating, women would stay in a hut: "The whole community knows. It's not something that's hidden. When she gets her cycle ... she leaves and she stays in her place ... until her cycle is finished, totally finished, then she can leave" (Suza Tsetso, pers. comm., February 12, 2004).

Power or Pollution?

Opinions falling into two categories are typically offered for the reasons behind Aboriginal women's exclusion from various activities during menstruation, especially from activities of religious and spiritual importance: impurity/pollution and power. Buckley and Gottlieb (1988, 4) found that most ethnographic reports of menstrual practices and beliefs record menstrual blood as being considered "symbolically dangerous and otherwise defiling." Buckley and Gottlieb further identified that these "analyses have great predictability, for again and again they center on the concepts of *taboo* (supernaturally sanctioned law) and *pollution* (symbolic contamination)" (4, emphasis in the original). Indeed, several authors have noted that, in some Aboriginal cultures, menstruation brings with it a connotation of impurity and religious defilement (see Irwin 1994; Ryan 1995; Goulet 1998).

Although notions of pollution and taboo have been used as the primary explanations for certain menstrual practices, Anderson (2000) asserts that Aboriginal women's segregation during menstruation is based not on the notion of impurity but on that of the enhanced power women have during this time. Indeed, some Aboriginal women take issue with menstruation being depicted as a "manifestation of female sin, contamination and inferiority" (ibid., 75). Suza Tsetso elucidated the power associated with menstruation: "If a part of your body is dying, going through a cycle, then you're closer to the spirit world than you are at your regular time" (pers. comm., February 12, 2004). Certainly, some of the participants in my research saw women's power during menstruation not as polluting but as possibly overpowering or clashing with men's power.

The role of menstrual practices has diminished considerably in recent years, yet these practices and beliefs continue to exert an influence on many aspects of life in some Dehcho communities. Today, only a few girls and women continue to follow the tradition of remaining in the home, separated from men, when menstruating. The tradition has changed because girls and women need to attend school or participate in paid or unpaid work. Instead of remaining segregated, those who continue to follow menstrual practices often do one or more of the following: avoid going anywhere that they do not have to go (e.g., recreational events); refrain from eating fish, birds, and berries; and refrain from boating while "on their time" (Anonymous, pers. comm., August 11, 2002).

Hand Games and Menstruation

Hand games are the Dene game most clearly linked to Dene menstrual practices. In the past, hand games were played on the land, often when two groups met on the trail while hunting. The stakes for these games were high, with the teams wagering important articles such as guns, knives, and blankets on the outcome. Losing such valuable materials could have a significant impact on a group's well-being; thus, in an attempt to ensure success, the male players would draw on their medicine power, sometimes described as drawing on powers from animal spirits, to influence the games' outcome. As these games contained an element of medicine power, menstruation needed to be managed in such a way as to not bring about an undesirable outcome (i.e., a loss) or damage a man's hunting capabilities, which could occur if a menstruating woman were present or playing. This belief in the game's spiritual component still shapes some peoples' involvement in hand games today. As one woman reported, "They say women can easily overpower men if they're not careful. I don't know, [the DTGA is banning women] just to keep the men safe, I guess" (Anonymous, pers. comm., July 16, 2002).

Thus, for some Dene, the failure to observe menstrual practices is believed to result in negative material consequences for community members. For these reasons, some interviewees took very strong stances against women's and girls' participation in Dene games. One woman from Sambaa K'e/Trout Lake stated:

> Hand games and drum dance ... it's strictly for the men ... It has something to do with spiritual legends and ... it's always said ... that it was for the men. So I think they should just keep the women out of it. (Anonymous, pers. comm., July 6, 2002)

Gender Equity

But why ban all women and girls, rather than only those who are menstruating? According to one participant, "Nowadays you can't tell when it's a woman's certain time of the month, you can't really tell" (Anonymous, pers. comm., March 20, 2004). By keeping all women out of Dene games, organizers are able to ensure that menstruating girls and women are not playing and thus not bringing about negative material consequences. However, banning women Dene games, as the DTGA proposed to do, runs counter to Canadian gender equity policies. The pressure to impose gender equity in sport stems from several fronts, including the Canadian Charter of Rights and Freedoms (1982) and the United Nations' Universal Declaration of Human Rights (1948), as well as from organization- and sport-specific gender equity policies. A case in point is Sport North Federation (1995), the Territorial Sport Organization for the Northwest Territories. It has a gender equity policy that states, "The Sport North Federation, in cooperation with the Territorial Sport Organizations will work towards an equitable distribution of resources and opportunities to girls and women when developing, delivering and evaluating its programs" (ibid., 2). Gender equity policies thus position traditional Dene practices as being out of date and morally wrong.

In light of this political context, it is not surprising that gender equity was a recurrent theme in my research. Many participants drew on discourses of gender equity during their interviews. For example, Liidlii Kue/Fort Simpson resident Walter McPherson stated:

> It's good that girls participate too, because some people say that women can't do just as good as men. I think they can do just as good as men. It's there for sport, I don't see why not. If everybody's willing and capable of playing the game, I don't see why not. (Pers. comm., March 19, 2004)

Elder Fred Norwegian from Thek'ehdeli/Jean Marie River stated:

> I always believe that things are changing these days. I watch TV, I now see women boxers and I also see women hockey players, which was not seen before ... so I would think that [Dene games] would change ... my belief is, sure, why not? (Pers. comm., August 18, 2003)

Wesley Hardisty, a young man in his twenties from Liidlii Kue/Fort Simpson argued:

> The whole question of if women deserve to play [Dene games] because of the gender equality thing is totally outrageous because, you know, women can do anything that a guy can do, as I can see, and I'd never say a woman can't do that because she's a girl. (Pers. comm., February 12, 2004)

Interestingly, some Dehcho residents believed that female participants were necessary to keep traditional games alive and so offered a utilitarian argument to justify their participation. Elder Dolphus Jumbo from Sambaa K'e/Trout Lake, framed the issue this way:

> How can you urge all these young people to keep these traditional games if you don't invite everybody to do it? Everybody has to do it to keep the traditional games going ... There are not very many Aboriginal people now that are into traditional [games]. If they choose all men to do the traditional [games], they won't have very much success at it. (Pers. comm., August 7, 2002)

In this particular case, the argument was made not on the grounds of what is just or traditional but on the grounds that in order for boys and men to play, women and girls need to play too.

Within Dene games, there are traditional elements that are seen by some as being unchangeable (e.g., participants' sex) and those that are seen as being changeable (e.g., the use of Kevlar and Crisco). But is there an obligation to maintain *all* aspects of a tradition in order to keep practices "traditional"? For instance, why did the DTGA view the introduction of some neo-traditional aspects of Dene games as unproblematic, yet viewed women's participation in hand games as problematic? Several women participants opposed the DTGA's view, arguing that girls and women should not be forced to maintain traditional practices that they feel are no longer relevant. One young woman stated:

> Things [have] changed now, you know. Nobody lives solely by the traditional way of life anymore ... [and] women should be allowed to play. Like, back then there were certain reasons why women couldn't play certain things because it's like the way of life, the way people live, the traditional way of life. If women participated in certain things it brought bad luck or nobody got any good luck or anything like that. But now nobody lives like that anyway ... so why bring [back] everything traditional when nobody lives like that now? (Pers. comm., July 11, 2002).

Stef Sanguez, a woman in her twenties from Thek'ehdeli/Jean Marie River, noted that Dene women should not be the only ones reproached for not upholding traditional practices:

> Women are always the ones who are cooking and cleaning, that's the traditional part ... as far as I know, men are [now] cooking and cleaning ... they're taking on the women's roles ... men shouldn't even say anything at all [about women playing the games]!" (Pers. comm., August 10, 2003)

Sanguez's statement suggests that women are being heavily critiqued for failing to follow tradition, even though some men are doing the same thing, albeit in a different sphere (i.e., domestic rather than sporting).

Another Explanation?

Although the majority of participants stated that menstrual practices were behind the tradition of non-participation of women and girls in Dene games, a counter-explanation was given by a few participants. According to elder Julie Punch, women "never had time to sit back. We were always keeping ourselves busy with moose hide, and moose meat, and the camp ... we never had time to [play Dene games], just the men who really didn't have much to do in the camp, they'd just go out and compete" (pers. comm., July 11, 2002).

Suza Tsetso provided a detailed oral account, given to her by her father, that makes similar assertions:

> This one gathering, women were getting food and watching the kids and the men were gone ... they'd be playing hand games, it went on for days and things needed to be done that didn't get done. Everyone had a role and w[as] needed, so the women were starting to get really upset. "This has gone on too long," they said. The women said okay ... stopped what they were doing, got together, went to where the men were playing hand games. They went over there and stopped in there and said, "Stop this game! You're needed over here. You need to go hunting, check the nets, do all these things. Dogs need to be fed. You have a lot of responsibility, you men have to take responsibility. Stop the game now, let's get back to life" ... So what happened was that the women challenged [the men]. They got in there. They were playing and playing and they beat the men at their own game. The game stopped right there and then they all went back to their work. And the only reason they didn't want the women to play is that there's nobody else to do the jobs at the camp. They didn't have anybody else to do

> it. If the women and the men [play hand games], nobody's going to raise the children or feed the dogs, so they left all the work to the women and the women said no. (Pers. comm., February 12, 2004)

The above two accounts differ quite markedly from the explanations provided by other research participants and suggest that women's and girls' lack of participation in the past could have been rooted in something other than menstrual practices: the division of labour.

From Research to Effective Programming

Dene menstrual practices can pose challenges for those unfamiliar with them. They can be particularly problematic for those who feel that gender equity demands that males and females be allowed to participate in the same activities. They are also a challenge for the Dene, many of whom are trying to maintain their traditional practices in a very different context from that within which they originally emerged. Research, however, can play an important role in helping to promote understanding between sport and recreation participants and organizers, as well as programmers' and policy makers' understanding of the cultural contexts in which they work, and in which the participants live and play. This, I realize, is not a groundbreaking insight, and is easier said than done, particularly in cross-cultural environments such as that of the Northwest Territories.

Paraschak (1985, 11) notes,

> The Government of the Northwest Territories [which, along with Sport North, manages various aspects of sport and recreation in the Northwest Territories] is made up mainly of people originating from southern Canada ... Since it is government workers who establish the programs and services for recreation, very often those programs end up being based on southern Canadian rather than native standards, even though they are created to meet native needs.

Almost three decades after she published these findings, they remain relevant. Importantly, differences between government services and community needs can become evident when research is conducted with community members. During the course of my research, it became clear that some residents of Sambaa K'e/Trout Lake, Thek'ehdeli/Jean Marie River, and Liidlii Kue/Fort Simpson felt resentment toward GNWT and AWGIC officials for attempting to control Dene games. Residents of these small communities felt that both non-Aboriginal and Aboriginal officials living in the territorial capital, Yellowknife, did not necessarily have an appreciation for the value of the cultural practices that some members of the small communities were attempting to maintain or the ways in which they were attempting to maintain them (e.g., disallowing female participants).

Indeed, whereas support for gender equity among sport and recreation policy makers and programmers is often widespread, the same cannot be said for the recognition of cultural self-determination. Clearly, based on cultural beliefs, some Dene residents of the Northwest Territories – for example, the DTGA and some of the individuals I interviewed during my research – feel that it is inappropriate and even potentially dangerous for women and girls to participate in Dene games. Nevertheless, for Euro-Canadian, southern-based sport and recreation organizers, efforts to add categories for women and girls to the Dene Games component of the AWG might seem like an appropriate response to a perceived inequity. Such an approach has been seen in various other conventionally masculine physical practices (e.g., boxing, the marathon), so why not do the same with Dene games?

If the goal of enabling girls and women to participate in Dene games at the AWG is to "empower" them, it would be ironic if the medicine power that some Dene individuals view as being associated with menstruation goes unrecognized. Moreover, as critical theorists (e.g., Freire 1972) have pointed out, it is impossible to empower others; they must empower themselves. For some Dene women, empowerment may mean privileging and respecting their medicine power and thus not participating in Dene games. For others, it might mean participating in Dene games, but only when not menstruating. For others yet, it might mean participating in Dene games no matter the circumstances.

Because of the differences in beliefs and practices concerning tradition, menstruation, and women's and girls' involvement in Dene games in general, but especially hand games, it becomes difficult to create rules and policies that will please everyone, Dene or non-Dene. Thus, finding ways in which to "develop" Dene games along culturally appropriate lines for women and girls becomes difficult, especially for the often white male sport and recreation professionals in the Northwest Territories who are often incredibly uncomfortable with discussions pertaining to Dene menstrual practices. The reverse is also true: some Dene women too are uncomfortable with having such discussions with men, be they Dene or non-Dene.

A Conclusion of Sorts

In his article "Der wilde Westen," Scanlon (1990) described the annual pilgrimage that thousands of German men, women, and children make to a field northeast of Koblenz, Germany, to essentially "play Indian" (Deloria 1989). As described in this article, an Aboriginal couple from Canada, Clifford and Vanora Big Plume, visit the field to take in the activities. Dressed in "a turquoise beaded vest over a blue plaid shirt, new blue jeans, beaded moccasins and a dark brown cowboy hat with an eagle feather" (Scanlon 1990, 59), Clifford Big Plume stands out from the other participants, most of whom are non-Aboriginal but are dressed in full Aboriginal regalia. Upon seeing Big Plume, a German participant "instantly dismisses the real Indian's outfit as too garish: 'When you do this, it has to be right'" (ibid., 60). Despite being alive and Aboriginal, Big Plume is labelled as untraditional for failing to live up to a prepackaged stereotype. Another example of indigenous peoples being dismissed as illegitimate or untraditional is the Yorta Yorta Aborigines' struggle in Australia in 2002: they lost a land claim dispute after the High Court ruled that the Yorta Yorta failed to prove they were still using their land in a "traditional" fashion, that is, in a way that matched their ancestors (Associated Press 2002).

So what do the Big Plumes and the Yorta Yorta have to do with women's and girls' participation in Dene games? I would suggest that these three cases all illustrate the same point: cultures change and, thus, so too do representations and understandings of cultures and cultural practices. The tendency to represent traditional cultural practices and history across Denendeh (or the Wild West or Australia) as static, uniform, and beyond debate results in a failure to acknowledge the fluidity of tradition and the people who live it. All of these examples also display the ways in which unequal power relations (e.g., between those in small and large communities, women and men, Aboriginal and non-Aboriginal peoples) and the rhetoric of "consultation" (Giles 2005b; Giles and Castleden 2008) have a profound, material impact on people's lives. Furthermore, they illustrate the ways in which people who live with the consequences of unequal power relations and their outcomes are often omitted from consultation processes.

Consultations with potential female participants concerning their *own involvement* in Dene games were conspicuously absent from the DTGA's and AWGIC's decision-making processes. What might such consultations have told DTGA and AWGIC members? Based on my research findings, Dene women's traditions, power, and empowerment can take many forms, and people are going to have a range of feelings about these forms. Indeed, there may be some very valid reasons, other than those relating to patriarchal control, for Dene women and girls to choose to – or choose not to – participate in Dene games. These reasons may very well push the limits not only of conventional Western liberal feminist understandings of equity and equality but also of static understandings of tradition. Certainly, Dene games provide a fascinating lens through which we can examine sport and recreation in a Canadian context. These games challenge us to think more carefully about the ways in which understandings of culture influence participation, and the ways in which participation influences culture.

ACKNOWLEDGMENTS

This research, which was completed for my doctorate (University of Alberta, 2005), was generously funded through direct funding or funding in kind from the following organizations: Social Sciences and Humanities Research Council's Doctoral Fellowship, Northern Scientific Training Program Grants (2), Walter H. John's Scholarship, Circumpolar/Boreal Alberta Research Institute Grants (2), an Aurora Research Institute Research Fellowship, Aurora Research Institute Research Assistant Grants (2), a Province of Alberta Doctoral Fellowship, a University of Alberta Master's Recruitment Scholarship, the Sport North Federation, the Aboriginal Sport Circle of the Western Arctic, the Mackenzie Recreation Association, the Government of the Northwest Territories, Sambaa K'e Dene Band, and the Jean Marie River First Nation. Several individuals deserve special mention for their support: my doctoral supervisor, Debra Shogan; my research assistants, Lousia Moreau and Suza Tsetso; and, finally, the residents of Sambaa K'e/Trout Lake, Thek'ehdeli/Jean Marie River, and Liidlii Kue/Fort Simpson for their guidance and generosity – *mahsi cho!*

Portions of this chapter previously appeared in Giles (2004).

NOTE

1 I capitalize "Dene Games" when referring to the name of the formal event in the Mackenzie Region of the Northwest Territories. Otherwise, "games" is lowercased.

REFERENCES

Abel, K. 1993. *Drum Songs: Glimpses of Dene History.* Montreal: McGill-Queen's University Press.

Anderson, K. 2000. *A Recognition of Being.* Toronto: Second Story.

Associated Press. 2002. Australia's High Court dismisses Aboriginal land claim. December 12. http://ap.tbo.com/.

Buckley, T., and A. Gottlieb, eds. 1988. *Blood Magic: The Anthropology of Menstruation.* Berkeley: University of California Press.

Deloria, P. 1989. *Playing Indian.* New Haven, CT: Yale University Press.

Freire, P. 1972. *Pedagogy of the Oppressed.* Harmondsworth, UK: Penguin.

Giles, A.R. 2004. Kelvar, Crisco, and menstruation: "Tradition" and Dene games. *Sociology of Sport Journal* 21(1): 18-35.

–. 2005a. A Foucaultian approach to menstrual practices in the Dehcho Region, Northwest Territories, Canada. *Arctic Anthropology* 42(2): 9-21.

–. 2005b. Letting stories loose in the world. In H. Castleden, R. Danby, A. Giles, and J.P. Pinnard, eds. *New Northern Lights: Graduate Work in Circumpolar Studies at the University of Alberta* (88-104). Edmonton: Canadian Circumpolar Institute Press.

–. 2008. Beyond "add women and stir": Politics, feminist development, and Dene games. *Leisure/Loisir* 32(2): 489-512.

–. 2010. Menstruation and Dene physical practices. In D. Holmes and T. Ridge, eds., *Abjectly Boundless: Boundaries, Bodies, and Health Work* (33-48). Farnham, UK: Ashgate.

Giles, A.R., and H. Castleden. 2008. Community co-authorship in academic publishing: A commentary. *Canadian Journal of Native Education* 31(1): 208-13.

Goulet, J.-G. 1998. *Ways of Knowing: Experience, Knowledge, and Power among the Dene Tha.* Vancouver: UBC Press.

Handler, R., and J. Linnekin. 1984. Tradition, genuine or spurious. *Journal of American Folklore* 97(385): 273-90.

Heine, M. 1999. *Dene Games: A Culture and Resource Manual.* Yellowknife: Sport North Federation and Department of Municipal and Community Affairs, Government of NWT.

Helm, J. 2000. *The People of Denendeh: Ethnohistory of the Indians of Canada's Northwest Territories.* Montreal: McGill-Queen's University Press.

Helm, J., and N.O. Lurie. 1966. *The Dogrib Hand Game.* National Museum of Canada bulletin no. 205. Ottawa: National Museum of Canada.

Irwin, L. 1994. *The Dream Seekers: Native American Visionary Traditions of the Great Plains.* Norman: University of Oklahoma Press.

Kay, C. 2002. Tradition gains the upper hand. *News/North,* June 17, B4, B19.

Paraschak, V. 1983. Discrepancies between government programs and community practices: The case of recreation in the Northwest Territories. PhD diss., University of Alberta.

–. 1985. A look at government's role in recreation in the Northwest Territories. In M.J. Patterson, ed., *Collected Papers on the Human History of the Northwest Territories* (11-27). Yellowknife: Prince of Wales Northern Heritage Centre.

Riphenburg, C. 1997. Women's status and cultural expression: Changing gender relations and structural adjustment in Zimbabwe. *Africa Today* 44(1): 33-55.

Ryan, J. 1995. *Doing Things the Right Way: Dene Traditional Justice in Lac La Martre, NWT.* Calgary: University of Calgary Press and Arctic Institute of North America.

Scanlon, K. 1990. Der wilde Westen. *Equinox* 53: 57-66.

Sport North Federation. 1995. *Gender Equity Policy.* Yellowknife: Sport North Federation.

7

Performance Indicators
Aboriginal Games at the Arctic Winter Games

MICHAEL HEINE

For Aboriginal people in Canada, often culturally displaced and economically marginalized, participation in sports offers an opportunity for meaningful physical activity, often providing important physical, cultural, and sometimes spiritual benefits (Aboriginal Sport Circle 2004).[1] Although considerable barriers to regular participation exist for many Aboriginal people (Skinner, Hanning, and Tsuji 2006; Findlay and Kohen 2007), the success of events such as the North American Indigenous Games (Forsyth and Miller 2005) and the national importance of forms of recognition such as the Tom Longboat Award, which is given to leading Aboriginal athletes in the Canadian amateur sport system, indicate the pervasive positive importance of sports for Aboriginal people across Canada.

Sports thus are an important cultural practice, typically viewed positively in both the dominant culture and marginalized Aboriginal communities. What is more, this positive understanding of sports often centres on a model for participation that is so familiar and taken for granted that people understand it as inherently meaningful and appropriate; I examine this model in more detail below. This sports model has been extended into northern Canada only during the past forty years (Paraschak 1982; Sport North Federation 2000); Aboriginal people in the northern communities now also widely understand this model to be meaningful. Across the Arctic and Subarctic, Aboriginal people play many sports, and they join recreational leagues and local competitions (Smith, Findlay, and Crompton 2010). On the other hand, before today's sports became such an important part of community life – in fact, before many of the communities came into existence – Aboriginal people engaged in their own physical activity practices and games (Heine 2006, 2007). They also knew these cultural practices to be inherently meaningful, and those meanings and the ways in which they were articulated sometimes differed from those expressed through many facets of sports participation today.

In this chapter, I examine how the games of northern Aboriginal people – specifically, the games of the Inuit and Dene[2] – are sometimes practised in ways that express their own inherent "meaningfulness" and cultural significance, even when they are played in the organizational context of a sports competition. And context is important: What forms of cultural meanings are expressed when Inuit and Dene games are organized like a sports competition? Some of these meanings will be influenced by the logic of practice of sports, others will refer to the earlier cultural contexts of Inuit and Dene games.

To untangle these issues, three analytical steps are required. First, a brief examination of the "logic of practice" (Bourdieu and Wacquant 1992) that informs much participation in today's sports is provided. An examination of the logic of a cultural practice, according to Bourdieu and Wacquant, seeks to understand the underlying principles and values that render that practice meaningful to participants, even though they may not necessarily be explicitly aware of those principles and values. It is a logic that becomes evident through what people do as much as through what they say about it. I argue that today's sports express a logic of practice that partially differs from the practical logic of Inuit and Dene games (although those two cultural practices, in turn, also express their own distinctly different cultural logics). Second, to make this argument, I describe the cultural logic and the cultural values that in a general way informed participation in Inuit and Dene games before the expansion of the settler state's sports system into the Arctic and Subarctic.[3] Third, I examine a cultural and sport festival, the Arctic Winter Games (AWG), which features mainstream sports as well as Inuit and Dene games, which are organized as sports competitions: it is during moments of such immediate contact of mainstream sports and Aboriginal games that their relative importance and viability for people in northern Aboriginal communities can be understood more clearly.

A Sporting Logic of Practice: The Performance Principle

Sports South to North: A "Heterotransplantation"

The present importance of sport for northern communities is the consequence of a process of "heterotransplantation" (Paraschak 1982; see also Paraschak 1985, 1991, 1996) from the urbanizations of southern Canada to the northern communities. Through the implementation of extensive recreation programming initiatives and facility development programs (Ayalik, Vikse, and Schofield 1991; Legaree, Schofield, and Hayden 1994), and the establishing of an administrative structure (Sport North Federation 2000), the organizational model of southern sports was "transplanted" to Aboriginal communities in northern Canada, especially the Northwest Territories as it then existed. Paraschak (1982, 1) metaphorically refers to this heterotransplantation process as "the transfer of an organ or tissue from one individual to another of a different species." She thereby makes the point that, initially, the sports system was transplanted from its original context, the urbanizations of the south, with little input from the northern communities concerned, and without regard for the "differences between Southern Canada and the NWT which have affected ... the transplantation of sport to the North" (ibid.). Although these differences have levelled off during the thirty years that have passed since Paraschak's initial observation, she makes clear that the ways in which a cultural practice is organized cannot be dissociated from the cultural values it has the potential to express. Organization and logic of a practice – the implicit and explicit values that inform it – are interdependent. The way in which sports are presently organized across the North also tends to emplace a dominant logic of practice that historically originated in the sports of urban southern Canada.

The Performance Principle

The dominant logic of practice in today's sports is so familiar to most people that they intuitively know participation in sports to mean something, without having to reflect on this fact: for most people, participation would not be meaningful without an element of competition, and for many, competitive involvement is simply the most important consideration when they participate in sports (Ingham 2004). This emphasis on competitive comparisons, on unequal outcomes, and a focus predominantly on winning have been referred to by authors such as Hoberman (1992), Eichberg (1998), and Ingham (2004) as an expression of the performance principle of sports. Participants in sports wish to perform – and continuously to improve their performance

– in order to realize the dominant objective of sports participation: winning. Competition and winning, and therefore an emphasis on outcome over process (Donnelly 1996), are at the core of the performance principle, the logic of practice that informs our assumptions about what constitutes meaningful participation in sport. An extreme example of this orientation is provided by those sports where a tied game is considered not to be an acceptable or meaningful outcome; participants are required to continue the contest until disequilibrium in the outcome has been secured.

Much organizational labour has to be expended to facilitate sports in this modality. Guttmann (2004; see also Parry 2006) has provided a detailed delineation of this model's historical development. In order to make differential performances comparable, and thus winning meaningful, organizational principles of division have to be in place that serve to define a state of initial equality between participants. Athletes are divided into performance classes or leagues, or segregated according to weight, size, age, or gender criteria. Performances and standings are recorded, and league tables are maintained. Records can be broken by athletes who do not need to be in direct competition with the opponent whose performance they improve on (Guttmann 2004). Were the organizational system of sports as we know it today not in place, the logic of competitive sporting practice might not find meaningful expression.

On the symbolic level, the values of the sporting logic of practice are reinforced by the effects of medals, trophies, victory awards podiums, championship rings, and the like. It is these symbolic validations in particular that serve to render inherently meaningful those norms of sport participation that centre on competition.

Olympic Performance

The dominant symbols to render meaningful the value of differential performance are the Olympic gold, silver, and bronze medals. The Olympics advance on a global scale a sports model whose meaningfulness is almost exclusively determined by its emphasis on winning and competition, while tending to "standardize [sport] cultures that were once distinct" (Whitson 1994, 1). Donnelly (1996, 23) observes that within this model, "the single-minded emphasis on the result almost completely dominates concerns with process, that is, the way a sport is played and the experience of the players." Donnelly further notes that this global expansion of the Olympic sports model serves to create a homogenized model of global sameness, while at the same time enabling marginalized groups to appropriate this model in the context of their own cultural practices. This, he argues, identifies sports as a site of cultural contestation: a specific logic of practice will temporarily be dominant, but it will also sustain challenges and be contested; cultural practices are always open to reinterpretation. Donnelly's argument is of considerable importance here. The AWG are designed as a sports competition that mirrors the organizational format of the Olympics. The AWG are therefore also constructed as a space that emplaces the dominant performance logic of sporting practice. At the AWG, Inuit and Dene games are placed in this organizational frame of reference, but they hold the potential to give expression to a different logic of cultural practice, and to enable forms of involvement not solely focused on competition. To clarify this point, the cultural position of Inuit and Dene games, as it existed before the development of the organized sports system, needs to be considered. Even though there are important differences between the Inuit and Dene games cultures, they shared certain cooperative principles that set them apart, both in their own way, from organized sports' competitive emphasis. These differences can be observed at the AWG.

Aboriginal Games of the Inuit and Dene and the Land-Based Way of Life

The principal variance from the performance principle of sport shared by Inuit and Dene traditional games relates to the embeddedness of both practices in the Aboriginal culture that existed at the time of contact between Aboriginal peoples and representatives of the settler state. In a general sense, Aboriginal peoples followed a land-based way of life, living in close connection to the land (e.g., see Helm and Damas 1963). Through its dependence on seasonally fluctuating food resources whose availability was not always certain, this way of life was highly flexible and relied on specific forms of cooperation, mutual support, and sharing. At the same time, the often demanding requirements of survival gave rise to a distinct emphasis on the value of individual self-reliance.

These cultural factors were expressed in the "internal grammar" (Sutton-Smith 1976) of Inuit and Dene games. Reflecting capabilities required for survival, many games tested technical skills and competencies also important for the land-based subsistence lifestyle. Target practice competitions such as the bow and arrow shoot and the spear throw (for both the Inuit and Dene), the harpoon throw (for the Inuit), and the axe-throw (for the Dene) were games understood to be directly relevant for the development of survival skills. Numerous games that served to develop strength, endurance, and the ability to withstand pain were seen to have similar practical significance. Inuit as well as Dene understood and valued an immediate and close link between traditional games and the practical necessities of the land-based way of life (Heine 2006, 2007).

It was their practical utility that embedded games activities in the land-based way of life, close to the fundamental link between people and the land. It also served to extend a cultural logic of practice that focused on cooperation in subsistence production and other domains of social life to the field of games. Cultural valuations bearing on the outcome of competitive endeavours in any domain of social life, therefore, tended to de-emphasize the symbolic importance attached to asymmetrical outcomes – to winning (and losing). Most people entered a games contest with the intent to compete, do well, and emerge as the winner, but there were limits to the too explicit symbolic validation of the outcome of games contests (e.g., see Blondin 1990b). Nobody was supposed to make too much of the fact that he or she had won: "You can't make a fuss about it, or you will upset everybody," as Inuit elder Edward Lennie, generally acknowledged to be a leader in the field of Inuit games, explained (quoted in Heine 1999, 16). In a general sense, Dene culture contained comparable implicit rules (e.g., see Blondin 1990a, 1990b).

The relationship to the land remains of enduring importance for northern Aboriginal people, even though most families now live in the communities more or less year-round. It goes without saying that the functional significance of games as preparation for the practical demands of a land-based lifestyle has decreased; however, the games cultures' expressive force to reference the cooperative elements of this lifestyle is undiminished. In this sense, participation in Inuit and Dene games, even in the context of an organized sports competition such as the AWG, remains informed by the cooperative logic of practice of the land-based way of life, and by the narratives that reference it. At the AWG, athletes in the sports competitions, and Aboriginal participants in Arctic Sports (as Inuit games are known in the AWG context) and Dene Games contests, may not necessarily perceive and express the meaning of competition in the same way. With their potential to evoke the values of the land-based lifestyles, the games of the Inuit and Dene have come to play an important role in the definition of Aboriginal identity positions, be it in the field of organized sports at events such as the AWG, or in the field of education (Northwest Territories 1993, 1997). A description of Inuit and Dene games, as played at the AWG, will make this clear. This is also the point where significant differences between Arctic Sports and Dene Games become apparent.

The Arctic Winter Games

The biennial AWG were established in 1970 to provide an opportunity for northern athletes to participate in high-level sports competitions without having to face the overpowering opposition provided by better-equipped and trained athletes from the urban centres of southern Canada. The AWG initially involved only teams from Alaska, Yukon, and the Northwest Territories. They have since grown into a prominent circumpolar gathering, attracting teams and athletes from Siberia, Alaska, Canada (Yukon, Northwest Territories, Nunavut, northern Quebec, and northern Alberta), Greenland, and northern Norway.

At the first AWG in 1970, Aboriginal games were not a part of the competition schedule, but the games of the Inuit were included as a cultural demonstration event. Inuit games were added as Arctic Sports to the official competition schedule of the third AWG, held in Anchorage, Alaska, in 1974. The games of the Dene were added to the program of the 1990 AWG, under

Figure 7.1 The ulu medal, a symbol of athletic prowess. *Source:* Government of the NWT.

the eponymous designation "Dene Games." Initially, only men's teams were included in a single "open male" age category; a subdivision into "junior" and "open" age categories was introduced at the 2002 AWG. Junior girls participated for the first time at the 2004 AWG in Wood Buffalo, Alberta; juvenile girls' teams at the 2006 Games in Kenai, Alaska. Arctic Sports and Dene Games are now among the most popular competitions at the AWG.

North of 55

For participants representing Canadian jurisdictions, admittance to the AWG is based on geographic criteria: athletes must reside north of 55 degrees latitude for a period of at least six months prior to registration (AWGIC 2010). The practical effects of this rule are thus limited to the province of Alberta. In keeping with the AWG's original intent, this regulation serves to preclude participation by athletes from the southern urban centres. A similar regulation was in effect for Anchorage, Alaska, the only large city with training facilities comparable to those in the larger cities of the south. Until the 2000 AWG, participation in the AWG by Division I university athletes from the University of Alaska was restricted in several sports. For capacity reasons, the general AWG eligibility criteria were tightened prior to the 2000 AWG. Adults, that is, those seventeen years or older, are now excluded from participation in all disciplines except Arctic Sports and Dene Games. This has made the special regulations for high-performance university athletes from Anchorage redundant; they are now too old to participate. The exception for Arctic Sports and Dene Games athletes was made out of a concern for capacity development. Outside of participation in the AWG, opportunities to attend competitive meets in Inuit and Dene games are few and far between. AWG organizers hoped that by allowing athletes in these events to compete as adults, their transition into coaching and instructional responsibilities subsequent to their athletic careers would be more likely. Coaches and instructors are in constant demand, and limited supply, in all of the remote northern communities. Inuit and Dene games have to compete for volunteer coaches with the sports played in the communities. Athletic disciplines that exclude certain athletes during an extended segment of their careers will find it difficult to attract such athletes as coaches or instructors. On the other hand, 55 degrees latitude pushes the boundary line sufficiently far south to include some of the smaller urban centres of central Alberta, which provides an opportunity to stage the Games in cities other than Fairbanks, Yellowknife, and Whitehorse. The 1994 AWG were held in the city of Slave Lake and the 2010 Games in Grande Prairie, both in central Alberta; geographically, these cities are located just north of the line of residential demarcation. The 2004 AWG were held in Wood Buffalo/Fort McMurray, also in Alberta.

At the AWG, the performance principle is thus in an ambiguous position. The festival's Olympic format emplaces the relevance of the performance principle, whereas the residency rules seek to contain its effects by excluding some athletes whose athletic and sport skills would make them well qualified to participate. The requirement that a state of initial equality between participants be established is temporarily suspended, overridden by residency considerations that in themselves have no bearing on the athletic merits that would determine admittance were the performance principle in effect.

Such geographical fracturing of the performance principle's coherence became an issue when two NWT figure skaters who had qualified for participation in the 1996 Games were removed from the team after concerns over their residential eligibility emerged; the skaters took the sports governing body to court to overturn the decision (Findlay and Corbett 2001). Although the outcome of this case is not significant for this discussion, it provides an example of the sometimes contradictory processes that influence the definition of legitimate participation in northern sports. In this instance, on the organizational level, geography, expressed as rules of residence, partially overrides the functioning of the performance principle. Arctic Sports and Dene Games also pose their own challenges to the legitimacy of the performance principle.

Aboriginal Games at the AWG

As mentioned above, at the Arctic Winter Games, elements of Aboriginal cultural identity are expressed in and through traditional games practices as they interact with the organizational constraints and signifying force of contemporary sports. Cultural meanings attached to traditional games practices owe much of their importance to the traditional antecedents of the present practice, and to the representations the participants hold thereof. At the same time, the position of the Aboriginal games is circumscribed by the interplay of the enabling and constraining conditions provided by the structure of the field of contemporary sports. In this context it becomes apparent that, in terms of the technical skills required for successful participation, the Arctic Sports are potentially more closely aligned with the logic of the performance principle than are the Dene Games. Participation in Arctic Sports, that is, Inuit games, requires the display of physical and technical movement skills that only adherence to a regular training regime – a habitually accepted prerequisite for successful participation in sports competitions – will develop. Participation in the Dene Games, technically less demanding and more easily accessible, implies no such prerequisite: a training regime will improve the chances for success, but it is not a prerequisite for participation.

Arctic Sports

Nine Inuit games, and two games of the Aboriginal people of Siberia, are combined into the Arctic Sports competition. They represent only a small inventory of more than 150 known Inuit games (Keewatin Inuit Association 1980; Heine 2007). At least 6 of the Arctic Sports games require the skilled execution of complex movement sequences (Gal 1996; Way 2005). Events such as the One-Foot High Kick, the Two-Foot High Kick, the Alaskan High Kick, and the Kneel Jump represent exceedingly difficult technical challenges. At the other end of the continuum, events such as the Airplane, the Arm Pull, the Head Pull, and the Knuckle Hop test athletes' maximal strength and pain resistance but do not provide an elaborate technical challenge (see CBC 2012 for video documentation of Arctic Sports and Dene Games).

Participants in the Arctic Sports competition have to master a broad range of skill sets, since they are required to participate in a minimum number of events of their own choosing. Senior male athletes must select at least seven from the ten games open to them; athletes in all other divisions are eligible to participate in seven events, and they must select at least four of these (see Table 7.1).

Enforcement of this rule at the Arctic Sports competition, however, can be quite flexible (Heine 2010). Athletes are sometimes permitted to participate in fewer than the stipulated number of events, but they are then not eligible to be considered for the All Around award (AWGIC 2011a, 2-3; 2011b, 3), which is given to the athlete in each age category who achieves the highest combined score in his or her three best disciplines. Similarly in the Dene Games: two of the events, the Pole Push and the Hand Game, require full teams of four participants to enter the competition. Should it so happen that a team is short a player, one of the coaches may fill the vacancy, as long as the player meets the age and gender eligibility criteria; this is explicitly stated in the rule manual (AWGIC 2011b, 2; AWGIC 2011a, 2). Such

TABLE 7.1

Age and gender divisions in Arctic Sports at the Arctic Winter Games

Sport	Women (< 17 years)	Open Women (17 years +)	Junior Men (< 17 years)	Open Men (17 years +)
Airplane				•
Alaskan High Kick	•	•	•	•
Arm Pull	•	•	•	
Head Pull				•
Kneel Jump	•	•	•	•
Knuckle Hop				•
One-Foot High Kick	•	•	•	•
One-Hand Reach				•
Sledge Jump	•	•	•	•
Triple Jump	•	•	•	•
Two-Foot High Kick	•	•	•	•
Minimum number of events required for All Around award placement	4	4	4	7

Source: AWGIC (2011a).

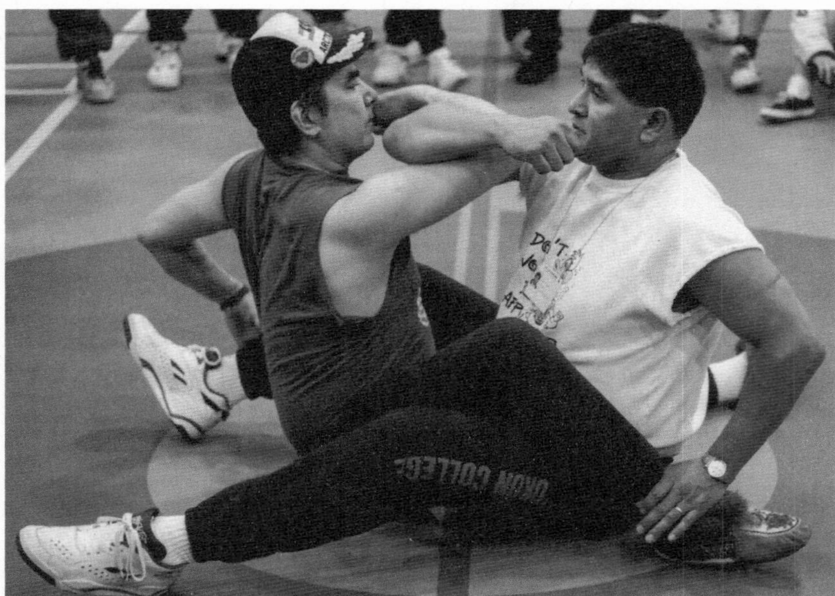

Figure 7.2 Arctic Sports at the 1992 Arctic Winter Games: Arm Pull.
Photo by Michael Heine.

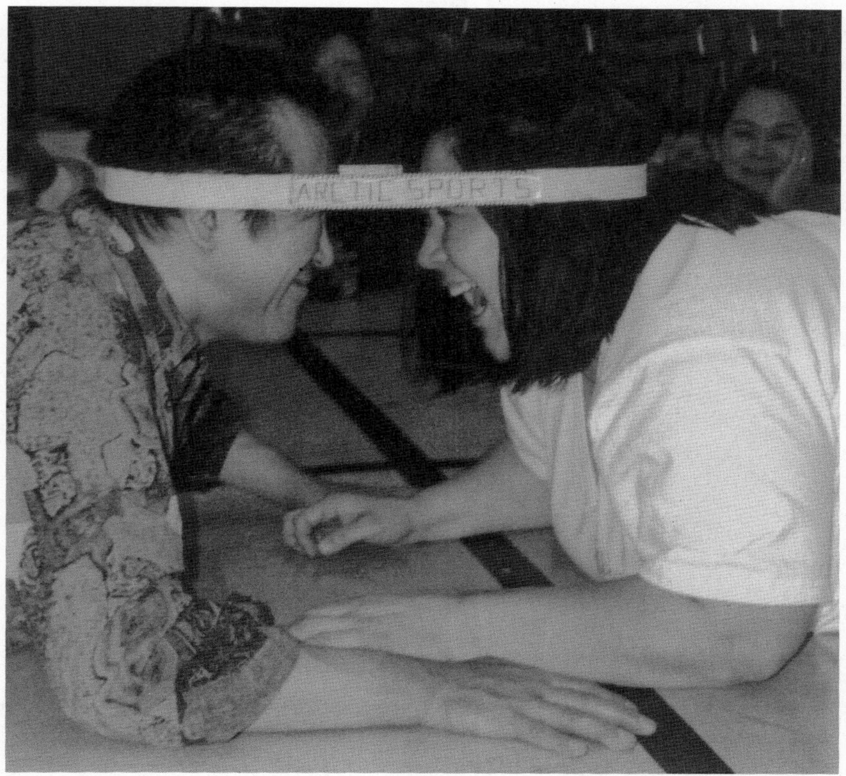

Figure 7.3 Arctic Sports at the 1999 Aurora College Aboriginal sport coaching development workshop: Head Pull. Photo by Vicky Paraschak.

a degree of flexibility as shown in the organization of these high-level circumpolar competitions would be considered unusual in most high-level sports events.

As mentioned, participation with the intent to do well requires adherence to a structured training regimen. This is also true of the Triple Jump and Sledge Jump, which, although not as technically difficult as the other games, still require regular systematic preparation for even entry-level skill development. Both of these games were introduced to the AWG by indigenous participants from Siberia. Only two of the Arctic Sports, lastly, are characterized by the kind of easy accessibility characteristic of the Dene Games described below: the Head Pull and the Arm Pull, both variations on the tug-of-war. Participation in these games does not require prior skill development (Heine 2007).

Extensive training and a willingness to perform is required to master the difficult technical skills of several Arctic Sports. Given that the activities originated in Inuit culture, they reference elements of traditional identity, yet competent mastery can be valued just as emphatically with reference to the symbolic expressions implied by the performance principle. To the extent that an appreciation of competitive performance in respect of the performance principle requires proof of athletic excellence, the Arctic Sports are much more closely aligned with contemporary sports than are the Dene Games. The very "grammar" (Sutton-Smith 1976) of Arctic Sports, from the point of view of the performance principle, can render meaningful a predisposition to "perform" in ways that the internal grammar of Dene Games does little to occasion.

Dene Games

Four of the five games of the Dene played as Dene Games at the AWG pose rather more manageable challenges than do the Arctic Sports. The fifth event, the Hand Game, is a complex game of chance and strategy. Participants take turns attempting to guess the location of a small object the players on the opposing team hide in either fist. Backed by the insistent sounds of drums and singers, the Hand Game is one of the most exciting events at the AWG. Participants think of the activity as a mind game (Heine 2010). The outcome is determined not by the display of physical skills but by the application of strategic knowledge and techniques of obfuscation that can be acquired only through much practice. Since it is not a contest of physical skill in the strict sense of a sports competition, this analysis focuses on the four remaining, more explicitly athletic, events: Pole Push, Finger Pull, Stick Pull, and Snowsnake. Participants are required to register in all five events; standings for the aforementioned All Around award are calculated based on the scores in the individual contests, that is, Finger Pull, Stick Pull, and Snowsnake (AWGIC 2011b, 2).

Three of the Dene Games – Stick Pull, Pole Push, and Finger Pull – are variations on the tug-of-war, strength contests that do not pose advanced technical demands. Only Snowsnake, reminiscent of the javelin throw, represents a certain degree of technical difficulty. Transforming a traditional subsistence hunting technique into an athletic distance competition, the game involves throwing a spear or javelin (the "snake") such that it glides along a packed snow surface. The competitor who scores the greatest distance wins the competition. This is the only Dene Games event in which a record distance can be registered, and this has been done since the 1998

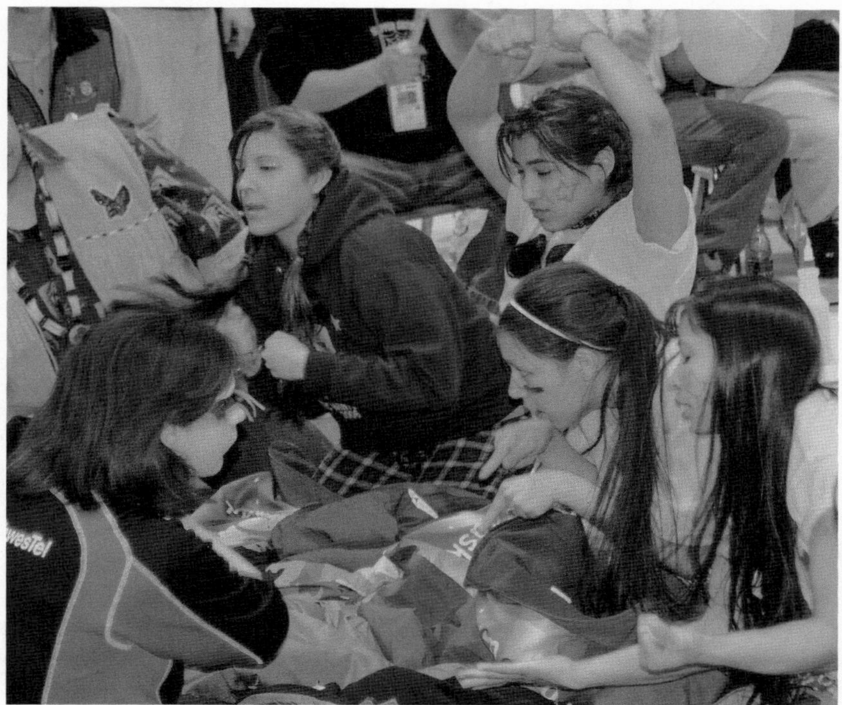

Figure 7.4 Dene Games at the 2006 Arctic Winter Games: Junior Women's Hand Games competition. Photo by Michael Heine.

AWG. Even in the Snowsnake competition, participation without prior practice is possible, but it is the one event where practised technique will result in superior scores. At the 1998 AWG in Yellowknife, one of the leading competitors in the Snowsnake was an Inuk from Barrow, Alaska, who attributed his advanced technical skills to regular practice during the whale hunt (Heine 2010). In general, however, as mentioned, participation in the Dene Games does not necessarily require sustained athletic or technical training. Practice will increase the probability of success, but lack of training does not preclude participation, even at a high-level athletic gathering such as the AWG.

The Finger Pull is a strength contest in which two opponents interlock middle fingers of one hand. One opponent, the "offence," attempts to break the opponent's finger lock by pulling backward as strongly as possible. The opponent, the "defence," attempts to maintain the finger lock and arm position for a set period. This contest is to equal degrees a test of strength and

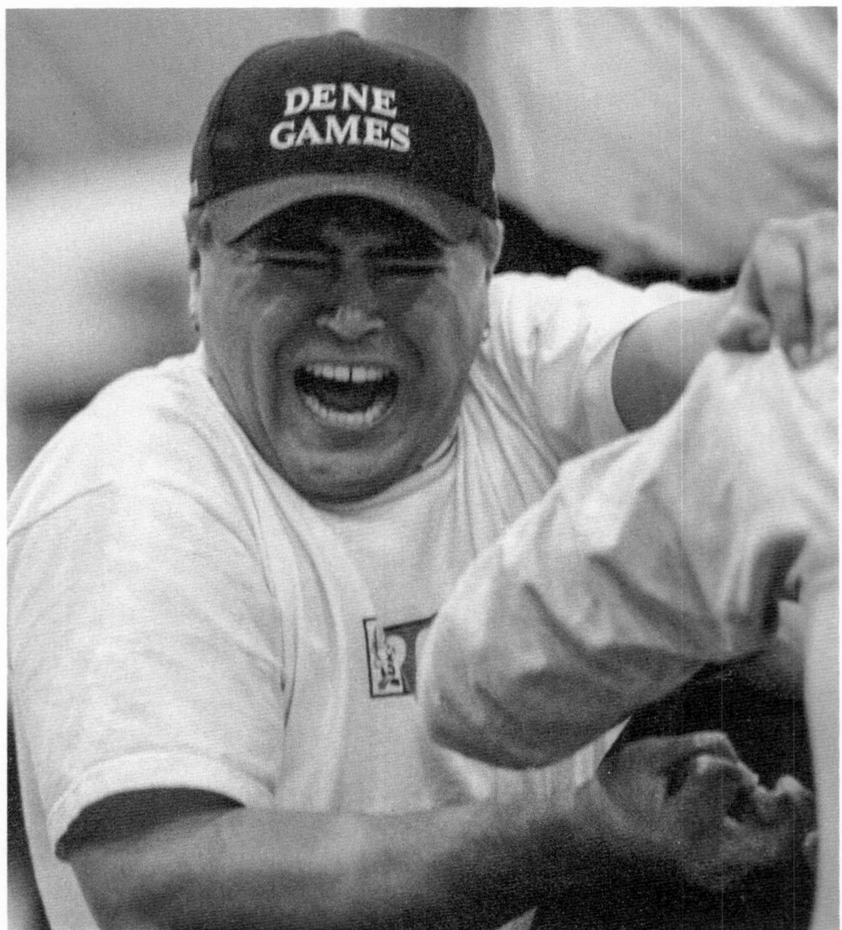

Figure 7.5 Dene Games at the 2000 Arctic Winter Games: Finger Pull.
Photo by Michael Heine.

a test of pain resistance. To weaken the opponent's resistance, a competitor will attempt to exert considerable pressure on the opponent's middle finger during the pull. All competitors consider this to be a rational strategy, not an unfair manoeuvre, and it may not even be visible to the spectators present. Often, an ice bucket is kept close at hand during the competition so that competitors may cool their aching finger joints after a particularly vigorous (and painful) contest (Heine 2010). In the Stick Pull, both opponents grasp one end of a conically shaped stick with one hand. On the referee's signal, each attempts to pull it out of the opponent's hand. To make the contest

Figure 7.6 Dene Games at the 2000 Arctic Winter Games: Snowsnake.
Photo by Michael Heine.

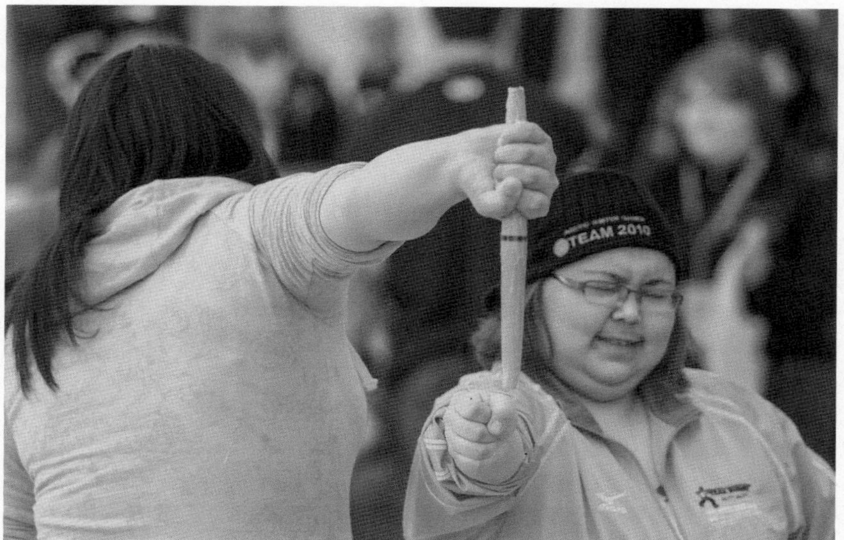

Figure 7.7 Dene Games at the 2010 Arctic Winter Games: Stick Pull.
Photo by Michael Heine.

Figure 7.8 Dene Games at the 2010 Arctic Winter Games: Girls' Pole Push competition. Photo by Michael Heine.

more difficult, the stick is coated with grease before each match. Lastly, there is Pole Push, a contest that is the mirror image of a tug-of-war. Two teams of four players each grasp one end of a smoothed tree trunk and attempt to push the other team out of the playing area.

Sports, Games, and Competition

Judged by the exacting standards of the performance principle (Ingham 2004), the Dene Games, as athletic activities of relatively minor technical complexity, offer a more limited range of symbolic validations for successful engagement. Participation is not necessarily dependent on the mastery of difficult athletic or movement skills, which is the criterion for validation implied by the performance principle. It is also true that many of the Aboriginal participants in Dene Games competitions at the AWG, unlike their fellow competitors in Arctic Sports, are not trained athletes. Thus, the positive validation that comes with the awarding of medals is often complemented by narratives delineating the significance of the activities in the traditional culture. Such narratives tend to elaborate two dominant themes:

1 The games' functional significance for the development of physical skills deemed important in the Dene land-based way of life. Examples of this were given by Tlingit elder Sam Johnston at the 2006 Arctic Winter Games, where he acted as supervisor of the Dene Games events. He pointed out that both Finger Pull and Stick Pull may have served to develop the specific kind of finger strength required for pulling fish – which are hard to grip, especially when still alive – out of the water, or for removing them from a net (Heine 2010).
2 The emphasis on the games' cooperative orientation, understood as an expression of the inherently cooperative nature of the land-based way of life. This second element of the narrative tends to emphasize the games' cooperative aspects in explicit contradistinction from the competitive elements of contemporary sports: it expresses cultural values – an implicit logic of practice – that, in the view of Aboriginal participants, distinguish Dene Games from an ordinary sports competition (Heine 1994, 2010).

By virtue of the activities' considerable technical difficulty, narratives positioning the Arctic Sports are more easily aligned with the performance logic of competitive sports. Yet, Arctic Sports as well effect a distancing from the sporting logic of practice. This is accomplished by an explicit and habitual emphasis on cooperation in the course of the competition in a form that is rarely encountered at contemporary sports contests; it would be quite unimaginable in the context of a high-level competitive meet (and it has to be kept in mind that, the World Eskimo-Indian Olympics and the Northern Games excepted, the AWG represent the highest level of competition in both Inuit games and Dene games). Of relevance here is the fact that most Arctic Sports events are individual, self-testing games. The individual demonstration of athletic skills at the centre of the gym very much invokes the atmosphere of a dramatic performance during which the audience is continually enjoined to remain quiet so as not to disturb the competitor's concentration. It is all the more remarkable, then, when this self-contained demonstration of athletic accomplishment is temporarily disrupted by competing athletes, coaches from all participating teams, and elders, all of whom volunteer advice on how to improve a specific skill execution. These interventions always occur in between attempts and in full view of everybody present. It is in such demonstrative elements of cooperation that athletes and spectators alike recognize a fundamentally cooperative principle at the very centre of a contemporary sports competition.

Paradoxically, the intervention also further energizes the competitive process, inasmuch as competing athletes and coaches cooperate in an attempt to improve an opponent's athletic performance. The significance of asymmetrical competitive outcomes, as implied by the performance principle, is acknowledged, but it is at the same time elegantly transmuted into a cooperative frame of reference that connects to a narrative about the importance of games in Inuit culture – without diminishing the importance of the sporting competition. It is no exaggeration to suggest that this unique form of cooperation within competition occupies pride of place among Arctic Sports athletes, coaches, and spectators. One can invariably observe it throughout the Arctic Sports events, and a competitor showing a disinclination to follow its imperative will be looked on with some disapproval. Even though there is not a single competitor who does not desire to win a gold ulu (the AWG equivalent of the Olympic gold medal), this approach mediates the ambiguities that can occur when Arctic Sports express the values of a sporting competition and of an Inuit cultural practice at the same time (Heine 2005).

The potential of Arctic Sports and Dene Games to transform, at least partially, the sporting logic of practice does not detract from the importance that winning ulu medals holds for the winners of the competitions. In its Olympic modality, the ulu medal represents the symbolic value of winning a sports contest, and it is what brings temporary notoriety to the winner of a gold ulu back in his or her home community. In addition to the sheer excitement they generate, it is this simultaneous confirmation of the significance of sports, and of Inuit and Dene culture, that makes Arctic Sports and Dene Games the most popular events at the AWG. Their present vitality as physical activity practices is largely due to their success at the AWG. It also depends on the continuing ability of Inuit and Dene games practices to negotiate, each in their own way, the effects of the emplacement of organized sports. These effects can be felt in Dene Games competitions, when contestations over the participation of girls and women must be resolved (Giles 2005), and they become visible when the winner of an Arctic Sports demonstration event at the 2007 Canada Winter Games (a national-level high performance multi-sport event) receives a considerable monetary reward from an industrial sponsor (Tapardjuk 2007) for winning a gold medal, that reward multiplied by the number of medals won (Heine 2010). It is within the context of the pervasive presence of organized sport and the performance principle that Arctic Sports and Dene Games, the games of the Inuit and

Dene, will find new forms of expression and develop their own logic of practice.

NOTES

1 In this chapter, I use the terms "Aboriginal" and "indigenous" interchangeably, though I acknowledge that in Canadian English usage they connote differing political positions. Note further that Inuit do not use "Aboriginal" as a self-reference, and "indigenous" only rarely. I use the terms merely for convenience of presentation.

2 In Alaskan acceptable English usage, Inuit are referred to as "Eskimo," the Dene people as "Athabascan Indians." Both terms are no longer acceptable Canadian usage, where "Inuit" and "Dene" are accepted terms of self-identification. "Dene" is a term taken from the Slavey language. It was used as a term of self-identification by the people of the Northwest Territories during their recent struggles over land rights and political self-determination (Asch 1984). At the AWG, the term is used to reference the games of the Dene eponymously as "Dene Games."

The Inuit are the most northerly Aboriginal culture on earth. Inuit traditional land use areas extend from the coast of Siberia east through Alaska and Canada, to include all of Greenland. The Dene are the Inuit's southern neighbours. Dene traditional land use areas extend from interior Alaska, across Yukon Territory, east to the Hudson's Bay coast. On the Canadian side, the tree line is sometimes seen as an approximate indicator of the slow transition from Inuit to Dene land use areas.

3 I wish to emphasize again that Inuit and Dene games must be understood as distinct cultural practices. What they have in common is that both are affected by the development of a system of organized sports across the Arctic and Subarctic.

REFERENCES

Aboriginal Sport Circle. 2004. *Aboriginal Coaching Manual*. Ottawa: Aboriginal Sport Circle.

Asch, M. 1984. *Home and Native Land: Aboriginal Rights and the Canadian Constitution*. Toronto: Methuen.

AWGIC (Arctic Winter Games International Committee). 2010. *Arctic Winter Games Policies: 9.01: Athlete Eligibility*. http://www.arcticwintergames.org.

–. 2011a. *2012 Arctic Winter Games: Technical Package for Arctic Sports*. Yellowknife: AWGIC. http://www.arcticwintergames.org/.

–. 2011b. *2012 Arctic Winter Games: Technical Package for Dene Games*. Yellowknife: AWGIC. http://www.arcticwintergames.org/.

Ayalik, C., D. Vikse, and D. Schofield. 1991. Recreation facility development in Canada's Arctic. *Recreation Canada* 49(1): 41-45.

Blondin, G. 1990a. Traditional Dene games. *Dene Yati* 4(4): 1-4.

–. 1990b. *When the World Was New: Stories of the Sahtu Dene*. Yellowknife: Outcrop.

Bourdieu, P., and L. Wacquant. 1992. *An Invitation to Reflective Sociology*. Cambridge: Polity Press.

CBC. 2012. *Topic: Arctic Winter Games*. Video files. http://www.cbc.ca/archives/categories/sports/.

Donnelly, P. 1996. Prolympism: Sport monoculture as crisis and opportunity. *Quest* 48(1): 27-41.

Eichberg, H. 1998. *Body Cultures: Essays on Sport, Space, and Identity.* London, UK: Routledge.

Findlay, H.A., and R. Corbett. 2001. The rights of athletes, coaches and participants in sport. In M. Holman, D. Moriarty, and J. Forsyth, eds., *Sports, Fitness and the Law: North American Perspectives*, 2nd ed. (101-20). Toronto: Canadian Scholars' Press.

Findlay, L.C., and D.E. Kohen. 2007. Aboriginal children's sport participation in Canada. *Pimatisiwin: A Journal of Aboriginal and Indigenous Community Health* 5(1): 185-206.

Forsyth, J., and B. Miller. 2005. *The 2002 North American Indigenous Games: Celebrating Our Achievements.* Winnipeg: North American Indigenous Games Host Society.

Gal, J. 1996. Mechanical analysis of Artic sports. Unpublished manuscript. Faculty of Kinesiology, University of Calgary.

Giles, A. 2005. The acculturation matrix and the politics of difference: Women and Dene games. *Canadian Journal of Native Studies* 25(1): 355-72.

Guttmann, A. 2004. *From Ritual to Record: the Nature of Modern Sport.* 2nd ed. New York: Columbia University Press.

Heine, M. 1994. Cognitive dichotomies: Games, sports, and Dene cultural identity. *Communication and Cognition* 27(3): 321-36.

–. 1999. The 1999 Aurora College Aboriginal Sport Coaching Development Workshop: Final report. Inuvik, NWT: Aurora College.

–. 2005. It's a competition, not a show! Inuit and Dene games at the Arctic Winter Games. *Stadion: International Journal of the History of Sport* 31(1): 145-59.

–. 2006. *Dene Games: An Instruction and Resource Manual.* 2nd ed. Yellowknife: Sport North Federation.

–. 2007. *Inuit Games: An Instruction and Resource Manual.* 3rd ed. Yellowknife: Sport North Federation.

–. 2010. Field notes, 1991-2010. In author's possession.

Helm, J., and D. Damas. 1963. The contact-traditional all-Native community of the Canadian north: The upper Mackenzie "bush" Athapaskans and the Igluligmiut. *Anthropologica* 5(1): 9-21.

Hoberman, J. 1992. *Mortal Engines: The Science of Performance and the Dehumanization of Sport.* New York: Free Press.

Ingham, A. 2004. From the performance principle to the developmental principle: Every kid a winner? *Quest* 54(4): 303-31.

Keewatin Inuit Association. 1980. *Inuit Games.* Rankin Inlet: Department of Education Regional Resource Centre, Government of NWT.

Legaree, I., D. Schofield, and L. Hayden. 1994. Developing recreation leaders in Canada's Arctic. *Recreation Canada* 52(5): 4-7.

Northwest Territories. 1993. *Dene Kede: Education; A Dene Perspective.* Yellowknife: Education, Culture and Employment, Government of NWT.

–. 1997. *Inuuqatigiit: The Curriculum from the Inuit Perspective.* Yellowknife: Education, Culture and Employment, Government of NWT.

Parry, J. 2006. The idea of the record. *Sport in History* 26(2): 197-214.

Paraschak, V. 1982. The heterotransplantation of organized sport: A Northwest Territories case study. In School of Physical Education, University of Toronto, ed., *Proceedings of the Fifth Canadian Symposium on the History of Sport and Physical Education* (424-30). Toronto: University of Toronto.

–. 1985. A look at government's role in Northwest Territories recreation. In M.J. Patterson, C.D. Arnold, and R.R. Janes, eds., *Collected Papers on the Human History of the Northwest Territories: Occasional Papers of the Prince of Wales Northern Heritage Centre,* vol. 1 (11-27). Yellowknife: Prince of Wales Northern Heritage Centre.

–. 1991. Sport festivals and race relations in the NWT of Canada. In G. Jarvie, ed., *Sport, Racism and Ethnicity* (74-93). London, UK: Falmer Press.

–. 1996. Native Canadians in sport: A clash of cultural values. In L.U. Uche, ed., *North-South Information Culture: Trends in Global Communications and Research Paradigms* (99-113). Lagos: Longman Nigeria.

Skinner, K., R.M. Hanning, and L. Tsuji. 2006. Barriers and supports for healthy eating and physical activity for First Nation youth in northern Canada. *International Journal of Circumpolar Health* 65(2): 148-61.

Smith, K., L. Findlay, and S. Crompton. 2010. Participation in sports and cultural activities among Aboriginal children and youth. *Canadian Social Trends,* no. 90. http://www.statcan.gc.ca/.

Sport North Federation. 2000. History of organized sports in the NWT, 1967-2000. Unpublished manuscript. Yellowknife: Sport North Federation.

Sutton-Smith, B. 1976. Structural grammar of games and sports. *International Review for the Sociology of Sport* 11(2): 117-37.

Tapardjuk, L. 2007. Minister's statement 013-2(4): Inuit and Dene games. In Nunavut, Legislative Assembly, *Hansard,* 4th session, 2nd assembly, March 9 (p. 107). http://www.assembly.nu.ca/hansard.

Way, D. 2005. Traditional Arctic sports: A biomechanical analysis of the One Foot and Two Foot High Kick. MA thesis, University of Manitoba.

Whitson, D. 1994. Olympic sport, global media and cultural diversity. In R.K. Barney, ed., *Global and Cultural Critique: Proceedings of the Fourth International Symposium for Olympic Research* (1-9). London, ON: International Centre for Olympic Studies.

The Quality and Cultural Relevance of Physical Education for Aboriginal Youth
Challenges and Opportunities

JOANNIE HALAS, HEATHER McRAE,
AND AMY CARPENTER

In 2000, at the National Recreation Roundtable on Aboriginal/Indigenous Peoples, the delegates produced the Maskwachees Declaration, which described physical education (PE), along with physical activity, sport, and recreation, as a vehicle for improving Aboriginal peoples' health, wellness, cultural survival, and quality of life (Federal-Provincial/Territorial Advisory Committee on Fitness and Recreation 2000). The declaration also highlighted the need to ensure quality PE in schools. The recognition of the potential benefits of PE, as well as the need for quality PE, speaks to this chapter's major purpose: to identify both challenges and opportunities influencing Aboriginal children's and youth's access to quality PE. Much of our discussion draws upon examples of the delivery of Aboriginal education and PE in Manitoba schools; however, we feel that there are commonalities of experience that can be shared across other jurisdictions in Canada. While acknowledging that challenges do exist and shape the delivery of PE for Aboriginal children and youth, we also see opportunities for enhancing student achievement in PE through provision of culturally relevant PE.

In developing a framework for culturally relevant PE, we draw upon the work of Ladson-Billings (1995a, 1995b, 2001). A foundational component of Ladson-Billings's conception of culturally relevant pedagogy is the notion of student academic achievement. When we speak of academic achievement within a PE context, we are referring to the development of physical literacy, which Whitehead (2001) defined as a wholistic means by which an individual can draw upon a rich repertoire of established movement responses, thus enabling success within a wide range of challenging movements.[1] Within culturally relevant pedagogy, student academic success (i.e., physical literacy) is achieved in ways that affirm students' cultural identities within their school spaces. Although Ladson-Billings's research has predominantly involved African American children in US schools, her theories of culturally relevant pedagogy fit well when considering the context of Aboriginal youth learning within the intercultural spaces of Canadian schools.

In recent years, the benefits of a quality PE program and its relationship to sport development from "playground to the podium" (Mulholland 2008, iv, 7) have been acknowledged outside the education sector. The Canadian Sport Policy (Canadian Heritage 2002, 6) states that "access to quality physical education, physical activity and school sport provides many benefits for children, including better health and quality of life, psychological well-being, improved behaviour and ability to learn." As with the Maskwachees Declaration and Whitehead's definition of physical literacy, the Canadian Sport Policy adopts a wholistic perspective in describing the potential benefits of PE. Given PE's contribution to physical literacy and the role that culturally relevant educational practices can play in affirming Aboriginal youth's identities, an underlying assumption of our discussion is that quality and culturally relevant PE can positively contribute to the enhancement of Aboriginal youth's physical literacy, thus contributing to the development of Aboriginal sport in Canada.

From the "Playground to the Podium": Sport Development through PE

For many Canadian children, participation in sport begins in a school-based PE program. This is particularly the case for children and youth who do not have access to safe, enjoyable, organized, or informal sport and recreation opportunities within their neighbourhoods or communities. In Coté, Baker, and Abernathy's developmental model of sport participation (2007), the value of sampling a variety of sports and physical activities as an early pathway to elite sport performance is noted, as is the need for PE teachers "to ensure that children learn skills and stay motivated to continue their participation in sport at either an elite or a recreational level" (198). Given the identified factors outside the school environment that might present barriers to Aboriginal participation in sport (e.g., lack of awareness of the benefits of sport and the costs of registration fees and equipment for organized sport [see Canadian Heritage 2005]), access to a quality PE program as a pathway to later sport participation is particularly important for Aboriginal children and youth.

A quality PE program provides children with the opportunity to develop the knowledge, skills, and habits they need to lead physically active lifestyles (PHE Canada 2009). According to Physical and Health Education (PHE) Canada, a national advocacy group that promotes healthy living for all Canadians, a quality PE program has several features:

- daily curricular instruction for all students (K-12) for a minimum of 30 minutes
- well-planned lessons incorporating a wide range of activities
- a high level of participation by all students in each class
- an emphasis on fun, enjoyment, success, fair play, self-fulfillment, and personal health
- appropriate activities for the age and stage of each student
- activities that enhance cardiovascular systems, muscular strength, endurance, and flexibility
- a participation-based intramural program[2]
- qualified, enthusiastic teachers
- creative and safe use of facilities and equipment.

In sum, quality PE programs ensure that students are offered the opportunities to develop wholistically, thus promoting healthy child development.

In terms of specific learning outcomes related to sport, a quality PE program provides curricular instruction that is developmentally appropriate, which thus enables students to acquire the knowledge and skills of how to move effectively (e.g., Manitoba Education and Training 2000). As with Sport Canada's Long-Term Athlete Development model (2009), children in quality PE programs are encouraged to develop physical literacy through carefully designed programs that are based on developmental age, that is, maturation. At the kindergarten to grade four level, quality PE enables children to develop the fundamental movement skills that are the foundation of all activity; once the basic movement skills are acquired, they can be applied and refined through a well-planned curricular program of instruction related to the specific sport skills (from grade five onward). Although children and youth can acquire basic movement and sport-specific skills outside school (e.g., by watching and playing with older family members [see Halas 2001b], or by taking part in community-organized teams and sport camps), it is within a quality PE program that all children who attend school have opportunities to develop the physical literacy that enables them to participate actively in a wide variety of health-enhancing physical activities. In this regard, we agree with Whitehead (2007) when she states, "Physical literacy is a right of every individual and it is a denial of human freedom to inhibit its development."

Who Can Access Quality PE?

The United Nations Educational, Scientific and Cultural Organization (UNESCO 1999) stated that it is the right of all children to have access to sport and PE; yet, we intuitively know that this right is not distributed equally across population groups. Currently, schools that meet the criteria described in the list of features above are eligible for PHE Canada's national Quality Daily Physical Education recognition award (PHE Canada 2009); however, there is little information that tracks access to quality PE across Canada. Furthermore, there is little information about Aboriginal children and youth's ability to access quality PE in their home communities, and emerging evidence suggests that Aboriginal students' experiences of PE in high school can be negative (Champagne and Halas 2003; Champagne 2006).

Within Canada, questions about the quality of PE for Aboriginal children and youth also need to be raised in light of the many barriers to sport participation for Aboriginal peoples, as identified in *Sport Canada's Policy on Aboriginal Peoples' Participation in Sport* (Canadian Heritage 2005). Of the programs that do exist, little attention is focused upon the cultural relevance of the activities offered (Forsyth, Heine, and Halas 2006). Further complicating the issue of Aboriginal students' access to quality and culturally relevant PE is the socio-historical context of education for Aboriginal peoples in Canada. In this regard, Canada's colonial history has deeply influenced the experiences of Aboriginal students in schools, particularly through the disgraced residential school system. As such, the experience of PE for Aboriginal students needs to be understood within the context of the overall school experience, which continues to be shaped by unequal relations of power and issues of race within schools (van Ingen and Halas 2006).

As a means to address Aboriginal children and youth's access to quality PE, we begin by discussing a key challenge affecting the delivery of quality PE programs for Aboriginal students: the systemic underfunding of Aboriginal education in Canada. We then show how this underfunding of education has many consequences, particularly in relation to (1) the provision of quality PE facilities and equipment, and (2) quality of instruction in PE. In the final section of the chapter, we shift the focus from challenges to opportunities as we present approaches to culturally relevant PE for Aboriginal students. By focusing on culturally relevant teaching practices, we advocate for improved teacher education in PE, so that culturally relevant PE programs will be available for greater numbers of Aboriginal children and youth. By doing so, we hope that the "podium" dreams of Aboriginal children on the playgrounds can be more fully realized.

Systemic Underfunding of Aboriginal Education and Implications for PE

Although we wish to avoid essentializing Aboriginal experiences in today's schools, any discussion of the quality of PE for Aboriginal youth must begin with an acknowledgment of the larger social, economic, and historical context of colonization and the pervasive use of "education as an instrument of oppression" (Mendelson 2008a, 3) of Aboriginal peoples within Canada. Even though the last residential school closed in 1996 (Truth and Reconciliation Commission 2009), the harmful legacy of the residential school system continues to affect Aboriginal children and youth in schools today (Hare and Barman 2000; Miller 1996). Issues of academic performance must also be understood in relation to the intersecting factor of socio-economic status. As illustrated in a large Manitoba study, there is a strong correlation between income level and educational outcomes; the lower the family income of a student, the lower the academic achievement (Brownlee et al. 2004). Aboriginal youth lag behind their non-Aboriginal peers in terms of school attendance and high school graduation rates (HRDC 2002; Mackay and Miles 1995), a trend that shows little signs of improvement (Mendelson 2008b). The high number of Aboriginal children and youth living in poverty (Campaign 2000 2009), combined with the systemic underfunding of Aboriginal education (Richards 2008; Wilson and Wilson 2008), continues to place many Aboriginal children and youth at a disadvantage compared with their non-Aboriginal counterparts. This is not to say that Aboriginal peoples are "uniformly disadvantaged" (Canadian Centre for Policy Alternatives 2001). Rather, as the Canadian Centre for Policy Alternatives indicates, the reality for Aboriginal peoples is complex, and complicating factors such as geographic location (on-reserve, in rural and urban areas) and income level (from poor to middle class to wealthy) make it very difficult to generalize to the Aboriginal population as a whole.

Many of Canada's First Nations federally funded on-reserve schools are under-resourced, and provincially funded public schools are generally better funded than on-reserve schools (Mendelson 2008b). As noted by James Wilson, former director of education for the Opaskwayak Cree Nation (OCN) in Manitoba, First Nations schools that are funded by the federal government receive approximately 30 percent to 40 percent less funding than public schools that are provincially funded (Opaskwayak Cree Nation, Public Services n.d.). According to figures presented by Wilson on the OCN website (ibid.), the Manitoba average provincial spending per pupil is $8,950, whereas the funding per student at OCN is $6,400. Funding for public schools derives from at least three sources: provincial support (for operating and capital expenses), local taxation support (i.e., a special levy raised by school divisions), and other revenue (i.e., support received by school divisions through external agencies) (Manitoba Education, Citizenship and Youth 2009). First Nations schools are funded by Aboriginal Affairs and Northern Development Canada, a branch of the Canadian federal government, which, despite many promises to support Aboriginal education over successive governments, has routinely underfunded Aboriginal schools.[3] In both on-reserve and provincially funded schools, further resources are located within the fundraising efforts of parents, students, and community members who volunteer to raise money for particular school projects.[4] The level of economic wealth and strength of social networks within a community can influence the success of these volunteer fundraising efforts.

The amount of funding available at each provincially funded school off-reserve depends on the strength of the economic tax base from which school divisions draw their education funding, as well as the size of the student population. Given that schools receive provincial funding per student, larger schools with higher student populations will receive more overall funding than smaller schools. As such, Aboriginal students on- and off-reserve in rural or smaller schools may encounter educational contexts that are once again under-resourced in comparison with the larger, provincially funded schools, many of which are located in urban centres. Transportation costs can be significantly higher for school divisions in rural and remote areas (Seven Oaks School Division 2009). A further challenge for students living in such communities is the impact on student mobility. Although it is not always the case, youth living on reserves may be required to leave home to attend high school in a larger community in order to carry on past grade eight (Mendelson 2008b). Indeed, it is not uncommon for Aboriginal students to move hundreds of kilometres from home to complete their high school education (Halas 2006).

In the next section, we discuss the impact of the disparities in funding and how inequitable resources can influence the delivery of quality PE for Aboriginal students in two significant ways: access to infrastructure (facilities) and equipment, and the quality of instruction.

Implications for Infrastructure and Equipment

Regarding capital expenditures that provide for the physical infrastructure (i.e., the building, the gym), a recent report by the Office of the Parliamentary Budget Officer (2009) stated that of Canada's 803 on-reserve schools, only 49 percent (approximately one in two) were in good condition.[5] By comparison, many provincially funded schools provide good facilities and equipment, including full-sized gymnasiums. Although not addressing PE specifically, the 1957 MacFarlane Royal Commission on Education (Province of Manitoba 1959) resulted in the consolidation of public schools throughout Manitoba into forty-eight districts; the reorganization of school districts paved the way for larger public schools to be built, particularly in rural areas. Consequently, better school gyms were built (ibid.). Having said that, there are currently some provincially funded school gymnasiums that are old and too small, and need replacing.

This state of infrastructure is current, yet the facility deficit for Aboriginal communities has been long-standing. In a comprehensive study of physical activity, recreation, and sport relevant to Aboriginal peoples in Canada (Winther, Nazer-Bloom, and Petch 1995), with few exceptions, a lack of adequate community facilities was identified as a significant participation barrier in many Aboriginal communities. Exceptions were identified as those communities able to build recreational facilities because of flood settlements or extraction of natural resources. Where facilities did exist, it was noted, a lack of space for spectators "limited the social benefit physical activity can bring to a community" (ibid., 133). Most communities had school gyms, but these were often closed after school hours. In *Sport Canada's Policy on Aboriginal Peoples' Participation in Sport* (Canadian Heritage 2005), on-reserve Aboriginal communities are identified as lacking adequate sport and recreation infrastructure, as capital projects such as schools, roads, and housing were seen to take precedence. Within this context, the need for school officials to provide community members with access to the school gymnasium after the school day ends cannot be overstated. When the school and community work together, the school gym can become the hub of community sport and recreation activities.

Impact on Access to Quality PE

When funding for infrastructure needs is limited, offering a quality PE program becomes very challenging (Morgan and Hansen 2008): the quality of the facility and equipment readily available for use will affect the diversity of sports and physical activities that can be offered as part of the school program, thus shaping the type of learning opportunities available for students. With adequate yearly operating budgets, teachers can maintain an ongoing inventory of equipment and plan for replacing or adding to the inventory; the provision of adequate funding ensures that a wide range of curricular, intramural, and interschool offerings are supported.

Resourceful teachers in schools without a gym can access community facilities, if they are available and in good working order, such as a community hall or centre, the hockey and curling rinks, as well as outdoor fields, thus providing opportunities for many sports to be played. Used equipment can be purchased or acquired at low to no cost, which adds to the variety of activity options for students. Equipment costs increase for remote and rural communities that rely upon fly-in or long winter roads for transport. Another interesting point related to the smaller schools (predominantly on-reserve or rural schools) stands out in relation to the delivery of quality PE: although there may be less funding for infrastructure and equipment, in some cases it has been noted how the smaller size of a school may create opportunities for increased PE time, as physical educators may have greater flexibility to schedule time for PE within the daily curriculum (e.g., Halas 1998).

Issues surrounding the lack of availability of high-quality facilities and a wide variety of equipment can be alleviated by ensuring a quality experience in a few activities, provided they are meaningful and relevant for students (Halas 2002). A variety of curricular activity options contributes to the breadth of physical literacy skills that can be introduced, practised, developed, and acquired, yet depth of learning can still take place when students are highly motivated to engage in a select few activities that are personally and socially meaningful (e.g., Halas 2001a, 2002, 2003). For example, one PE teacher working at a school with an undersized and under-resourced gymnasium recognized and respected the high interest of Aboriginal students in two sports that the gym could accommodate: basketball and volleyball. As a result, the teacher developed a curricular program that focused on these activities, which in turn attracted and engaged a high number of Aboriginal youth (Halas 2002).

As a final consideration pertaining to the inequities in school funding, we should also account for the high levels of mobility of Aboriginal children and youth (Social Planning Council of Manitoba 2008). A high proportion of Aboriginal families change residences; thus, it is reasonable to expect Aboriginal students to experience differences in the quality of facilities and equipment they are exposed to depending on the schools they attend. For those students who move from an under-resourced to a better-equipped school, the apparent difference in the quality of the facility (or equipment) provides an experiential lesson about the inequities in our society. When Aboriginal students and/or student athletes travel to differently resourced schools, their experiences of one facility being so much nicer than the other teach them lessons about who and what type of school is valued in society. These messages can be internalized and thus reinforce racialized beliefs about who is valued in our society and who is not, based simply upon the quality of infrastructure available.

Implications for Provision of Quality Instruction in PE

PHE Canada (2009) defines a "qualified" physical educator as a provincially certified teacher who holds a bachelor of physical education, or a bachelor of education or kinesiology with a concentration in physical education, and follows provincial curriculum using sound pedagogical principles. Across Canada, most public schools designate a qualified PE teacher at the middle and high school levels, whereas generalist teachers often teach PE at the early years (Janzen 2003/2004).[6] In Manitoba, a lack of a specialized education in PE for teachers working in smaller, rural schools is not uncommon, particularly at the early years level (Manitoba Education and Training 1995; Fitzpatrick 1998).

In schools that do not have adequate funding to designate a PE teacher, the quality of instruction by the classroom generalist can be diminished by the teacher's lack of content knowledge (i.e., what to teach) and pedagogical content knowledge (i.e., how to teach content specific to PE) regarding developmentally appropriate, safe, and inclusive instruction that will provide enjoyable experiences for children (DeCorby et al. 2005). As well, the lack of time that classroom teachers have to prepare lessons or exercise leadership for the overall PE program can diminish opportunities for students (ibid.), as can one's confidence in teaching PE (Morgan and Hansen 2008). In addition, as Mendelson (2008a) points out, many First Nations schools are isolated and have little professional support typically associated with the educational "system" that organizes and shares educational resources across schools. For example, a teacher working on-reserve may not have access to the curricular support provided by a physical education and health consultant that many public school divisions offer. Lack of professional support can be particularly challenging for those teachers who lack knowledge and confidence to teach PE. In this case, opportunities to enhance the quality of instruction for students are diminished.

Intramural programming is considered a key aspect of the overall quality of a PE program (PHE Canada 2009). The depth and breadth of an intramural program often depends upon the willingness of teachers to voluntarily organize sports and activities. If teachers lack knowledge of how to plan and organize a wide variety of sports and physical activities, it is possible that the quality of the intramural program will be diminished, or, as was the case in one small rural school (DeCorby et al. 2005), the program will not be offered at all. Extracurricular programming can be similarly affected: if there are too few teachers volunteering to coach teams, it becomes difficult to offer the full range of sports typically offered in the interschool program. An advantage of larger schools at the middle years and high school level is that the responsibility for the interschool and intramural programs can be shared among a team of teachers, who often collaborate to offer a wide variety of activities for students of all abilities and interests. Consequently, students attending larger schools may have greater access to a wider variety of extracurricular physical activity opportunities.

An example of a highly successful extracurricular sport program is the Frontier School Division Games (Frontier School Division 2010). Offered annually, students from grades six to nine compete in team sports (basketball, volleyball, floor hockey, soccer), racquet sports (badminton, tennis), snowshoeing, cross-country skiing, and trap setting. The division's coordinator of health, wellness, and physical education assists with the delivery of the Games, which involves schools representing approximately 75 percent of Manitoba's territory. The Frontier Games has become a much-anticipated winter tradition for students, staff, and community members. It is an example of how athletic endeavours can be used to promote participation, friendship, and leadership for students living in rural and remote areas.

For Aboriginal students attending larger, urban schools, the wide repertoire of physical activity offerings does not guarantee that the activities are accessible. In a study investigating the experience of Aboriginal youth in high school PE, Aboriginal students attending a large multicultural school were not familiar with the culture of the PE program, which inhibited their participation (Champagne and Halas 2003). That is, they were neither familiar with what an intramural program offered by the PE teachers was, nor understood the structures and processes governing participation. As a result, they did not participate in intramurals because they did not know how to become a participant.[7] PE teachers need to be aware of those students who may be unfamiliar with this aspect of the school's PE program and should ensure that all students (including those arriving from countries other than Canada) are aware of the benefits of intramural and interschool programs and how to join a team. Without this awareness of the need to communicate how the extracurricular programs are run, some Aboriginal students who are unfamiliar with the culture of interschool sports might miss out on opportunities to play both recreational (e.g., intramurals) and competitive sport, thus affecting their sport development.

Teachers coaching interschool teams at schools with small student populations may face additional challenges of having adequate numbers of students interested in playing interschool sports. It may be easier for students to make the team when there are fewer players; it may also become more difficult to field a competitive team. This situation can be addressed in creative ways. In one Winnipeg high school with a small overall student population (i.e., two hundred mostly Aboriginal students in grades nine to twelve), the school division's Athletic Council permits varsity players (grades eleven and twelve students) to play on the junior varsity team (grades nine and ten) as long as they are still eligible to play high school sports (Elke Wurr, pers. comm., February 10, 2010). Given the governance policies of various school divisions' athletic systems, this type of accommodation can be very difficult or impossible, or it can meet with resistance from other schools' coaches, who see the older students as providing an unfair advantage. Key to our point here is that it may take a highly dedicated PE teacher or coach who is willing to take on some of the challenges of advocating for her or his team in order to create greater sport opportunities for students.

In those schools without a PE specialist, organizing the intramural or interschool teams may be more challenging, given that generalist teachers may not have the planning skills, often acquired in PE methods courses offered in teacher education programs (e.g., learning to schedule tournaments, and to organize weight rooms in a safe manner). Finally, the greater the geographic isolation of a community, the greater the cost of travel, which thus requires that the teacher or coach be resourceful in finding opportunities for engagement in interscholastic activities. Participation in field trips might also be affected by the availability of substitute teachers (again, with a

PE background) and the associated financial implications for under-resourced schools. This is particularly true for Aboriginal students given the remoteness of many First Nations and Métis communities in Manitoba.

Regarding quality of instruction, a further consideration is the intercultural skills of the PE teacher – the majority of Canadian PE teachers have middle-class, white backgrounds (Douglas and Halas 2008). The demographic increase in the numbers of Aboriginal children and youth, in addition to immigration patterns, which have increased the number of racialized minority youth, has transformed the character of many public schools. These demographic changes are taking place within a public education system that remains predominantly white in terms of teaching and support staff, as well as curriculum (Howard 2003). With a majority white student population in university teacher education programs (see ibid.; Ladson-Billings 2001), the demand for Aboriginal teachers in Aboriginal communities cannot be met (Hare and Barman 2000). Within faculties of physical education and kinesiology in Canada, only a handful of Aboriginal students are studying to become physical educators (Douglas and Halas 2011). As well, the lack of accessible, well-resourced initiatives to recruit and retain Aboriginal students at the postsecondary level in PE limits the numbers of Aboriginal role models as physical educators.[8]

Many PE teachers may lack awareness of the issues affecting Aboriginal children, youth, and their families and communities (Champagne 2006). Some feel inadequately prepared to work with Aboriginal populations (ibid.), and few have developed a white race consciousness that enables them to understand the social and historical impacts of colonization and racism that continue to influence the experience of Aboriginal students in schools today (Halas 2006). Consequently, as Champagne notes, educators lose out on opportunities to be effective allies in support of Aboriginal youth. What's more, a teacher's lack of understanding of the cultural context affecting Aboriginal youth might adversely affect his or her relationships with students, resulting in lower Aboriginal student engagement in PE (e.g., Champagne and Halas 2003; Halas 2006). The need for Aboriginal cultural awareness is an issue that applies to educators working in all types of schools (Hare and Barman 2000).

Finally, quality of instruction is affected by the high level of teacher mobility within Aboriginal communities (Taylor 1995). For teachers hired to work at on-reserve schools, the financial constraints (i.e., lower salary, inadequate space and facilities, and inability to implement and develop new curriculum [see Wilson 2007]) and the isolated location of many Aboriginal communities, as well as the cultural disconnect that many non-Aboriginal teachers may experience when living on a reserve for the first time, can result in high teacher turnover (Taylor 1995). To be effective community educators, teachers must avoid being "triangle" teachers (limiting their movement in the community from home to the school to the local store) and become "triangulating" teachers, whereby they make great efforts to get to know the community and see community members as both individuals and members of a racial group (Wyman and Kashatok 2008). In this regard, the ability to offer a high-quality, sustainable PE program will depend upon a community's ability to attract dedicated, caring teachers who will make efforts to fit into the culture of the community (e.g., Taylor 1995; Champagne 2006).

Culturally Relevant or Culturally Irrelevant? Aboriginal Students' Experiences of PE

Given the expressed value of quality PE as a pathway for Aboriginal sport development, fundamental to Aboriginal children and youth benefiting from PE is that they want to be actively engaged and that their experiences are positive. As one study involving Aboriginal youth at an adolescent parent centre/school and a second involving Aboriginal high school students made evident, when students felt supported by their teachers, they were more likely to participate in and enjoy their PE experience (Orchard, Halas, and Stark 2006; van Ingen and Halas 2004). In a series of focus group interviews with Aboriginal high school students, many youth commented on their love of PE in elementary school (Champagne and Halas 2003). Yet, these positive feelings diminished as students moved into the middle and high school years, about which many spoke of "irrelevant" activities that they were "forced" to do in gym class. It was evident that for the youth to be more engaged in PE, they needed to value the activities they were asked to perform. Examples of meaningful curricular activities included cultural activities, such as the construction of a trap line that incorporates snowshoeing and hunting (van Ingen and Halas 2006); extended activity units (e.g., basketball or volleyball [Halas 2002, 2003]); fitness-oriented, low-competition games and activities (Orchard, Halas, and Stark 2006); and free play (Halas 2004a). The diversity of these activity choices for different groups of Aboriginal students illustrates the importance of teachers getting to know their students' activity preferences.

In programs where Aboriginal students felt unsupported or disrespected by their PE teachers, they refused to take part in class (Champagne and

Halas 2003). Their resistance, which can be viewed as a survival strategy (Brant Castellano 2009) or cultural resilience (Hampton 1995), often took the form of not showing up for class, not changing for class, participating selectively in class, or not taking part in extracurricular activities. Furthermore, the enduring context of racism toward Aboriginal peoples within Canadian society in general, including sport environments (Robidoux 2004), can be very painful for students. For example, in one large multicultural school, the presence of racial stereotyping affected an Aboriginal student, who felt pressured to know how to do archery, even though he had never tried it before (Champagne and Halas 2003). Physical educators need to be cognizant of how Aboriginal students are experiencing their schools, communities, and classes (Champagne 2006; Halas 2006). Given how difficult conversations about race can be (Fox 2001; Solomona et al. 2005), the need for PE teachers to build respectful, supportive relationships with Aboriginal youth cannot be overstated. These relationships can be strengthened by a teacher's race consciousness, which enables him or her to recognize racial inequalities while respectfully getting to know more about individual students and the day-to-day cultural landscape that shapes who they are (Halas 2006).

Another factor is the change room and how teachers understand the dynamics within it. Although changing for PE is an accepted practice in PE programs, many Aboriginal students avoid PE because of how uncomfortable they feel changing in front of others before and after PE class (Champagne and Halas 2003; Halas 2004a). In PE programs where students are expected to change into gym clothes, participation by Aboriginal youth may be limited in the absence of strategies by the teacher to understand and accommodate this discomfort (Halas 2006). These strategies include allowing students to wear gym clothes (e.g., sweats) to school, arranging flexible change spaces or time for changing for students, and allowing students to play in their street clothes (Halas 2004b).

The above examples from the research literature that investigates Aboriginal youths' experiences of PE indicate both the complexity of the issues affecting Aboriginal student participation in PE and the potential benefits of a quality PE program when teachers work to build supportive relationships with their Aboriginal students. Conversely, when teachers do not take into consideration the diverse cultural landscapes of Aboriginal children and youth whom they teach, even a quality PE program might fail to actively engage Aboriginal students, thus creating more barriers for Aboriginal sport development. In the final section of this chapter, we identify the characteristics of culturally relevant programming that we believe will create opportunities for more Aboriginal children and youth to succeed in PE and sport.

Toward Culturally Relevant PE

Culturally relevant education is a wholistic and contextually based approach to education and therefore resists easy definition. At its broadest definition, culturally relevant education can be understood as a sociological approach to education that examines intercultural relationships between the macro-level social context (e.g., those social forces that shape the cultural landscapes of educators and racialized minority students), mid-level organizational issues (e.g., the educational practices and policies that shape educator-student relationships), and micro-level interactions (e.g., the immediate space of contact where teachers and racialized minority students and youth interact) (Irvine 1990). Culturally relevant education acknowledges the prevalence of deficit-based thinking that influences "traditional school thinking, practices, and placement" (Howard 2003, 198), including teachers' thoughts, actions, and behaviours (Ladson-Billings 1995a; Halas and Hanson 2001). To counter deficit-based thinking, one of the principles of culturally relevant education is that teachers believe in racialized minority learners as capable and successful learners (Ladson-Billings 2001; Howard 2003). Culturally relevant pedagogy is not a new idea: critical education scholars interested in the demographic divide between an increasingly homogeneous teaching population and heterogeneous student population have addressed similar ideas and goals (for examples see multicultural education scholars such as Banks [2001], anti-racism educators such as Fox [2001], or more specific examples such as Sable's culturally interactive science curriculum [2005] with Mi'kmaq students in Atlantic Canada). However, it is an educational theory and practice that is garnering increasing attention, as it directly links teacher training and practices to the individual and collective empowerment of racialized minority students.

Culturally relevant education is based on three key principles: "(a) students must experience academic success; (b) students must develop and/or maintain cultural competence; and (c) students must develop a critical social consciousness" (Ladson-Billings 1995a, 160). Aboriginal communities and educators have long argued for a culture-based approach to education and teaching (Hampton 1995); in fact, many scholars credit the 1972 Red Paper, formally known as *Indian Control of Indian Education,* as a landmark policy for Aboriginal peoples to reclaim their inherent right for local control

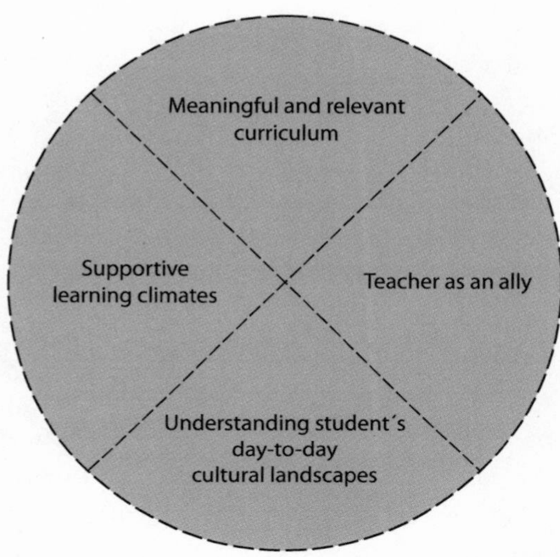

Figure 8.1 Culturally relevant physical education

of education. Stairs (1995) notes that in educational spaces in Aboriginal settings, change has typically been directed at the curricular level and has resulted in little change to teacher practices, which then places the responsibility on Aboriginal students, rather than teachers, to mediate cultural tensions and conflict between the students' home and community culture and the culture of the school and teacher (see also Sable 2005). An example of how unrealistic expectations are placed on Aboriginal students is found in the comment made by a male PE teacher who, upon learning that one of his students did not feel comfortable changing for gym class, suggested that the student just come and tell him when she feels this way (Halas 2006). To assume that students will have the confidence and communication skills to negotiate sensitive topics such as how they feel about their bodies in relation to others, particularly given the shyness of many Aboriginal youth when encountering new teachers in a new school, is to be mistaken. Teachers need to be aware of the potentiality of such issues and have proactive strategies to ensure all students feel supported in their classes.

In PE contexts, culturally relevant PE can be described as four interrelated constructs: (1) the teacher as an ally, (2) who understands the students and their day-to-day cultural landscapes, (3) in order to provide a supportive learning environment, (4) that includes a meaningful and relevant curriculum. Each of these aspects is interconnected and relational (see Figure 8.1).

The model of culturally relevant PE is designed to be applied interculturally across diverse student populations; it is not meant to be an Aboriginal approach to PE. In an Aboriginal context it would be directed by and embedded within Aboriginal world views, perspectives, and cultural values.[9] It is used to ensure that Aboriginal students in PE are taught by educators who have the knowledge, skills, and confidence to deliver effective lessons, while also taking into consideration the cultural landscapes of the children and youth in their classes.

An example of a culturally relevant approach to PE programming can be found in the Rec and Read Mentor Programs (known by the more familiar name Rec and Read) developed at the University of Manitoba (Carpenter et al. 2008; Carpenter 2009). Set within the bachelor of physical education degree program, Rec and Read involves Aboriginal and non-Aboriginal university students and Aboriginal high school students, who collectively plan and deliver a culturally relevant physical activity, nutrition, and education program for early years students at a neighbouring school. Rec and Read is designed to build on the strengths, energy, and talents of Aboriginal youth. The strengths-based approach immediately situates the university students as allies and co-learners within the program, as the mentors learn from each other (and the children) how to deliver effective programs. Both university and high school students can receive course credit for their involvement in the program. In addition, high school mentors are invited to work in the program once they graduate.

A core component of the Rec and Read mentor programming is intercultural relationship building based on Kirkness and Barnhardt's conception (1991) of the four Rs – respect, relevance, reciprocity, and responsibility (Carpenter and Halas 2011). University and high school mentors take time to get to know each other prior to initiating any activity programming for the early years students. Many of the university mentors are non-Aboriginal, have middle-class backgrounds, and have grown up in the suburbs or rural Manitoba; a majority of the high school participants are Aboriginal and live in inner-city or north-end (i.e., lower income) neighbourhoods. It is during this time of relationship building that mentors work together to create an inclusive community of learners (Ladson-Billings 1995b) where the power relations and leadership exercised by the high school and university mentors are always shifting within the group (Carpenter 2009). In one of the introductory leadership activities, all of the mentors are asked to take turns teaching each other a favourite game or activity from their childhood. As the games are played, the mentors are encouraged to think about the types of students who might be reluctant, shy, or less confident to play the game, and strategize how to maximize the active engagement of everyone involved.

Once programming with the early years children begins, the university and high school mentors work together to deliver the games and activities they have planned for the students. Each activity day ends with a sharing circle, where the mentors debrief among themselves as they critically reflect upon how their activity plans unfolded. It is a non-hierarchical, communal approach to mentoring that has thus far succeeded in actively engaging hundreds of inner-city and urban Aboriginal children and youth in games and activities. As a culturally relevant approach, it has also provided university students with unique opportunities to develop their intercultural competencies in working with diverse populations.[10] Rec and Read provides university and high school students with opportunities to develop their knowledge and skills related to the delivery of safe, inclusive physical activity environments for urban Aboriginal children, while contributing to enhanced leadership capacity that is "culturally sensitive, flexible and adaptive to the diverse needs of Aboriginal populations" (Canadian Heritage 2005, 7). In addition, Rec and Read connects high school mentors with summer employment in their own communities, offering urban sport providers a wider pool of experienced Aboriginal youth leadership to draw upon when looking to hire quality instructors. By widening the repertoire of physical activity opportunities for Aboriginal children and youth, physical literacy at the grassroots level is enhanced. As an extension of a school's PE program, the AYM programs open up new, early, and more equitable pathways for aspiring Aboriginal athletes and activity leaders to follow.

Conclusion

Our understanding of the quality and cultural relevance of PE is meant to provide a background that PE teachers (and sport coaches) can use when attempting to understand "where their Aboriginal students are at" when they enter their school gyms. It is our hope that by applying a contextual understanding of the challenges and opportunities that shape Aboriginal students' access to quality and culturally relevant PE programs, physical educators across Canada will draw upon a more informed approach when seeking to build meaningful relationships with Aboriginal children and youth. Each student has a particular experience; as a starting point, we recommend that teachers take the time to get to know the student they are working with, and in doing so, create supportive environments that affirm the cultural identities of everyone in their programs. Although it will take sustained, funded efforts to enhance Aboriginal children's and youth's access to quality PE, particularly in schools that do not have adequate infrastructure, equipment, and quality of instruction, the potential to provide culturally relevant PE exists in every school. It is the route that we believe will lead to enhanced physical literacy as the foundation for Aboriginal sport development in Canada.

NOTES

Funding for Joannie Halas's research program was provided by the Social Sciences and Humanities Research Council of Canada, the Manitoba Health Research Council, and the University of Manitoba. Funding for Heather McRae's doctoral research is provided by the Social Sciences and Humanities Research Council and Sport Canada's Doctoral Award Supplement – the Sport Participation Research Initiative Award, the Network Environments for Aboriginal Health Research (NEAHR), and the PhD Studies for Aboriginal Scholars (PSAS) Fund. Amy Carpenter's graduate research was supported by a grant from the Aboriginal Capacity and Developmental Research Environments.

1 We purposefully spell the term "wholistic" rather than the more common "holistic" to accentuate the connection between the meaning of "whole" and "wholistic." *Canadian Dictionary of the English Language* defines "Whole" as "1. Containing all components; complete. 2. Not divided or disjointed; in one unit" (s.v. "whole").

2 Intramurals are recreational sports organized *within the walls* of a school. They are typically planned by the PE teacher, often with the support of other school teachers or student leaders. Offered mostly at lunchtime (but in some cases before and after school), a quality intramural program provides students of all skill levels and interests with opportunities to be physically active in a variety of sports throughout the school year.

3 As but one example, see *Attawapiskat School Fight* (Bozlo 2008), a video that depicts a northern Cree community's struggle for a new school that had been repeatedly promised but not delivered by successive federal governments (YouTube 2008, Attawapiskat School Fight video). After years of lobbying efforts, Attawapiskat finally broke ground for a new school on June 22, 2012 (Carpenter 2012).

4 In Manitoba in 2007/08, there were 684 provincially funded public schools, and 72 First Nations schools (Manitoba Education, Citizenship and Youth 2009).

5 The Office of the Parliamentary Budget Officer (2009, 8) report also highlighted that it is currently "impossible to determine how much Parliament intended to appropriate for school infrastructure funding and consequently, how much was actually spent on schools," which helps to explain why and how inadequate funding for on-reserve schools remains a systemic issue.

6 In Manitoba, kindergarten to grade five constitutes the early years, grades six through eight the middle years, and grades nine through twelve the high school years.

7 Coalter (2007, 3) states that the major methodological limitation of sports-related research is the "lack of understanding of what processes produce what effects, for which participants, in what circumstances." Thus, if the participation and engagement levels of Aboriginal students in intramural programs or physical education classes are lower than that of non-Aboriginal youth, this may suggest that the normalized structures and processes governing these programs are unfamiliar or hostile to Aboriginal youth, and need to be adapted accordingly.

8 Although the Faculty of Kinesiology and Recreation Management at the University of Manitoba has made some gains in this regard, the process of change is very slow. Aboriginal teacher education programs (e.g., the Brandon University Northern Teachers Education Program, and the Community Based Aboriginal Teacher Education Program offered in Winnipeg) often provide limited curricular instruction in physical education.

9 Our use of the term "culturally relevant" is different from its usage in an Aboriginal approach to physical education, one that would be informed by Aboriginal teachings, world views, and perspectives. Given the wholistic nature of physical education, it is an educational context that would greatly benefit from the application of Aboriginal cultural approaches. See Brenda Kalyn's PhD dissertation (2006) for an example of a curricular model that applies Aboriginal perspectives to PE. For examples of curricular activities based on Aboriginal traditions (e.g., dance, traditional games and activities), see Keillor, Cle-alls (John Medicine Horse Kelly), and von Rosen (2007) and the Native Drums Teachers Homepage (Carleton University 2007).

10 For more information about the Rec and Read Mentor Programs, contact the Faculty of Kinesiology and Recreation Management at the University of Manitoba.

REFERENCES

Banks, J.A. 2001. *Cultural Diversity and Education: Foundations, Curriculum, and Teaching.* 4th ed. Toronto: Allyn and Bacon.

Brant Castellano, M. 2009. *Terra Nullius: The Enduring Myth of Canada's Origins.* Keynote address at the Canadian Society for the Study of Education conference, Carleton University, Ottawa, May 23.

Bozlo, B. 2008. Attawapiskat School Fight. Video file, February 25. http://www.youtube.com/.

Brownlee, M., N. Roos, R. Fransoo, A. Guevremont, L. MacWilliam, S. Derksen, M. Dik, et al. 2004. *How Do Educational Outcomes Vary with Socioeconomic Status? Key Findings from the Manitoba Child Health Atlas 2004.* Winnipeg: Manitoba Centre for Health Policy.

Campaign 2000. 2009. *2009 Report Card on Child and Family Poverty in Canada: 1989-2009.* http://www.campaign2000.ca/.

Canadian Centre for Policy Alternatives. 2001. *Aboriginal Peoples and Social Classes in Manitoba.* Winnipeg: Canadian Centre for Policy Alternatives.

Canadian Heritage. 2002. *The Canadian Sport Policy.* http://www.pch.gc.ca/.

–. 2005. *Sport Canada's Policy on Aboriginal Peoples' Participation in Sport.* Catalogue no. CH24-10/2005. Ottawa: Minister of Public Works and Government Services Canada.

Carleton University. 2007. Native dance. http://www.native-dance.ca/.

Carpenter, A. 2009. Rec and Read: Stories of an Aboriginal youth mentor program. MA thesis, University of Manitoba.

Carpenter, A., and J. Halas. 2011. "Rec and Read" mentor programs: Building on the strengths, talents and energy of Aboriginal youth. *Reclaiming Children and Youth Journal* 20(1): 20-24.

Carpenter, L. 2012. Attawapiskat celebrates new school sod-turning. *Wawatay News Online*. http://www.wawataynews.ca/archive/.

Carpenter, A., A. Rothney, J. Mousseau, J. Halas, and J. Forsyth. 2008. Seeds of encouragement: Initiating an Aboriginal youth mentorship program. *Canadian Journal of Native Education* 31(2): 51-69.

Champagne, L. 2006. Teachers as allies for Aboriginal youth. MA thesis, University of Manitoba.

Champagne, L., and J. Halas. 2003. "I quit!" Aboriginal students negotiate the "contact zone" in physical education. In V. Paraschak and J. Forsyth, eds., *North American Indigenous Games Research Symposium Proceedings* (55-64). Winnipeg: Health, Leisure and Human Performance Research Institute.

Coalter, F. 2007. *A Wider Social Role for Sport: Who's Keeping the Score?* New York: Routledge.

Coté, J., J. Baker, and B. Abernethy. 2007. Practice and play in development of sport expertise. In R. Eklund and G. Tenenbaum, eds., *Handbook on Sport Psychology*, 3rd ed. (184-202). Hoboken, NJ: Wiley.

DeCorby, K., J. Halas, S. Dixon, L. Wintrup, and H. Janzen. 2005. Generalist teachers and the challenges of teaching quality physical education. *Journal of Educational Research* 98(4): 208-20.

Douglas, D., and J. Halas. 2011. The wages of whiteness: Confronting the nature of ivory tower racism and the implications for physical education. *Sport, Education and Society*, DOI:10.1080/13573322.2011.602395.

Federal-Provincial/Territorial Advisory Committee on Fitness and Recreation. 2000. *Maskwachees Declaration*. Gatineau, QC: Federal-Provincial/Territorial Advisory Committee on Fitness and Recreation.

Fitzpatrick, D. 1998. Survey of Selected Manitoba Physical Education, and Health Teaching Variables: Preliminary Report. http://www.uwinnipeg.ca/.

Forsyth, J., M. Heine, and J. Halas. 2006. A cultural approach to Aboriginal youth sport and recreation: Observations from year 1. In J.P. White, S. Wingert, D. Beavon, and P. Simon, eds., *Aboriginal Policy Research: Moving Forward, Making a Difference*, vol. 4 (93-100). Toronto: Thompson Educational.

Fox, H. 2001. *When Race Breaks Out: Conversations about Race and Racism in College Classrooms*. New York: Peter Lang.

Frontier School Division. 2010. Frontier games. http://www.frontiersd.mb.ca/.

Halas, J. 1998. "Runners in the gym": Tales of resistance and conversion at an adolescent treatment center school. *Canadian Native Education Journal* 22(2): 210-22.

–. 2001a. Playtime at the treatment center: How physical activity helps troubled youth. *AVANTE* 7(1): 1-13.

–. 2001b. Shooting hoops at the treatment centre: Sport stories. *Quest* 53(1): 77-96.

–. 2002. Engaging alienated youth in physical education: An alternative program with lessons for the traditional class. *Journal of Teaching in Physical Education* 21(3): 267-86.

–. 2003. Culturally relevant physical education for students who have emotional and behavioral difficulties. In R. Steadward, G. Wheeler, and E.J. Watkinson, eds., *Adapted Physical Activity in Canada* (285-303). Edmonton: University of Alberta Press.

–. 2004a. Engaging reluctant students in physical education: Is there more to student resistance than meets the eye? *Manitoba Physical Education Teachers' Association* 27(4): 20-21.

–. 2004b. Questioning our assumptions: Unconventional lessons from the "swamp of practice." *JOPERD* 75(4): 14-21.

–. 2006. Developing a white race consciousness: A foundation of culturally relevant physical education for Aboriginal youth. In E. Singleton and A. Varpalotai, eds., *Stones in the Sneaker: Active Theory for Secondary School Physical and Health Educators* (155-82). London: Althouse Press.

Halas, J., and L. Hanson. 2001. Pathologizing Billy: Enabling and constraining the body of the condemned. *Sociology of Sport Journal* 18(1): 115-26.

Hampton, E. 1995. Toward a redefinition of Indian education. In M. Battiste and J. Barman, eds., *First Nations Education in Canada: The Circle Unfolds* (5-46). Vancouver: UBC Press.

Hare, J., and J. Barman. 2000. Aboriginal education: Is there a way ahead? In D. Long and O.P. Dickason, eds., *Visions of the Heart: Canadian Aboriginal Issues,* 2nd ed. (330-59). Toronto: Harcourt Canada.

Howard, T.C. 2003. Culturally relevant pedagogy: Ingredients for critical teacher reflection. *Theory into Practice* 42(3): 195-202.

HRDC (Human Resources Development Canada). 2002. *Aboriginal People in Manitoba.* Winnipeg: HRDC.

Irvine, J. 1990. *Black Students and School Failure: Policies, Practices, and Prescriptions.* Westport, CT: Greenwood Press.

Janzen, H. 2003/2004. Daily physical education for K-12: Is government legislation in sight? *Physical and Health Education Journal* 69(4): 4-12.

Kalyn, B. 2006. A healthy journey: Indigenous teachings that direct culturally responsive curricula in physical education. PhD diss., University of Saskatchewan.

Keillor, E., Cle-alls (John Medicine Horse Kelly), and F. von Rosen, eds. 2007. Native dance – Native dance. http://www.native-dance.ca/.

Kirkness, V., and R. Barnhardt. 1991. First Nations and higher education: The four R's – respect, relevance, reciprocity, responsibility. *Journal of American Indian Education* 30(3): 1-15.

Ladson-Billings, G. 1995a. But that's just good teaching! The case for culturally relevant pedagogy. *Theory into Practice* 34(3): 159-65.

–. 1995b. Toward a theory of culturally relevant pedagogy. *American Educational Research Journal* 32(3): 465-91.

–. 2001. *Crossing over to Canaan: The Journey of New Teachers in Diverse Classrooms.* San Francisco: Jossey-Bass.

Mackay, R., and L. Myles. 1995. A major challenge for the education system: Aboriginal retention and dropout. In M. Battiste and J. Barman, eds., *First Nations Education in Canada: The Circle Unfolds* (157-78). Vancouver: UBC Press.

Manitoba Education and Training. 1995. *Manitoba Physical Education Assessment 1993: Final Report; English Language Schools.* Winnipeg: Manitoba Education and Training.

–. 2000. *Kindergarten to Senior 4 Physical Education/Health Education: Manitoba Curriculum Framework of Outcomes for Active Healthy Lifestyles.* Winnipeg: Manitoba Education and Training.

Manitoba Education, Citizenship and Youth. 2009. *A Statistical Profile of Education in Manitoba September 2003 to June 2008.* Winnipeg: Manitoba Education, Citizenship and Youth.

Mendelson, M. 2008a. *Improving Education on Reserves: A First Nations Education Authority Act.* Ottawa: Caledon Institute of Social Policy. http://www.caledoninst.org/.

–. 2008b. Poor educational outcomes for Aboriginal students threaten Canada's prosperity. *Maytree Policy in Focus* 5: 1-7.

Miller, J. 1996. *Shingwauk's Vision: A History of Native Residential Schools.* Toronto: University of Toronto Press.

Morgan, P., and V. Hansen. 2008. Classroom teachers' perceptions of the impact of barriers to teaching physical education on the quality of physical education programs. *Research Quarterly for Exercise and Sport* 79(4): 506-16.

Mulholland, E. 2008. *What Sport Can Do: The True Sport Report.* Ottawa: True Sport.

Office of the Parliamentary Budget Officer. 2009. *The Funding Requirement for First Nations Schools in Manitoba.* http://www2.parl.gc.ca/.

Opaskwayak Cree Nation. Public Services. *n.d.* Education Directors Meeting. http://www.opaskwayak.ca/.

Orchard, T., J. Halas, and J. Stark. 2006. Minimizing the *Maxim* model? Interpreting the sexual body rhetoric of teenage moms through physical education. In L.K. Fuller, ed., *Sport, Rhetoric, and Gender: Historical Perspectives and Media Representations* (131-42). New York: Palgrave/Macmillan, Global Publishing at St. Martin's Press.

PHE Canada (Physical and Health Education Canada). 2009. Quality daily physical education: About QDPE. http://www.cahperd.ca/eng/.

Province of Manitoba. 1959. *Report of the Manitoba Royal Commission on Education.* Winnipeg: Queen's Printer.

Richards, J. 2008. *Closing the Aboriginal/non-Aboriginal Education Gaps.* October. http://www.cdhowe.org/.

Robidoux, M. 2004. Narratives of race relations in southern Alberta: An examination of conflicting sporting practices. *Sociology of Sport Journal* 21(3): 287-301.

Sable, T. 2005. Emerging identities: A proposed model for an interactive science curriculum for First Nations students. PhD diss., University of New Brunswick.

Seven Oaks School Division. 2009. Two tiered education: Fact or fiction? http://www.7oaks.org/.

Social Planning Council of Manitoba. 2008. *Manitoba Child and Family Poverty Report Card.* Winnipeg: Social Planning Council of Manitoba.

Solomona, P.R., J.P. Portelli, B.-J. Daniel, and A. Campbell. 2005. The discourse of denial: How white teacher candidates construct race, racism, and "white privilege." *Race Ethnicity and Education* 8(2): 147-69.

Sport Canada. 2009. *Long-Term Athlete Development Model.* Ottawa: Sport Canada.

Stairs, A. 1995. Learning processes and teaching roles in Native education: Cultural base and cultural brokerage. In M. Battiste and J. Barman, eds., *First Nations Education in Canada: The Circle Unfolds* (139-53). Vancouver: UBC Press.

Taylor, J. 1995. Non-Native teachers teaching in Native communities. In M. Battiste and J. Barman, eds., *First Nations Education in Canada: The Circle Unfolds* (224-44). Vancouver: UBC Press.

Truth and Reconciliation Commission. 2009. Residential school locations. http://www.trc-cvr.ca/.

UNESCO. 1999. Declaration of Punta del Este. http://www.unesco.org/.

van Ingen, C., and J. Halas. 2004. What works? Lessons learned from the experiences of Aboriginal youth in high school physical education classes. *Manitoba Association of School Superintendents Journal* 4(1): 26-28.

–. 2006. Claiming space: Aboriginal students within school landscapes. *Children's Geographies* 4(3): 379-98.

Whitehead, M. 2001. The concept of physical literacy. *European Journal of Physical Education* 6(2): 127-36.

–. 2007. Squaring the circle: Women, physical literacy and Western patriarchal culture. *British Philosophy of Sport Association.* http://www.physical-literacy.org.uk/.

Wilson, J. 2007. First Nations education: The need for legislation in the jurisdictional gray zone. *Canadian Journal of Native Education* 30(2): 248-56.

Wilson, S., and P. Wilson. 2008. Editorial: First Nations' education at a critical juncture. *Canadian Journal of Native Education* 31(1): 1-3.

Winther, N., L. Nazer-Bloom, and V. Petch. 1995. *A Comprehensive Overview of Physical Activity and Recreation/Sport Relevant to Aboriginal Peoples in Canada.* Winnipeg: Fitness Directorate of Health Canada.

Wyman, L., and G. Kashatok. 2008. Getting to know students' communities. In M. Pollock, ed., *Every Day Anti-Racism: Getting Real about Race in School* (299-304). New York: The New Press.

Two-Eyed Seeing
Physical Activity, Sport, and Recreation Promotion in Indigenous Communities

LYNN LAVALLÉE AND LUCIE LÉVESQUE

"Two-eyed seeing," a term coined by Mi'kmaq elder Albert Marshall, relates to seeing the world through two perspectives: Indigenous and Western or European. In this instance, the term "Western" refers to the dominant ideology of the western hemisphere (predominantly North America) and "indigenous" refers to the ideology traced to the earliest known inhabitants of a geographical region. Although the earliest inhabitants of North America were indigenous peoples, the current dominant ideology is that of the early European settlers. For the purpose of this chapter, when referring to the Aboriginal or indigenous peoples of Canada, we are referring to the First Nations, Métis, and Inuit. Two-eyed seeing requires an attentiveness to bicultural ways of knowing, which, in this case, means incorporating the strengths of indigenous and Western perspectives to create a hybridized understanding of how to address a particular issue, for example, health promotion. It involves using both eyes together, weaving back and forth between perspectives without one perspective dominating the other, to the benefit of all (Kitchikeesic 2005; Marshall and Bartlett 2009). In this chapter, we use two-eyed seeing to discuss and integrate two perspectives related to physical activity, sport, and recreation promotion: the medicine wheel teachings of the Anishinaabek and the socio-ecological model as conceptualized by Western scholars. Parallels are drawn between medicine wheel teachings and the Western socio-ecological approach to health promotion. Using a two-eyed seeing approach, an integrated indigenous-ecological model for promoting physical activity, sport, and recreation is presented. Illustrations and examples show how the model can be used to promote physical activity, sport, and recreation, as well as how this model represents a means to convey the medicine wheel teachings.

Bringing together the strengths of Aboriginal and Western approaches through a two-eyed seeing approach is both relevant and essential for the promotion of physical activity, sport, and recreation in Aboriginal communities. It is relevant because of the contemporary and westernized contexts in which many Aboriginal peoples in Canada live and play. For instance, hockey and basketball, two Western-derived sports, are very popular among Aboriginal youth (NAHC n.d.; Anderson 2006), as are activities of indigenous origin, such as lacrosse, hand games, and dancing. Two-eyed seeing is relevant because non-Aboriginal and Aboriginal practitioners work with Aboriginal peoples to promote physical activity, sport, and recreation; thus, adopting a two-eyed seeing approach can create opportunities for new understanding by requiring the conscious and constant reflection of the merging of ideas and philosophies. Using a framework that fosters the integration of indigenous and Western perspectives for the promotion of well-being is essential because it acknowledges and addresses colonization's impact on Aboriginal people's health and well-being. The next section explains why this view represents a critical starting point for reclaiming Aboriginal well-being.

Colonization and Aboriginal Well-Being

Indigenous sport has a complex history. At times extolled for its virtuous proffering of spiritual reward, it has also been used toward other ends. For example, lacrosse has been termed "the little brother of war" because it was used as a surrogate for war; in this context, lacrosse would be played violently, involving the maiming of opposing players (Cohen 2002). The potential for sport to offer both positive and negative experiences is not unique to indigenous sport but can be found in many cultures and across a diversity of sports (Coakley 2002).

In a more positive incarnation, and its most typical application, indigenous sport has been used to teach personal and social values, such as "honesty, courage, respect, personal excellence, and gratitude for the guidance of parents, elders, and communities, [which] prepared children and youth for the responsibility of adulthood" (Canadian Heritage 2003, para. 1). For many indigenous people, sport and physical activity are considered to hold medicinal value and healing potential. For example, Culin (1907) noted that

Aboriginal people saw the playing of lacrosse as spiritual; the Huron Indians would play it as a way of praying for a sick man or sick country, with medicine men often serving as officials during lacrosse games.

The notion of sport and physical activity as medicine has been argued as a right for Aboriginal peoples in a contemporary interpretation of Treaty 6, which, in 1876, stipulated that "a medicine chest shall be kept at the house of each Indian Agent for the use and benefit of the Indians, at the direction of such Agent" (Haslip and Edwards 2002, 38). Haslip (2001) contends that similar clauses exist in Treaties 7, 8, 10, and 11, which cover a geopolitical area spanning much of western Canada, and argues that the medicine chest includes the right to have access to sport and physical activity. The Maskwachees Declaration of 2000 echoes Treaty 6 by recognizing sport and physical activity as a central means to promote wholistic health (Canadian Heritage 2006). ("Wholistic" is spelled with a "w" to emphasize the concept of wholeness when the four areas of health – physical, mental, emotional, and spiritual – are in balance. See Antone, Gamlin, and Provost-Turchetti 2003.) Further, the Aboriginal Sport Circle, the national body for Aboriginal sport and recreation development in Canada, considers sport and recreation "powerful medicine that can prevent many of the social ills facing Aboriginal peoples, and foster community healing" (ASC n.d.). Evidence of the positive impact that sport and physical activity involvement can have on Aboriginal people's health and well-being is found in the many stories offered by Aboriginal communitiy members throughout Canada. This seems to be especially true where community members have participated in recognized events, such as the North American Indigenous Games; received recognition for their accomplishments, as with the Tom Longboat Awards; had their elite status validated in the dominant sports system, for instance, in the Olympic Games (e.g., Alwyn Morris, who won gold and bronze medals in pairs kayaking at the 1984 Summer Games, and Waneek Horn-Miller, who competed in water polo at the 2000 Summer Games in Sydney, Australia) (ASC n.d.); have represented their communities on national sports teams; or have become role models in their communities for healthy lifestyles (Macaulay et al. 2005).

Regular involvement in sport and physical activity has been found to have a beneficial impact on the physical, mental, and emotional dimensions of health. For example, in children and youth, physical activity is inversely related to obesity (Tremblay and Willms 2003; Janssen et al. 2004), cardiovascular disease risk factors (Katzmarzyk, Malina, and Bouchard 1999; Eisenmann 2004; Strong et al. 2005), and various physical and psychological health complaints (Haugland, Wold, and Torsheim 2003; Janssen et al. 2004). Reviews of literature have also revealed an association between physical activity and higher levels of good mental health in youth (e.g., self-esteem [Mutrie and Parfitt 1998], as well as academic achievement [Field, Diego, and Saunders 2001; Taras 2005]). Moreover, some evidence suggests that children and youth involved in physical activity tend to carry positive behaviours into adulthood (Malina 2001; Boreham et al. 2004; Telama et al. 2005). Finally, studies show that adult participation in sport and physical activity results in similar benefits for the physical, mental, and emotional dimensions of health. For adults, regular involvement in sport and physical activity helps to prevent chronic diseases, including cardiovascular diseases, ischemic stroke, hypertension, certain cancers, obesity, type 2 diabetes, and osteoporosis (Camacho et al. 1991; Giovannucci et al. 1995; Lee, Hsieh, and Paffenbarger 1995; Wannamethee and Shaper 1999, 2001; Hu et al. 2000; Sesso, Paffenbarger, and Lee 2000; Hu, Leitzmann, et al. 2001; Hu, Manson, et al. 2001; Warburton, Nicol, and Bredin 2006).

Given the demonstrated health benefits of physical activity, sport, and recreation, and the notion of sport and physical activity as medicine for indigenous peoples, the absence of such activities can have significant detrimental effects. Aboriginal people face a number of challenges that limit their ability to gain access to and maintain their involvement in sport, recreation, and physical activity. Many of these challenges can be linked to barriers established during colonization. When European settlers arrived in North America, they fundamentally and forever altered Aboriginal ways of life – for example, by appropriating Aboriginal traditional lands and resources (Wesley-Esquimaux and Smolewski 2004). With the creation of Indian reserves in the late eighteenth and early nineteenth century, many First Nations were forced to move to new and unfamiliar territory, which had serious implications for their hunting, fishing, and farming methods. In addition, many Aboriginal children were removed from their homes and communities and placed in residential schools, where they often lived throughout the year (ibid.; Warry 1998). As Janice Forsyth discusses in Chapter 1, efforts to "take the Indian out" of the children through the residential school system included prohibiting all Aboriginal forms of expression, such as sport, physical activity, dance, and play (Barron 1984; Paraschak 1997; Waldrum 1997; Giles 2004; Forsyth and Wamsley 2006). For instance, potlatch and powwow ceremonies involved the coming together of Aboriginal people to celebrate, dance, and play sports like lacrosse and games of chance and dexterity (Culin 1907; Waldrum 1997). Some of the games were interpreted by non-Aboriginal observers, such as Culin, Kohl, and de Brébeuf, as involving the use of "superior cunning skill or magic" to "please the gods" (Culin 1907, 32-34). The missionaries generally viewed these practices as abominations and counterproductive to their religious projects and thus campaigned to have the government ban them. The Potlatch Law of the 1884 Indian Act banned the potlatch and "spirit dancing" (Waldrum 1997, 6). In 1895, the government revised the Potlatch Law to provide more specific legislation banning illegal components of the potlatch, including the grass and sun dance (Waldrum 1997). As such, successive generations of Aboriginal peoples were prohibited from engaging in their traditional physical practices and the lifelong lessons that stemmed from them.

Assimilation strategies included the use of Euro-Canadian sports to inculcate a new set of cultural values (e.g., individualistic, capitalistic values) among Aboriginal peoples (Forsyth and Wamsley 2006). Recent events are glaring reminders that this historical pattern continues well into the present day. One need only look to the federal Native Sport and Recreation Program (1972-81) as an example of how the Canadian government privileged the Euro-Canadian structure of sport and the values taught through that system over indigenous sports and the values embraced in those contexts (Paraschak 1997). Funding for the Native Sport and Recreation Program was withdrawn by the federal government in 1981. The rationale for this move was that Native sports programs would not produce elite (national, international) level athletes, which was a priority area for government at that time. Such action continued the colonial legacy of the Canadian government attempting to eliminate traditional Aboriginal cultural practices while, at the same time, imposed a Western world view of how to organize sports so as to produce elite-level athletes, all the while discrediting indigenous approaches to sport.

The Canadian government's repression of indigenous physical activities has had a lasting impact on Aboriginal peoples' participation in physical activity and sport. Data from the Canadian Community Health Survey show that 57.2 percent of Aboriginal adults and 65.8 percent of Aboriginal youth are not active enough to obtain health benefits. These numbers mirror self-reported physical activity data from non-Aboriginal adult and youth (Katzmarzyk 2008). In addition, an increasing number of Aboriginal children and youth are spending their free time engaged in sedentary activities such as watching television, playing video games, or sitting at the computer (NAHO 2005). Findings from the Aboriginal Peoples Survey 2001 (children's component) reveal that only 26 percent of Aboriginal children participate in sports on most days of the week, though a total of 65 percent participate at least once per week. Given Aboriginal peoples' low levels of regular involvement in sport and physical activity, a strong rationale exists for the development of relevant strategies to engage Aboriginal people in sport and physical activity. Increased participation in positive activities has the potential to enhance physical, mental, emotional, and spiritual health. Furthermore, sport and physical activity settings offer an ideal context through which medicine wheel teachings can be passed on. The next section discusses the medicine wheel teachings as they relate to physical activity and health.

The Medicine Wheel, Sport, and Health

In Canada, 1982 constitutional amendments acknowledged three distinct groups of Aboriginal peoples: First Nations, Métis, and Inuit. Within these three groups there are diverse ways of knowing, customs, and traditions. The medicine wheel teachings discussed in this chapter represent some First Nations and Métis peoples' teachings and provide an example of how indigenous teachings can be integrated with Western knowledge. Not all Aboriginal people follow the teachings of the medicine wheel. For instance, Inuit people do not have teachings related to the medicine wheel. Nor do all First Nations and Métis people practise the medicine wheel. This chapter merely provides an example of how a specific indigenous teaching can be integrated with a Western model of health promotion. The intent is not to offer a definitive iteration of two-eyed seeing; rather, the intent is to provide one way of framing an approach to sport and physical activity promotion in Aboriginal communities. The rationale for the selection of the medicine wheel teachings is based on author Lavallée's Anishinaabe and Métis culture.

Many of the references for the medicine wheel teachings in this chapter come from Lavallée's personal experiences with elders and people who carry the knowledge of traditional and ceremonial practices. The elders referenced here are recognized in their communities for their cultural knowledge and have allowed the authors to use their knowledge in this chapter. The teachings discussed here are not sacred or familial knowledge, and can thus be used for educational purposes (Kovach 2009). From an academic standpoint, proper citation of original ideas involves crediting the original author; however, traditional teachings are normally shared orally and passed down through generations (Brant Castellano 2000). As such, medicine wheel teachings are not the intellectual property of one person; rather, teachings emanate from specific nations, cultures, or families. As other Aboriginal authors have done (e.g., Green 2009; Kovach 2009), in this chapter we acknowledge the person who originally shared the teaching with author Lavallée.

The medicine wheel and related teachings are often used to discuss and analyze Aboriginal ways of knowing; this chapter focuses on teachings related to health and well-being. Teachings related to the medicine wheel are vast and cannot be fully understood even in an entire lifetime (K. Wheatley, pers. comm., August 10, 2005). The teachings are thousands of years old and have been passed down orally through the generations, in this case, among the Anishinaabek (G. Antone, pers. comm., October 2, 2004). One of the fundamental values and beliefs of the Anishinaabek, and many indigenous peoples globally, is the connection of humans and animal life to the natural world (NAHO 2005). This connection is often depicted by a complete circle. Since many things in nature are circular, such as the sun, earth, and moon, circles take on sacred meaning for some Aboriginal peoples (Stevenson 1999).

The medicine wheel (see Figure 9.1) – a circle – represents life, which has no beginning and no end because, according to this belief system, we are all spiritual beings living in the physical world who will return to the spirit world after death (V. Harper, pers. comm., November 20, 2004). A complementary teaching is the four directions, which express a relationship that helps us to understand various ideas that can be expressed in groups of four,

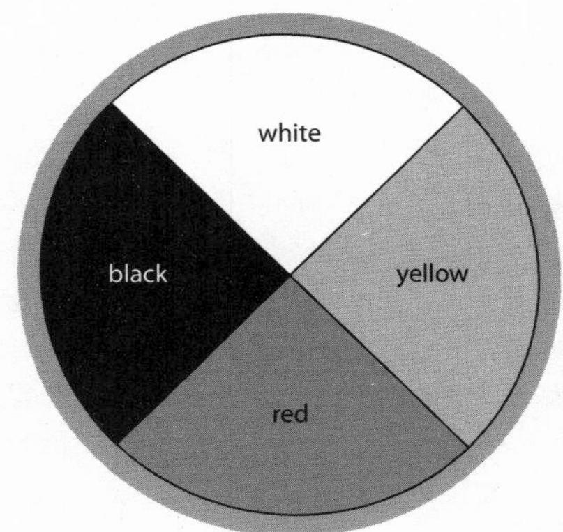

Figure 9.1 Medicine wheel

and also demonstrate the interrelatedness of ideas (Lane et al. 2003). Different Aboriginal groups use different colours and vary the order of the colours; the Anishinaabek teachings of the four directions show east in yellow, south in red, west in black, and north in white. There are many teachings related to the medicine wheel. For instance, one of the teachings of the medicine wheel is that all races (yellow, red, black, and white) are equal and all people are related or interconnected (W. Commanda, pers. comm., January 19, 2008).

Although the circle may be divided into four or more quadrants, a fundamental understanding of the medicine wheel is that everything within the circle is equal and interconnected. The circle promotes a wholistic way of viewing life and emphasizes the interconnectedness of all living things and the interconnectedness within the individual; this is sometimes visually depicted with the use of feathers between each quadrant and also recognized by the four quadrants joining in the centre.

The medicine wheel is composed of four interrelated aspects of life (i.e., the physical, mental, emotional, and spiritual) and is frequently used to broaden and enhance our understanding of Aboriginal health. Overall well-being stems from balance and harmony among these four aspects, and health is viewed as wholistic and integral to other aspects of a person's life (NAHO 2005; Royal Commission on Aboriginal Peoples 1996). The teachings related to health also emphasize the importance of balance to all other life forms. An individual's health and well-being is interconnected with the health of his or her family, community, people worldwide, the earth, the universe, the known, and the unknown (NAHO 2005). The interconnectivity of the medicine wheel teachings implies that if one aspect is out of balance or unhealthy, it impacts the entire system.

Due to the extent that sport and physical activity contribute to this balance, both individually and collectively, sport and physical activity are elements in the health equation. Although all four quadrants of the medicine wheel can be influenced by sport and physical activity, sport and physical activity outcomes may not always be viewed through the lens of medicine wheel teachings. Likewise, sport and physical activity opportunities available to Aboriginal peoples may not always integrate medicine wheel teachings. It is hoped that this discussion will encourage reflection on how sport and physical activity are integral to the medicine wheel.

An indigenous understanding of health emphasizes balance and interconnection of humans to all other life forms, to Mother Earth, and to all of creation, including the known and unknown. For instance, the pollution of the earth directly impacts the health of all living creatures. At the individual level, the medicine wheel teachings stress the importance of balance between physical, mental, emotional, and spiritual health. In this conceptualization, the physical is the body that encompasses physiological homeostasis, eating healthy, and being physically active. The mental refers to intellect. Feelings encompass the emotional aspects of the self. Finally, the spiritual is the most difficult to explain. It is about one's relationship with the Great Mystery, the Creator, the unknown; the connection to the ancestors through blood memory; the connection to the land, plant life, animals, other humans, and the winds from the four directions. These four dimensions are joined at the centre of the circle, emphasizing their interconnectedness. This is the wholistic view toward health – interconnectedness within and with all of creation.

Furthermore, the wholistic indigenous understanding of health emphasizes a balance between the four realms (Anishnawbe Health Toronto 2006; NAHO 2005). Unlike certain Western conceptualizations of health that focus on the physical body or deal separately with the different aspects of the self, some indigenous cultures believe that sickness permeates a person's four realms. In this view, sickness begins in the spirit and then affects the mind, the emotions, and finally the body (Anishnawbe Health Toronto 2006). Healing from trauma and grief must thus address the four areas to re-establish balance. In the physical realm, physical activity, sport, and recreation are powerful medicines that can be healing tools to balance physical health with mental, emotional, and spiritual well-being.

The Ecological Model

The concepts of relatedness of the self with the external world can be found in a Western conceptualization of health and related human behaviours known as a socio-ecological model of health. An ecological model offers a way of conceptualizing the pathways of influence between people and their environments that is useful for understanding health (McLeroy et al. 1988; Stokols 1992, 1996; Green, Richard, and Potvin 1996; Sallis and Owen 2002). It is rooted in human development research by Bronfenbrenner (1977, 1979), who viewed the growing human organism as influenced by multiple nested systems: the microsystem, the mesosystem, the exosystem, and the macrosystem.

In this view, the first and lowest level, *microsystem,* represents the settings in which the developing person interacts with his or her immediate interpersonal environment (e.g., home, school, workplace). The microsystem is nested within the *mesosystem*, which encompasses the connections that exist between the multiple settings that the person inhabits. The *exosystem* that envelops the mesosystem represents the environment that influences the lower-order settings of the system (e.g., the media, government). Finally, the most distal level, *macrosystem*, represents the explicit and implicit institutional (e.g., economic, educational, political) and cultural environments that influence all of the other system levels (Bronfenbrenner 1977, 1979).

The nesting of systems and/or interconnectivity between environments described by Bronfenbrenner can be likened to medicine wheel teachings. Although the specific systems identified by Bronfenbrenner in the ecological model and those of the medicine wheel may not be completely aligned, a two-eyed seeing approach highlights the similarities of their strengths. For instance, the microsystem might represent the self and family; the mesosystem might reflect the connection to community or nation; and the exosystem and macrosystem might link to humankind, plant and animal life, the earth, and the universe. The medicine wheel differs from the ecological model in that it privileges relationships to the land and to human, animal, and plant life. One can interpret aspects of the exosystem and macrosystems, such as political institutions, as relating to community and other humankind (i.e., political systems within Aboriginal communities and that of the broad political environment – federal, provincial, territorial). Although the concepts of exosystem and macrosystem depicted in the ecological model might be closely related to the family and community aspects of the medicine wheel, the macrosystem, seemingly more distant from the individual, might be interpreted as residing closer to the individual in the medicine wheel.

Criticizing systems-based ecological models for their lack of specificity, McLeroy and colleagues (1988) adapted Bronfenbrenner's model by identifying five levels of influence of human behaviour and health: intrapersonal, interpersonal, institutional, community, and policy. Intrapersonal level factors consist of the individual's traits and characteristics, whereas the interpersonal level represents close networks (e.g., friends and family). Institutional factors are the organizational and regulatory aspects of social institutions, whereas community factors refer to networks that exist between institutions. The policy level reflects the influence of policies and legislation upon individuals (ibid.). These five levels of influence are the leverage points for health promotion.

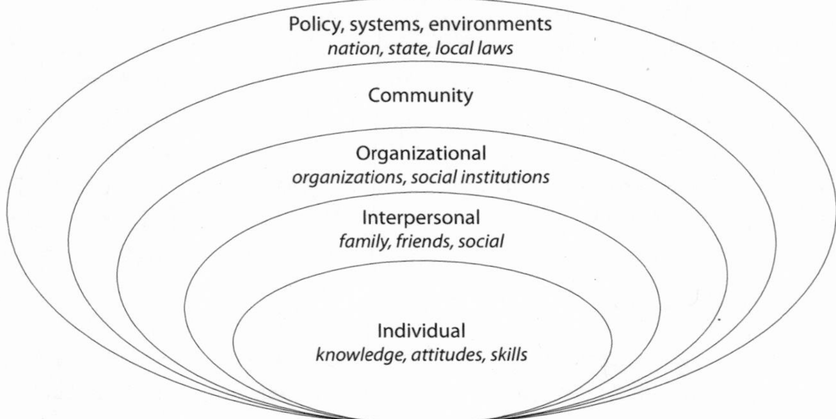

Figure 9.2 Socio-ecological model

Mostly used in health promotion, the contemporary version of the ecological model, illustrated in Figure 9.2, is often referred to as the socio-ecological model. This version includes input by McLeroy and colleagues (1988) and Stokols (1992), who made explicit the essential qualities of health-promoting environments. Stokols specified how aesthetic qualities and environmental controllability are essential for mental and emotional well-being. He outlined that physically non-toxic, comfortable environments are resources necessary to physical health. At the organizational and community levels, he deemed that social support networks and participatory processes are key elements of social cohesion. Stokols was most interested in the ways in which the environment could be leveraged to promote health, and he developed a set of guidelines to aid in the translation of socio-ecological theory into community health promotion.

In sum, an ecological approach to health stipulates that overall health is determined by the interconnectedness of all environmental systems. Over the past twenty years, health promotion efforts in general, and physical activity promotion efforts in particular, have increasingly been modelled on the premise that these systems should be leveraged in a way that ensures a consistent health message is broadcast widely throughout society (Smedley and Syme 2000; Booth et al. 2001; French, Story, and Jeffery 2001; Gauvin, Lévesque, and Richard 2001; Lavizzo-Mourey and McGinnis 2003). Given its intuitive appeal, many interventions to promote youth involvement in physical activity are now founded on an ecological approach, and physical activity-specific models that incorporate individual and environmental levels have been proposed (Sallis and Owen 1999; Spence and Lee 2003). To date, however, there is no specific evidence confirming the optimal degree of integration of ecological principles in physical activity programming.

An Integrated Indigenous-Ecological Model

The socio-ecological model (see Figure 9.2) closely parallels the medicine wheel teachings in its recognition of the reciprocal influence that exists between family, friends, community, and the physical environment. Once again, however, the medicine wheel teachings privilege connectivity to the land, whereas the ecological model does not explicitly recognize this relationship. The convergence and divergence of the medicine wheel and ecological approach are discussed in this section.

Ecological theory is rooted in indigenous knowledge inasmuch as it views environmental settings of living as determinants of human behaviour and health. Sometimes referred to as Traditional Ecological Knowledge (TEK), anthropologists recognized the contribution of knowledge by indigenous peoples to the development of ecological theory, specifically their understanding of the environment (Inglis 1993). Suzuki (2002) contended that Western science needs to more fully consider indigenous peoples' traditional knowledge, specifically the intricate interconnection of all aspects of the world and universe. Western science has begun this process through modern ecological theoretical approaches. In spite of the dearth of explicit examples of how medicine wheel teachings have informed the Westernized ecological view of human behaviour and health, the compatibility of these two approaches shows tremendous potential.

Incorporating Marshall and Bartlett's two-eyed seeing approach (2009), which was referenced near the beginning of this chapter, we recognize the strengths of the medicine wheel with one eye and the strengths of the ecological model with the other. Bringing the two together provides an avenue to consider a sport and physical activity promotion model with Aboriginal peoples. The strengths of the two views are where they converge, such as with the concepts of relatedness, the reciprocal influence of people and settings, and the importance of environments. Yet, there remain areas of divergence between the ecological model and the medicine wheel. A case in point is the lack of recognition by Western ecological approaches concerning the spiritual aspects of indigenous knowledge.

Spiritual knowledge is a concept that is discussed within indigenous knowledge, specifically the notion of revelations (Brant Castellano 2000).

Indigenous knowledge has been characterized as encompassing three processes: empirical observation, traditional teachings, and revelations (ibid.). Empirical observation within the context of indigenous knowledge is not based on quantitative inquiry in controlled settings. Rather, indigenous empirical knowledge is a representation of "converging perspectives from different vantage points over time" in real life, not in laboratory settings (ibid., 24). Traditional teachings encompass knowledge that has been passed down mostly orally from previous generations. Finally, knowledge through revelations such as dreams, visions, and intuitions is sometimes regarded as spiritual knowledge. Spiritual knowledge is sometimes seen as that coming from the spirit world and ancestors. This is sometimes called cellular or blood memory (G. Antone, pers. comm., February 20, 2002; V. Harper, pers. comm., April 12, 2002) because it is believed that indigenous thoughts, beliefs, and actions are transmitted from generation to generation through blood, that is, biologically. The notion of cellular memory in the field of DNA and human evolution genetics is still an emergent field, yet recent research validates what Aboriginal people have long understood as blood memory (Holmes 2000).

The spiritual aspect of the "self" is tied closely to one's cultural understanding of identity. When asked what the spiritual dimension represents, some people describe it not as religion but as a connection to everyone and everything, including a connection to the land because everything has a spirit and many indigenous people connect spiritually as spiritual beings living in a physical world (Lavallée 2007). An elaborate discussion on spiritual knowledge is beyond the scope of this chapter; however, spiritual knowledge is one of the key differences between an ecological approach and the medicine wheel that needs to be considered in physical activity and health promotion in Aboriginal communities: as one of the four interrelated aspects of life, spiritual health cannot be ignored. As noted previously, some indigenous people believe sickness begins in the spirit and then affects the mind, the emotions, and finally the body (Anishnawbe Health Toronto 2006). In this view, it is essential that the promotion of wholistic health through physical activity and sport include spirituality as a way to reclaim and promote wellness.

The strengths of an indigenous and Western approach are depicted in an integrated model of the medicine wheel and ecological model (see Figure 9.3). In this model, sport, recreation, and physical activity opportunities delivered using a decolonizing approach at each ecological leverage point (i.e., intrapersonal, interpersonal, organizational, community, policy, systems,

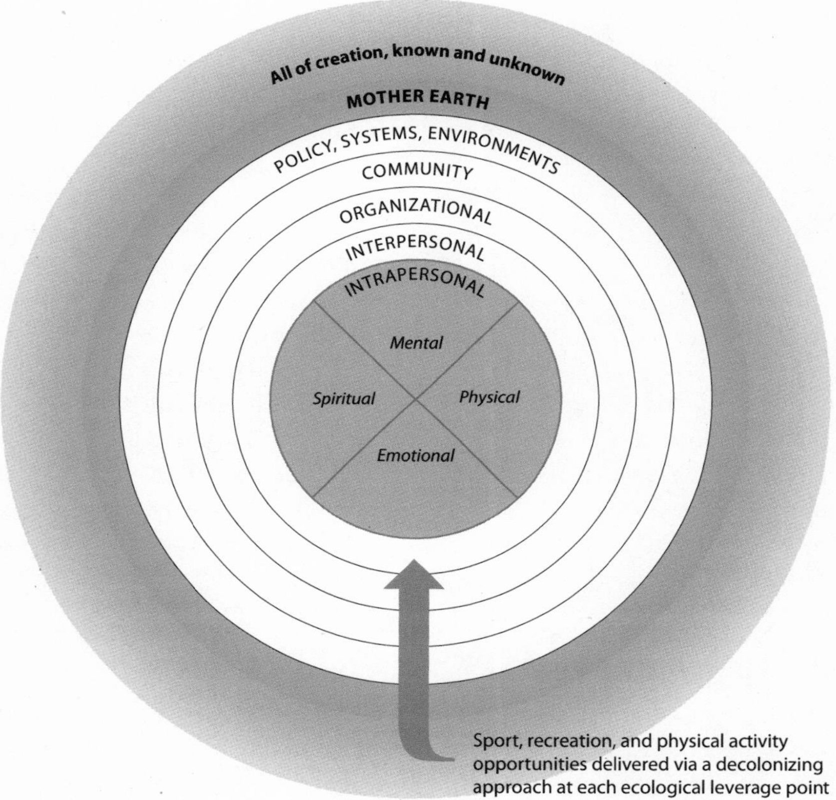

Figure 9.3 Integrated indigenous-ecological model for sport and physical activity promotion in Aboriginal communities. *Source:* Adapted from Lavallée (2006).

environments, and all of creation) serve to enhance and strengthen each of the four realms of wholistic health. Given the previous discussion about the impact of colonization on sport, and the paradox of sport's potential to provide both positive and negative opportunities, this model highlights the importance of positive, decolonizing activities to promote wholistic health.

An integral aspect of the integrated indigenous-ecological model is Morrissette, McKenzie, and Morrissette's contention (1993, 91-92) that an "Aboriginal framework of practice rests on four key principles": (1) the recognition of a distinct Aboriginal world view, (2) empowerment as a method of practice, (3) the development of Aboriginal consciousness about the impact of colonialism, and (4) cultural knowledge and tradition as an active component of retaining Aboriginal identity and collective consciousness.

These principles can provide a decolonizing approach to physical activity and sport promotion by requiring that an Aboriginal community's core values, beliefs, and healing practices be incorporated in promotion strategies. For the Anishinaabek, incorporating core values and beliefs might include the medicine wheel.

Decolonizing activities are the antithesis to activities that have been imbued with imperial and colonial practices. Often cast within the context of knowledge pursuit and research (Smith 2002), decolonizing activities offer a way for indigenous peoples to reclaim knowledge and practices that are rightfully their own. Applied to physical activity and health promotion, decolonizing activities are used to redress balance and harmony between the spiritual, mental, physical, and emotional domains of the self. They represent a means to resist and challenge dominant knowledge and practices imposed through colonization. The integrated indigenous-ecological model offers a decolonizing framework for sport and physical activity promotion by ensuring that each ecological leverage point and environmental level is addressed and can yield outcomes at one or more of the medicine wheel quadrants.

Working with the Model

The integrated indigenous-ecological model for sport, recreation, and physical activity promotion (see Figure 9.3) has multiple interconnected layers. The arrow in the model depicts the inputs (i.e., decolonizing sport, recreation, and physical activity opportunities) occurring at each ecological level. The ringed layers identify the different leverage points (intrapersonal, interpersonal, organizational, community, policy/systems/environments) at which interventions to promote sport, recreation, and physical activity can occur. These layers are set on Mother Earth (planet Earth) and cast within the infinite cosmos of known and unknown – or all of creation – to reflect the Anishinaabek traditional teaching of the medicine wheel. The nucleus of the model depicts the four realms (mental, physical, emotional, and spiritual) that make up the whole person. Physical activity and sport effects can transpire within each realm, ideally in a way that is balanced to achieve wholistic health. These effects represent the outputs of the model.

Providing positive, decolonizing sport and physical activity opportunities at each ecological leverage point is an important consideration of the integrated model. For instance, involving family members in the development of physical activity programs for Aboriginal youth is a strategy to leverage the interpersonal environment (e.g., family) to influence the individual (e.g., youth). Engaging family members in a medicine walk led by an elder who can teach participants about the traditional healing properties of herbs and plants offers a way to reconnect with the land (Karihoo 2009). Following Anderson's notion (2006, 1) of using the "master's tools" to resist "colonization through colonial sports," Western sport can be a venue to bring indigenous communities together. An example is the North American Indigenous Games where the majority of the sports are Western in origin; however, the Games weave in indigenous cultural activities, such as traditional dancing, which spectators can watch or, in many cases, participate in.

Moreover, the integrated indigenous-ecological model avoids a deficit approach that typically characterizes physical activity and sport promotion for youth. A deficit approach is based on a medical model and begins with the premise that something is wrong and needs to be fixed, for example, "deviant" youth behaviour. The integrated indigenous-ecological model differs from a deficit approach in that it attempts to achieve balance and harmony of the self through sport and physical activity rather than focusing on the use of sport to curb the deviant behaviour of at-risk youth (Coakley 2002). A focus on balance between the four realms (physical, mental, emotional, and spiritual) means that program delivery will integrate activities that touch upon each of the realms. The holistic sport model (Thorne and Thorne 2008) for coaches involved in Aboriginal sport is an example of how these four realms come together in sport. Thorne and Thorne (2008) highlight the spiritual realm of the medicine wheel to convey the importance of using sacred traditional preparation methods as the foundation of wholistic balance in coaching.

Involving the community from the conceptualization of a program to its delivery and evaluation addressed Morrissette, McKenzie, and Morrissette's principle of empowerment (1993) and is highlighted as a leverage point in the integrated model. Community members know best what is needed and wanted. Involving constituents in the entire process of designing and delivering programs can be empowering. For example, if a program for youth is the goal, then, using this approach, involving youth in the development and delivery of the program is imperative. Similarly, if the program is for pregnant mothers or seniors, these particular groups need to be involved in all aspects of programming.

The development of Aboriginal consciousness about the impact of colonialism (Morrissette, McKenzie, and Morrissette 1993) through sport and recreation can also be fostered by using the integrated indigenous-ecological model. Strengths of the Western ecological model that are depicted in the integrated model are the inclusion of the leverage points of policies, programs, the environment, and organizations. Using sport, recreation, and physical activity to educate individuals and organizations about the problems associated with assimilation of colonial practices, or advocating for policy change to re-engage participants in culturally relevant practices, would be strategies consistent with the integrated model. An example of a decolonizing approach to health promotion is Lavallée's research (2007, 2008) at a martial arts program at the Native Canadian Centre of Toronto, where the Cree instructor incorporated indigenous knowledge, such as the medicine wheel and the seven grandfather teachings (of respect, love, humility, bravery, truth, honesty, and wisdom) into his martial arts practice. In addition to learning the cultural teachings, program participants were provided with the opportunity to meet and identify with other Aboriginal people, which is an important consideration in the urban context, where Aboriginal people are often scattered throughout the city with few opportunities to gather as a collective. In this way, the martial arts program was much more than a physical activity program. It was a wholistic program delivered in a cultural way in an Aboriginal gathering place. The instructor also regularly included informal discussion sessions about the impact of colonization on the health and well-being of Aboriginal people today.

Learning about wholistic health and how other systemic and societal factors play a significant role in the health of Aboriginal people can be empowering for Aboriginal peoples because of the shift from blaming the individual to recognizing wider social factors as contributing to ill health. Coaches and instructors of physical activity and sport programs delivered to Aboriginal people are an excellent source for developing this consciousness about colonialism's impact. Sport and physical activity can thus be used as a tool to reintroduce Aboriginal people to cultural teachings that have been unlearned through colonization. This reclamation of Aboriginal identity through the inclusion of cultural knowledge in sport, recreation, and physical activity incorporates Morrissette and colleagues' final principle (1993): inclusion of cultural traditions.

These examples of a positive, decolonizing approach to sport and physical activity program delivery in Aboriginal communities illustrate how the elements of the integrated model can be applied. Although the method of delivering culturally relevant sports programs may differ across nations, sports, and physical activities, the examples noted above and the integrated model of the medicine wheel and the Western ecological model provide a framework from which to begin. This framework may be especially relevant in the context of Aboriginal and non-Aboriginal partnerships to promote sport, recreation, and physical activity (e.g., the Active Circle [n.d.], a partnership between Aboriginal Sport Circle and Motivate Canada) because its representation of concepts is meaningful to a diversity of peoples.

Conclusion

Sport and physical activity offer a way for Aboriginal people to re-establish balance in the cycle of their own lives and the lives of future generations. By drawing on traditional teachings such as the medicine wheel, Aboriginal peoples can begin to reclaim what was taken through colonization. The healing potential of sport and physical activity is powerful medicine that can touch all dimensions of wholistic health: the physical, the mental, the emotional, and the spiritual. The principles outlined by Morrissette and colleagues (1993) offer a way to conceptualize the delivery of physical activity and sport programs through a decolonizing lens; this approach allows physical activity and sport to be used as a tool to promote indigenous knowledge and enables indigenous knowledge to be used as a tool to promote physical activity and sport.

Similarly, the medicine wheel and the ecological approach, through an indigenous-ecological integrated model, provide a decolonizing framework from which to promote sport and physical activity in a way that enables Aboriginal peoples to reclaim their knowledges and cultures. Integrating Western and indigenous world views allows for the strengths of each to be united (two-eyed seeing) to benefit Aboriginal peoples.

Two-eyed seeing, the acknowledgment of the strengths of different approaches, is critical for the development of sport and physical activity promotion tools and initiatives in Aboriginal communities. One cannot ignore the abundance of knowledge that exists in communities that will help engage the community. By the same token, Western approaches to engage people in sport, recreation, and physical activity offer insight into program development within the context of the policies, systems, and environments that are critical in understanding how a program may flourish or flounder. Two-eyed seeing can provide a comprehensive lens that captures all of the relevant elements to successful mobilization of communities in sport, recreation, and physical activity promotion.

Bringing together the ecological model and the medicine wheel provides an example of how to frame a common understanding of wholistic health promotion. The bringing together of indigenous and Western knowledge might at first glance appear contradictory, yet existing synergies between the medicine wheel and ecological approaches suggest there are bridges of common understanding that can be leveraged to deliver culturally relevant programs to engage Aboriginal peoples in physical activity and sport and once again harness their powerful medicine.

REFERENCES

Active Circle. n.d. Welcome to the Active Circle. http://www.activecircle.ca.

Anderson, E.D. 2006. Using the master's tools: Resisting colonization through colonial sport. *International Journal of History of Sport* 23(2): 247-66.

Anishnawbe Health Toronto. 2006. *Anishnawbe Health Toronto.* Toronto: Anishnawbe Health.

Antone, E., P. Gamlin, and L. Provost-Turchetti. 2003. *Literacy and Learning: Acknowledging Aboriginal Holistic Approaches to Learning in Relation to Best Practices' Literacy Training Programs Final Report.* Toronto: Literacy and Learning.

ASC (Aboriginal Sport Circle). n.d. About the ASC. http://www.aboriginalsport circle.ca/.

Barron, F.L. 1984. A summary of federal Indian policy in the Canadian west, 1867-1984. *Native Studies Review* 1(1): 28-39.

Booth, S.L., J.F. Sallis, C. Ritenbaugh, J.O. Hill, L.L. Birch, L.D. Frank, K. Glanz, et al. 2001. Environmental and societal factors affect food choice and physical activity: Rationale, influences, and leverage points. *Nutrition Reviews* 3: 21-39.

Boreham, C., C.J. Robson, A.M. Gallagher, G.W. Cran, J.M. Savage, and L.J. Murray. 2004. Tracking of physical activity, fitness, body composition and diet from adolescence to young adulthood: The Young Hearts Project, Northern Ireland. *International Journal of Behavioural Nutrition and Physical Activity* 1: 14. http://www.ijbnpa.org/.

Brant Castellano, M. 2000. Updating Aboriginal traditions of knowledge. In G. Dei, B. Hall, and A. Goldin-Rosenberg, eds., *Indigenous Knowledges in Global Contexts* (21-36). Toronto: University of Toronto Press.

Bronfenbrenner, U. 1977. Toward an experimental ecology of human development. *American Psychologist* 32(7): 513-31.

–. 1979. *The Ecology of Human Development.* Cambridge, MA: Harvard University Press.

Camacho, T.C., R.E. Roberts, N.B. Lazarus, G.A. Kaplan, and R.D. Cohen. 1991. Physical activity and depression: Evidence from the Alameda County Study. *American Journal of Epidemiology* 134: 220-31.

Canadian Heritage. 2003. *North American Indigenous Games (NAIG) Funding Framework for 2008 and Onwards Hosting Component.* http://www.pch.gc.ca/.

–. 2006. *Maskwachees Declaration of 2000.* http://www.canadianheritage.gc.ca/.

Coakley, J. 2002. Using sports to control deviance and violence among youths: Let's be critical and cautious. In M. Gatz, M.A. Messner, and S.J. Ball-Rokeach, eds., *Paradoxes of Youth and Sport* (13-30). Albany, NY: SUNY Press.

Cohen, K. 2002. A mutually comprehensible world? Native Americans, Europeans, and play in eighteenth-century America. *American Indian Quarterly* 26(1): 67-93.

Culin, S. 1907. *24th Annual Report of the Bureau of American Ethnology: Games of North American Indians*. Washington, DC: US Government Printing Office.

Eisenmann, J.C. 2004. Physical activity and cardiovascular disease risk factors in children and adolescents: An overview. *Canadian Journal of Cardiology* 20(3): 295-301.

Field, T., M. Diego, and C. Saunders. 2001. Exercise is positively related to adolescents' relationships and academics. *Adolescence* 36: 105-10.

Forsyth, J., and K.B. Wamsley. 2006. "Native to Native ... we'll recapture our spirits": The World Indigenous Nations Games and North American Indigenous Games as cultural resistance. *International Journal of the History of Sport* 23(2): 294-314.

French, S.A., M. Story, and R.W. Jeffery. 2001. Environmental influences on eating and physical activity. *Annual Review of Public Health* 22: 309-25.

Gauvin, L., L. Lévesque, and L. Richard. 2001. Helping people initiate and maintain a more active lifestyle: A public health framework for physical activity promotion research. In R.N. Singer, H.A. Hausenblas, and C.N. Janelle, eds., *Handbook of Sport Psychology*, 2nd ed. (718-39). New York: Wiley.

Giles, A.R. 2004. Kevlar©, Crisco©, and menstruation: "Tradition" and the Dene Games. *Sociology of Sport Journal* 21(1): 18-35.

Giovannucci, E., A. Ascherio, E.B. Rimm, G.A. Colditz, M.J. Stampfer, and W.C. Willett. 1995. Physical activity, obesity, and risk for colon cancer and adenoma in men. *Annals of Internal Medicine* 122: 327-34.

Green, J. 2009. Gyawaglaab (Helping one another): Approaches to best practices through teachings of Oolichan fishing. In R. Sinclair, M.A. Hart, and G. Bruyere, eds., *Wicihitowin: Aboriginal Social Work in Canada* (222-33). Halifax: Fernwood.

Green, L.W., L. Richard, and L. Potvin. 1996. Ecological foundations of health promotion. *American Journal of Health Promotion* 10(4): 270-81.

Haslip, S. 2001. A treaty right to sport? *Murdoch University Electronic Journal of Law* 8(2): paras. 48-57. http://www.murdoch.edu.au/.

Haslip, S., and V. Edwards. 2002. Does sport belong in the medicine chest? Paper presented at the North American Indigenous Games Research Symposium, Winnipeg, July 25-26.

Haugland, S., B. Wold, and T. Torsheim. 2003. Relieving the pressure? The role of physical activity in the relationship between school-related stress and adolescent health complaints. *Research Quarterly for Exercise and Sport* 74(2): 127-35.

Holmes L. 2000. Heart knowledge, blood memory, and the voice of the land: Implications of research among Hawaiian elders. In G. Dei, B. Hall, and D. Rosenberg, eds., *Indigenous Knowledges in Global Contexts: Multiple Readings of Our World* (37-53). Toronto: University of Toronto Press.

Hu, F.B., M.F. Leitzmann, M.J. Stampfer, G.A. Colditz, W.C. Willett, and E.B. Rimm. 2001. Physical activity and television watching in relation to risk for type 2 diabetes mellitus in men. *Archives of Internal Medicine* 161: 1542-48.

Hu, F.B., J.E. Manson, M.J. Stampfer, G. Colditz, S. Liu, C.G. Solomon, W.C. Willett. 2001. Diet, lifestyle, and the risk of type 2 diabetes mellitus in women. *New England Journal of Medicine* 345: 790-97.

Hu, F.B., M.J. Stampfer, G.A. Colditz, A. Ascherio, K.M. Rexrode, and W.C. Willett. 2000. Physical activity and risk of stroke in women. *Journal of the American Medical Association* 283: 2961-67.

Inglis, J.T. 1993. *Traditional Ecological Knowledge: Concepts and Cases.* Ottawa: International Development Research Centre.

Janssen, I., P.T. Katzmarzyk, W.F. Boyce, and W. Pickett. 2004. The independent influence of physical inactivity and obesity on health complaints in 6th to 10th grade Canadian youth. *Journal of Physical Activity and Health* 1(4): 331-43.

Karihoo, E. 2009. Reframing physical activity programs for Aboriginal communities. *WellSpring* 20(6): 1-4.

Katzmarzyk, P.T. 2008. Obesity and physical activity among Aboriginal Canadians. *Obesity* 16: 184-90.

Katzmarzyk, P.T., R.M. Malina, and C. Bouchard. 1999. Physical activity, physical fitness, and coronary heart disease risk factors in youth: The Quebec family study. *Preventive Medicine* 29: 555-62.

Kitchikeesic, L. 2005. Meeting of the minds over two eyed seeing. Press release, University College of Cape Breton. http://www.canadian-universities.net/.

Kovach, M. 2009. *Indigenous Methodologies: Characteristics, Conversations, and Contexts.* Toronto: University of Toronto Press.

Lane, P., M. Bopp, J. Bopp, and L. Brown. 2003. *The Sacred Tree.* Lethbridge, AB: Four Worlds International Institute for Human and Community Development.

Lavallée, L. 2006. Threads of connection: Healing historic trauma through cultural recreation programming. Paper presented at the Canadian Institutes of Health Research, Aboriginal Capacity and Development Research Environments (ACADRE) Gathering of Graduate Students in Aboriginal Health, Hamilton, June 22.

–. 2007. Physical activity and healing through the medicine wheel. *Pimatisiwin: A Journal of Aboriginal and Indigenous Community Health* 5(1): 127-53.

–. 2008. Balancing the medicine wheel through physical activity. *Journal of Aboriginal Health* 4(1): 64-71.

Lavizzo-Mourey, R., and J.M. McGinnis. 2003. Making the case for active living communities. *American Journal of Public Health* 93: 1386-88.

Lee, I.M., C.C. Hsieh, and R.S. Paffenbarger. 1995. Exercise intensity and longevity in men: Harvard Alumni Health Study. *Journal of the American Medical Association* 273: 1179-84.

Lockard, V. 2000. Native American Sports Council gets honor. *Canku Ota: A Newsletter Celebrating Native America.* February 12. http://www.turtletrack.org/.

Macaulay, A.C., M. Cargo, S. Bisset, T. Delormier, L. Lévesque, L. Potvin, and A.M. McComber. 2005. Kanien'kehá:ka (Mohawk) ways for the primary prevention of type 2 diabetes: The Kahnawake Schools Diabetes Prevention Project. In M.L. Ferreira and G.C. Lang, eds., *Indigenous Peoples and Diabetes: Community Empowerment and Wellness* (407-34). Durham, NC: Carolina Academic Press.

Malina, R.M. 2001. Physical activity and fitness: Pathways from childhood to adulthood. *American Journal of Human Biology* 13(2): 162-72.

Marshall, A., and D. Bartlett. 2009. *Co-Learning Re: "Talking and Walking Together" of Indigenous and Mainstream Sciences.* http://www.brasdorcepi.ca/ (accessed September 2011).

McLeroy, K.R., D. Bibeau, A. Steckler, and K. Glanz. 1988. An ecological perspective on health promotion programs. *Health Education Quarterly* 15: 351-77.

Morrissette, V., B. McKenzie, and L. Morrissette. 1993. Toward an Aboriginal model of social work practice. *Canadian Social Work Review* 10(1): 91-107.

Mutrie, N., and G. Parfitt. 1998. Physical activity and its link with mental, social and moral health in young people. In S. Biddle, J. Sallis, and N. Cavill, eds., *Young and Active? Young People and Health-Enhancing Physical Activity; Evidence and Implications* (49-68). London, ON: Health Education Authority.

NAHO (National Aboriginal Health Organization). 2005. *First Nations Regional Longitudinal Health Survey (RHS) 2002/03: The Peoples' Report.* Ottawa: NAHO.

NAHC (National Aboriginal Hockey Championships). n.d. About NAHC. http://www.nahc2009.com.

Paraschak, V. 1997. Variations in race relations: Sporting events for Native peoples in Canada. *Sociology of Sport Journal* 14: 1-21.

Royal Commission on Aboriginal Peoples. 1996. *Looking Forward, Looking Back: Report of the Royal Commission on Aboriginal Peoples.* Vol. 1. Ottawa: Minister of Supply and Services Canada. http://www.collectionscanada.gc.ca/.

Sallis, J.F., and N. Owen. 1999. *Physical Activity and Behavioral Medicine.* Thousand Oaks, CA: Sage.

–. 2002. Ecological models. In K. Glanz, F.M. Lewis, and B.K. Rimer, eds., *Health Behaviour and Health Education: Theory, Research and Practice,* 3rd ed. (403-24). San Francisco: Jossey-Bass.

Sesso, H.D., R.S. Paffenbarger, and I.M. Lee. 2000. Physical activity and coronary heart disease in men: The Harvard Alumni Health Study. *Circulation* 102: 975-80.

Smedley, B.D., and L. Syme. 2000. *Promoting Health: Intervention Strategies from Social and Behavioral Research.* Washington, DC: Institute of Medicine.

Smith, L.T. 2002. *Decolonizing Methodologies: Research and Indigenous Peoples.* Dunedin, NZ: University of Otago Press.

Spence, J., and R.E. Lee. 2003. Toward a comprehensive model of physical activity. *Psychology of Sports and Exercise* 4: 7-24.

Stevenson, J. 1999. The circle of healing. *Native Social Work Journal* 2: 8-21.

Stokols, D. 1992. Establishing and maintaining healthy environments: Toward a social ecology of health promotion. *American Psychologist* 47: 6-22.

–. 1996. Translating social ecological theory into guidelines for community health promotion. *American Journal of Health Promotion* 10(4): 282-98.

Strong, W.B., R.R. Malina, C.J.R. Blimke, S.R. Daniels, R.K. Dishman, B. Gutin, A.C. Hergenroeder, et al. 2005. Evidence based physical activity for school-age youth. *Journal of Pediatrics* 146(6): 732-36.

Suzuki, D. 2002. *The Sacred Balance: Rediscovering Our Place in Nature*. Vancouver: Greystone Books.

Taras, H. 2005. Physical activity and student performance at school. *Journal of School Health* 75(6): 214-18.

Telama, R., X. Yang, J. Vilkari, I. Välimäki, O. Wanne, and O. Raitakari. 2005. Physical activity from childhood to adulthood: A 21-year tracking study. *American Journal of Preventative Medicine* 28(3): 267-73.

Thorne, D., and T. Thorne. 2008. Holistic sport model. Paper presented at the 2008 North American Indigenous Games Research and Education Symposium, Cowichan, BC, August 2-3.

Tremblay, M.S., and J.D. Willms. 2003. Is the Canadian childhood obesity epidemic related to physical inactivity? *International Journal of Obesity and Related Metabolic Disorders* 27(9): 1100-05.

Waldrum, J.B. 1997. *The Way of the Pipe*. Peterborough, ON: Broadview Press.

Wannamethee, S.G., and A.G. Shaper. 1999. Physical activity and the prevention of stroke. *Journal of Cardiovascular Risk* 6: 213-16.

–. 2001. Physical activity in the prevention of cardiovascular disease: An epidemiological perspective. *Sports Medicine* 31: 101-14.

Warburton, D.E., C.W. Nicol, and S.S. Bredin. 2006. Health benefits of physical activity: The evidence. *Canadian Medical Association Journal* 174: 801-9.

Warry, W. 1998. *Unfinished Dreams: Community Healing and the Reality of Aboriginal Self-Government*. Toronto: University of Toronto Press.

Wesley-Esquimaux, C., and M. Smolewski. 2004. *Historic Trauma and Aboriginal Healing*. Ottawa: Aboriginal Healing Foundation.

Conclusion

JANICE FORSYTH AND AUDREY R. GILES

One of our main objectives in producing this collection was to call attention to the significance of Aboriginal sport to Canadian culture. There are numerous reasons for doing so, including the fact that there is a national policy on Aboriginal sport in Canada, lacrosse is Canada's summertime national sport, and the Four Host First Nations played an integral part in Canada's winning the bid for the Vancouver 2010 Winter Olympic Games. Further, many of the best athletes in the mid-twentieth century came from the Indian residential schools, and the earliest days of Canadian sport were a success largely because of the involvement of Aboriginal male athletes, whose athleticism and exoticism drew large paying crowds. Certainly, as we have shown, Canada's rich and varied physical past – and present – is deeply tied to Aboriginal sport.

The chapters in this collection represent a broad array of responses to our objective. Altogether, they draw on insights from Aboriginal studies, history, sociology, psychology, political science, women's studies, gender studies, sport management, anthropology, social work, policy studies, physical education, and pedagogy. We believe that this heterogeneity is a positive feature and that what emerges from this collection is a stronger understanding of the key tensions that have shaped, and continue to shape, Aboriginal sport in Canada. Many of the tensions outlined in this text stem from cultural ideas that differ between Aboriginal and non-Aboriginal people, as well as among Aboriginal people, about what sport is, who should participate in it, and how it should be organized. Other conflicts emerge from the unequal power relations that influence the ability of some Aboriginal people and not others to implement their visions for sport. Still other frictions are tied to how Aboriginal people are attempting to make sport one venue through which to assert their cultural identities and to find a positive space for themselves and their future generations in contemporary Canadian society.

All of these issues make Aboriginal sport an important area of study; this is particularly true for our understanding of the enormous impact that colonialism has had on physical life in Canada, where all too often Aboriginal people have been on the losing end of the colonial project. Current attempts by Aboriginal people to tackle the problems associated with colonialism, problems that are often linked to a loss of identity, sometimes include efforts to revitalize their traditional games. But revitalizing traditional practices comes with a particular set of challenges. As Audrey Giles shows, ideas about tradition can be used to revitalize important facets of a culture while at the same time marginalizing certain segments of the population. As a result, those (Aboriginal and non-Aboriginal alike) who call for Aboriginal people to restore their traditions should also consider precisely what values are being promoted through such practices. Additional concerns include who has the ability to decide which values should be promoted and how. And what if those values do not align with the laws and legislation of the dominant Canadian state? Which values take precedent? Michael Heine also deals with the issue of tradition but from the perspective of modernity. His work highlights the challenge facing Aboriginal people who want use the dominant sports model to revitalize their traditional games and assert their identities on the national and international stage that competitive sport provides. When traditional games are remade to fit the framework of the dominant sports model, it allows greater access, more visibility, and presumably some funding for development. Attempts to fit into the dominant sports model, however, raise several questions: What happens to the values that were originally aligned with those activities? Are they overshadowed and thus lost given the emphasis on winning that characterizes the dominant sports model? Can people who do not belong to the cultural group from where the activity originates say they participate in a "traditional" Aboriginal sport? How can we use this knowledge to extend our understanding of what sport can be? Clearly, both tradition and modernity are highly politicized concepts, with very real practical effects in sport.

The future of Aboriginal sport in Canada is also contingent on students, researchers, practitioners, and the public engaging in more sustained and thoughtful discussions about the politics of Aboriginal involvement in sport. It is important that people develop a better understanding of the various ways Aboriginal men and women, boys and girls have participated in sport – and the contributions they have made to the Canadian system. The chapters by Janice Forsyth, Christine O'Bonsawin, and M. Ann Hall reveal Aboriginal people's extensive involvement in all forms and all levels of sport, from the residential schools to community leagues to the Olympic Games. Yet, there remains a great deal more research to be conducted in each area. Understanding how sport has been used to control Aboriginal bodies within the context of residential schools could shed much-needed light on issues of identity and health. For instance, how do residential school survivors who participated in sports understand the concept of health? Do they even equate sport with health? If Aboriginal women who attended residential schools were generally excluded from the structure of sport, what is their interpretation of health? How do their interpretations differ from that of the men, who generally had more opportunities to engage in organized physical activities? The Vancouver 2010 Olympics set a new precedent by officially involving Aboriginal people, through the Four Host First Nations, in the hosting of the event; might the Olympic Games, after several spectacular instances of stereotyping Aboriginal people and their cultures, be a model for appropriate inclusion? Given the unequal power relations that exist between the International Olympic Committee, the host society, and Aboriginal people, it seems fair to say that the model developed for Vancouver 2010 should be celebrated with caution. Above all else, the tangible benefits that were supposed flow to Aboriginal people after the Games were over have yet to materialize. This should lead readers to ask, who really benefits from the Olympic Games and how? The history of Aboriginal girls and women in sport is also an area waiting to be documented and analyzed, as Hall points out. Such information also holds the potential to change the gendered face of Canadian sport history – a history that all too often reflects only a small portion of Canadians' (usually men's) life experiences.

The institutionalization of Aboriginal sport in Canada should also be regarded tentatively. Vicky Paraschak's work demonstrates the extent to which sport policy and practice, when inattentive to Aboriginal cultural practices, can result in the systematic marginalization of Aboriginal people in unintended ways. Paraschak's work exposes the way that a national policy for Aboriginal people in sport, notable for being the first of its kind in the world, created barriers for its intended recipients by reinforcing ideas about race in sport. In this case, policy discourse can enable, as well as constrain, decision-making processes. This problem raises many challenging questions about how sport policies are constructed in Canada. Whose vision for Aboriginal sport is being privileged in these documents? To what extent do ideas about Aboriginality enable and constrain Aboriginal participants? Given that Aboriginal people represent less than 3 percent of the total Canadian population, and a large portion of the Aboriginal population has not obtained a high school diploma, who will occupy the decision-making positions that will help the federal government carry out its policy objectives? And as Paraschak rightly asks, why is there no action plan to the national policy, especially when the federal government expressed its commitment in the policy to bettering the lives of Aboriginal people through sport? This hardly speaks to a government fully committed to addressing the concerns of Aboriginal people through the medium of sport. Robert Schinke, Duke Peltier, and Hope Yungblut's chapter demonstrates that attention to Aboriginal culture needs to go beyond policy considerations and to extend to all aspects of sporting practices. A true commitment to supporting Aboriginal athletes' success at the highest levels will require not only culturally competent sport policy makers but also sport psychology consultants, coaches, athletic therapists, and so on. As researchers who also do consulting work for sport, Paraschak, as well as Schinke, Peltier, and Yungblut, provide a way forward in terms of how sport policy and practice can be revised to address Aboriginal people's self-identified needs.

Last but not least, students and scholars are beginning to explore how sport can be used as a tool for decolonization. It is an approach that requires people to engage in dialogue, see the possibilities, value alternatives, and be willing to work toward creating something new; certainly, this is a challenging task. We hazard a guess that most non-Aboriginal Canadians do not know what decolonization means or what it might even look like. Chances are that most will struggle to come up with any coherent understanding of the term, let alone present ideas about how it might work. Joannie Halas, Heather McRae, and Amy Carpenter tackle this issue from the point of physical education in Manitoba schools. They lead us to the conclusion that sporting practices need not be expressed through the dominant, Euro-Canadian model. Being accepting of and supportive of cultural differences opens up the possibility for the creation of new sporting opportunities – ones that more strongly align with Aboriginal cultures and values. Lavallée and Lévesque's chapter provides the tools for the use of a bicultural, decolonizing approach for physical activity and health promotion with Aboriginal communities: two-eyed seeing. Such an approach acknowledges the impact that Canada's colonial legacy has had on Aboriginal people's physical practices, but it also builds on the strengths of both Aboriginal and Euro-Canadian cultural practices. As a result, this approach provides a way to move forward that acknowledges the past but also seeks to find healthy, culturally relevant solutions for the future. It is reassuring that scholars are willing to tackle these issues directly and to map out potential promising practices for addressing those issues.

The chapters presented in this volume offer a strong platform for students and researchers who are willing to engage with and address the difficult issues that frame Aboriginal people's involvement in sport. They are but a starting point for the kinds of research that need to be conducted in the future. In particular, there is an urgent need to further our understandings of contemporary all-Native sporting events like the North American Indigenous Games, the various regional Aboriginal sporting competitions that take place annually throughout Canada, Aboriginal women's participation in sport, the resurgence of traditional sport forms, and sport's role in residential school life. In light of the dearth of information on Aboriginal sporting practices in Atlantic Canada, research in this region of the country is urgently needed to balance out the Canadian perspective. Research into these areas will not be easy, since information is often hard to find. Archives generally tell the tale of people in positions of power, not the marginalized and dispossessed. Fieldwork, including oral interviews, requires a significant amount of time and is costly – a deterrent for students on limited budgets and researchers who do the best they can to stretch their granting dollars. As a result, Aboriginal people's voices are often fragmented, distorted, muted, or altogether absent. That being said, as researchers, some of our greatest sources of information and our own personal research experiences have come from engaging with the people themselves – about their daily life experiences, the artifacts they keep, and the stories they tell of their families and communities, near or far, thriving or recovering, with challenges and all – but always working toward a better future. We hope this volume contributes to such change.

Contributors

Amy Carpenter is a Métis woman from the Red River region. She is a public high school educator with Seven Oaks School Division, in Winnipeg. Before teaching high school, Amy enjoyed five years teaching grades one to three in a multiage classroom. She completed her master's degree at the University of Manitoba in the Faculty of Kinesiology and Recreation Management. Her thesis and ongoing community efforts focus on culturally relevant education and community mentorship programs.

Janice Forsyth is the director of the International Centre for Olympic Studies and assistant professor in the School of Kinesiology, Faculty of Health Sciences, at the University of Western Ontario. Her primary research area is in Canadian sport history, with a specific interest in contemporary Aboriginal sport practices. Recent projects include Aboriginal people and the Olympic Games; the sporting experiences of Tom Longboat Award recipients; sports and games at residential schools; and Aboriginal women, work, and sport. She frequently provides leadership and direction to government and service organizations, including Sport Canada, the Aboriginal Sport Circle, Athletes CAN, and the Canadian Association for the Advancement of Women and Sport and Physical Activity. She is a member of the Fisher River Cree First Nation, Manitoba.

Audrey R. Giles is an associate professor in the School of Human Kinetics at the University of Ottawa. Her interdisciplinary anthropological research focuses on the discursive production of tradition, health, community, gender equity, and safety, all within a sport and recreation context, usually in the Canadian Arctic and Subarctic. She is especially interested in qualitative research, particularly emergent methodologies.

Joannie Halas is a professor in the Faculty of Kinesiology and Recreation Management at the University of Manitoba. A former public school physical education teacher, her teaching, research, and service are in the areas of culturally relevant physical education and access to postsecondary education for under-represented populations, including Aboriginal and racialized minority groups. She has conducted several community-based research projects that involve the design and delivery of meaningful and relevant physical activity and education programs for marginalized youth populations, including a recent multiage Aboriginal youth mentor program.

M. Ann Hall was educated at Queen's University (BA, BPHE), the University of Alberta (MA), and the University of Birmingham (PhD). In 1968, she joined the Faculty of Physical Education and Recreation at the University of Alberta, where she remained until her retirement in 1997 as Professor Emeritus. She is a former chair of the Women's Studies Program in the Faculty of Arts and continues to be an active scholar through writing, editorial work, occasional teaching, conference presentations, and volunteer work. Her most recent books include *The Grads Are Playing Tonight! The Story of the Edmonton Commercial Graduates Basketball Club*; *Immodest and Sensational: 150 Years of Canadian Women in Sport*; and *The Girl and the Game: A History of Women's Sport in Canada.*

Michael Heine, assistant professor, teaches sport sociology at the University of Western Ontario. His research interests include the games and physical activity practices of Alaskan and northern Canadian Aboriginal peoples. He collaborates with northern Aboriginal and governmental organizations in the development of instructional and coaching resources.

Lynn Lavallée is an associate professor in the School of Social Work at Ryerson University. She is Métis-Anishinaabe. Lynn holds an honours BA in psychology and kinesiology from York University and an MSc in community health from the University of Toronto. She completed her PhD at the University of Toronto's Faculty of Social Work. Her research interests include indigenous health; cultural, sport, and recreation programs; indigenous epistemology; and indigenous research methods. She is passionate about bringing indigenous ways of knowing into academia, both through teaching and research.

Lucie Lévesque is an associate professor in the School of Kinesiology and Health Studies at Queen's University in Kingston. She specializes in physical activity intervention evaluation, focusing her teaching and research on community-based interventions to enhance physical activity involvement through an ecological approach. A long-time member of the Kahnawake Schools Diabetes Prevention Project team, she has research experience working with Aboriginal communities within a community-based participatory research framework.

Heather McRae recently completed her PhD in the Faculty of Education at the University of Manitoba. She is Métis-Anishinaabe, with French and Scottish ancestry, and a member of the PhD Studies for Aboriginal Scholars at the University of Manitoba. Her doctoral research investigated and analyzed how a recognized and successful Aboriginal sport organizations used sport to address issues of social exclusion in mainstream sport and to provide experiences of empowerment by encouraging and developing the fitness, health, and life skills of urban Aboriginal youth.

Christine M. O'Bonsawin is an assistant professor in the Department of History and the director of the Indigenous Studies Program at the University of Victoria. She received her PhD from the University of Western Ontario, where she completed her master's thesis and doctoral dissertation at the International Centre for Olympic Studies. She specializes in indigenous sport history, focusing her research and teaching on indigenous politics and policy, Canadian sport, and Olympic history. She is a member of the Abenaki Nation at Odanak.

Victoria Paraschak is an associate professor in the Department of Kinesiology, Faculty of Human Kinetics, at the University of Windsor. She specializes in the sociology of sport, Aboriginal sport, government policy in sport and recreation, and marginalized groups and sport. She also has extensive experience working in Aboriginal sport in the Northwest Territories, where she leads research projects and strategic planning sessions for government and nonprofit organizations.

Duke Peltier is a band member residing at Wikwemikong Unceded Indian Reserve, Ontario. He has been a community co-researcher on funded projects pertaining to elite sport and Aboriginal youth sport participation. His co-authored work has been featured in the *International Journal of Sport and Exercise Psychology, The Sport Psychologist, Qualitative Inquiry, Journal of Sport and Social Issues, Qualitative Research in Sport, Exercise and Health,* and *Journal of Sport and Physical Activity*. He has also been a co-applicant on two projects funded by the Social Sciences and Humanities Research Council of Canada and one project funded by the Indigenous Health Research Development Program. He is a member of Wikwemikong's Band Council and is a former elite athlete in ice hockey.

Robert J. Schinke is a professor in the School of Human Kinetics at Laurentian University. Although his teaching area is sport psychology and social psychology, he also teaches graduate and doctoral research methods for the sport sciences. As the founder of cultural sport psychology, he actively engages in funded research with Canadian Aboriginal and new Canadian athletes. He was awarded the 2008 Sport Information Resource Centre's Canadian Sport Science Research Award for Community Research, and his work has been published in *Quest, The Sport Psychologist,* and *Journal of Clinical Sport,* among several other peer-reviewed journals. He has also edited and co-edited five textbooks and authored three applied sport psychology books. He travels extensively as a sport psychology consultant to professional boxers.

Hope Yungblut is a doctoral candidate in the Human Studies Program at Laurentian University. Her doctoral research was funded by the Social Sciences and Humanities Research Council of Canada and by Sport Canada. Her co-authored work has been published in the *Journal of Physical Activity and Health, International Journal of Sport and Exercise Psychology, Journal of Sport and Social Issues, Journal of Sport Science and Medicine,* and *Women and Sport and Physical Activity Journal*. She has also presented extensively at international academic conferences pertaining to female youth and physical activity.

Index

Printed and bound in Canada by Friesens

Set in Futura Condensed and Warnock
by Artegraphica Design Co. Ltd.

Copy editor: Judy Phillips

Proofreader: Francis Chow

Indexer: Annette Lorek